Oxford Paperback English T

14.99.

Sir Thomas Browne

**Religio Medici
Hydriotaphia**
and
The Garden of Cyrus

F. H. Van Houe. Sculp.

Effigies Viri Doc: tissimi Tho: Browne
Equ: Aur: et Med: Doctoris.

Sir Thomas Browne

Religio Medici
Hydriotaphia
and
The Garden of Cyrus

Edited by **R. H. A. Robbins**

Clarendon Press Oxford

Oxford University Press, Great Clarendon Street, Oxford OX2 6DP
Oxford New York
Athens Auckland Bangkok Bogota Bombay
Buenos Aires Calcutta Cape Town Dar es Salaam
Delhi Florence Hong Kong Istanbul Karachi
Kuala Lumpur Madras Madrid Melbourne
Mexico City Nairobi Paris Singapore
Taipei Tokyo Toronto Warsaw
and associated companies in
Berlin Ibadan

ISBN 0 19 871064 X

© *Oxford University Press 1972*

First published 1972
Reprinted with Corrections and Additions, 1982
Reprinted 1989, 1991, 1997

Printed in China

Preface

This volume presents those shorter works of Browne by which he is best known: *Religio Medici*, *Hydriotaphia*, and *The Garden of Cyrus*. I am deeply indebted to Professor L. C. Martin for the use of his critical text; to him and to his predecessors for their scholarly researches; to John Buxton for his kind and useful criticism; to Robert Venables for improving my versions of Browne's classical quotations; and to Balliol for supporting me.

Balliol College   R. H. A. R.
Oxford.

Contents

List of Illustrations

Introduction

As the greatest balsams, according to Browne, lie enveloped in the bodies of the most powerful corrosives, so the bitter conflicts of seventeenth-century England fostered his remedy of tolerance and moderation. *Religio Medici*—a doctor's religion—may be seen not only as an introduction to a wise, loving, and cultured personality, but also as a medicine for the religious dissensions which lent fiery banners to the social and economic forces of the English Revolution. Amid the austerity of the ensuing Commonwealth, Browne provided stately yet exuberant music in *Hydriotaphia* and *The Garden of Cyrus* —rich celebrations of ordered growth and chaotic decay.

'Even when we are dealing with a writer in whom mere style counts for so much as with Browne,' remarks Pater, 'it is impossible to ignore his matter.'[1] While Browne wrote 'as an artist, not as a preacher, to discover his own thought, not to instruct others', nevertheless 'he wrote because he enjoyed the play of mind and the power of language to reveal it.'[2] His writings are the distillation of a typical seventeenth-century, Christian, classical, and scientific education, through the mind—untypical in its range, sensitivity, and powers of expression—of a member of the English middle classes amid the turmoil in which they first realized their power in the community.

Born into the family of a pious London merchant in 1605, Browne went in 1616 to Winchester College, where 'Virgil, Horace and Homer formed the staple of the curriculum',[3] and the usual language of conversation was Latin. This thorough education in the classics was presumably extended at Broadgates Hall, Oxford, where, in 1624, he delivered the freshman's oration on its incorporation as Pembroke College. The literary and linguistic aspects of the B.A. course, however, were less emphasized than logical and moral philosophy, exemplified in the works of Aristotle and Plato, Cicero and Seneca. After graduating in 1626, Browne would have read for his M.A. not only the philosophers and rhetoricians, the dramatists, orators, and poets of Greece and Rome, but also, probably for the first time, the medical writers, Hippocrates and Galen, who provided the basis of his future career.

Thus, when he took his M.A. in 1629, Browne's ambition was presumably clear in his mind. There followed, however, one of those

---

[1] Walter Pater, *Appreciations* (London, 1900), p. 163.
[2] Joan Bennett, *Sir Thomas Browne* (Cambridge, 1962), p. 84.
[3] M. L. Clarke, *Classical Education in Britain 1500–1900* (Cambridge, 1959), p. 53.

interludes so usual between the termination of theoretical pursuits at university and taking up a practical vocation in the world at large. Although Browne may next have studied medicine for a short while, what seems certain is that, with his possibly somewhat belligerent stepfather, Sir Thomas Dutton, he visited turbulent Ireland, witnessing, if not the 'nightly bodrags' deplored by Spenser in *Colin Clout's Come Home Again*, at least their desolating results, and thereby, maybe, having planted in him the peaceable convictions expressed in *Religio Medici*.

Oxford in the 1630s was not distinguished for its medical course, which until a few years previously had been conducted entirely from books. The most famous faculty of medicine in Europe had for long been that of Montpellier—the university of Rabelais, whose cap and gown were donned by each candidate for the degree of doctor of physic. Thither Browne proceeded in 1630 or 1631 to listen to the lectures of Lazare Rivière, author of a standard work of long-lasting authority, the *Praxis Medica*. But while Montpellier gave a thorough grounding in botany and anatomy, the significant advances in surgery and medicine were being made elsewhere, so that Browne moved on, probably after a year, to Padua, pre-eminent in surgery and anatomy since the professorship of Andrea Vesale, author of a monumental study of the human body, *De Humani Corporis Fabrica* (1543). He had been succeeded by men as illustrious in their specialities: Gabriele Falloppio (after whom are named the Fallopian tubes), and Girolamo Fabrizio of Acquapendente, whose description of the valves in the veins was important in enabling his pupil William Harvey to demonstrate the circulation of the blood. This high clinical tradition was still alive at Padua in Browne's time, as was that university's ancient tradition of intellectual independence, protected from religious persecutors by the Venetian Republic's time-honoured disregard of papal pressures. Despite, however, the stimulus and academic substance of the course at Padua, Browne's eclecticism (and, perhaps, geographical convenience) led him to change again, this time to Leiden, where new ideas in chemical therapy were arising, and where, in 1633, he was granted his doctorate, more prestigious academically than that granted him by Oxford four years later, which signified little more than a licence to practise in England.

Thus Browne purposefully imbibed the best teaching available in his time. Incidentally, during his sojourn in three different countries, Protestant Holland, Catholic Italy, and France which, by the Edict of Nantes in 1598, extended a precarious toleration to Protestants in a mainly Catholic kingdom, he framed those broad views of men's

religious manners expressed in *Religio Medici*. The diverse and
crowded experiences of these years abroad may have left him un-
settled in mind, prompting that spiritual exercise in self-examination
which he presented to the world simply as a doctor's creed, but which
is both broader and more personal than its title implies in the richness
and complexity of its references to literature and experience.

Religio Medici is basically a devotional treatise arranged in two
parts which correspond broadly with the two great commandments
of Matthew 22:37-9. In the first and longer part Browne sets forth
his approach to God through the Anglican Church, treating of his
doubts, his conceptions of God's attributes and relations with his
creation, nature and fate, faith and reason, the truth of the Bible,
rival sects and religions, miracles, witchcraft, man the microcosm,
death, judgement, heaven and hell, resurrection and salvation. The
second part expresses Browne's love for his neighbour, be he
foreigner, beggar, or ignoramus, friend or enemy, good or bad. Each
of the two main parts is subdivided into sections—short essays on
topics more or less related to the general theme. The form seems to
have been modelled less on such modern writers as Montaigne, Bacon,
or Pierre Charron (whose treatise *Of Wisdome*, translated *c.* 1612,
Browne read), than on the moral treatises and letters of Cicero and
Seneca.

While, as would be expected in a religious disquisition, *Religio
Medici* is shot through with biblical allusions, it is none the less the
work of a classically educated man. If we accept Browne's protesta-
tion in his preface that it was penned without 'the assistance of any
good book whereby to promote my invention or relieve my memory',
we can gauge how firmly he retained a fondness for ancient authors
from his reading at Winchester and Oxford. Most frequently alluded
to is, predictably, that emperor of polymaths, Aristotle, followed by
those moralists favoured by Browne also for their form and style,
Cicero and Seneca. Substantial use is made of the historians, Livy,
Tacitus, Suetonius, Plutarch and Josephus, while Browne also shows
a taste for the stoic poetry of Lucan, the satire of Horace, and the
irreverent humour of Lucian. Surprisingly sparse in a treatise on a
doctor's religion are the mentions of Galen and Augustine. Apart
from Paracelsus, the importance for Browne of more modern writers
seems relatively small: the divines Thomas à Kempis, Suarez, and
Pineda, Dante and Du Bellay, Rabelais and Shakespeare, are each
used once to illustrate a point, then forgotten. But this diversity of
Browne's is one of his virtues: he is no strict humanist of the Renaissance such as Sir Thomas More, who in the first book of his *Utopia*

declares that 'There is nothing extant in Latin that is to any purpose
saving a few of Seneca's and Cicero's doings.' Browne has read even
more widely than he has travelled, and delights his readers' sensibili-
ties with what Basil Willey calls 'the inter-availability of all his
worlds of experience'.[1] This yoking of diversities is a favourite device:
he proceeds with his thesis, not in a straight line of argument,
dissecting and contrasting ideas, but turns toward whatever mental
horizon proffers an inclusive image in which contradictions may be
embraced if not resolved. As Leroy says, his world is a world not of
dialectic but of analogies, or, in his own words, he is 'content to
understand a mystery without a rigid definition, in an easy and
Platonic description'. Thus he blends the nominalist paradox that the
certitude of faith is not that of reason with the doctrine of three souls
in one body in his memorable image of man as 'that great and true
amphibium'.

Such an approach—rather aesthetic than analytical—to problems
of belief, invites the charge of intellectual levity. In pressing such an
accusation there is a danger that Browne's seriousness may be taken
for humour, and, inversely, his occasional teasing of the reader for
toying with things of gravity. In this quiet and private mode of
writing we lack those indications of irony, the twinkle in the eye, the
pause for a smile, that in his physical presence confirm a speaker's
ironical intent.

Conversational though it is, *Religio Medici* is the expression of a
peculiarly individual personality at a particular stage of his development as a scholar and a writer in a notably idiosyncratic age. In style
as in content, the work is rooted in both the Bible and classical
moralists. The influence of the former is immediately obvious. By
pointing out that parallelism and antithesis occur in inverse proportions in Hebrew and classical prose, Professor Whallon has
demonstrated the ancestry of Browne's frequent tautologies and
repetitive elaborations in the patterns of biblical prosody.[2] The
classical influences on Browne's style may be differentiated from
those affecting other prose-writers in his own or the following century.
As M. W. Croll puts it, between the Elizabethans and the Augustans
there intervened a century

in which Lucan had a more effective influence on the ideas and the style of
poetry than Virgil did; in which Seneca was more loved and much more

[1] Basil Willey, *The Seventeenth-Century Background* (London, 1934), p. 44.
[2] W. Whallon, 'Hebraic Synonymy in Sir Thomas Browne', *Journal of English Literary History*, 28 (1961), 335–52.

effectively imitated in prose-style than Cicero had been in the previous generations; in which Tacitus almost completely displaced Livy as the model of historical and political writing; in which Martial was preferred to Catullus, and Juvenal and Persius were more useful to the satirists than Horace; in which Tertullian, the Christian representative of the Stoic style of the Empire—*notre Sénèque*, as he was called—exercised a stronger power of attraction over the most representative minds than St. Augustine, who is the Cicero and the Ciceronian of patristic Latin.[1]

Browne's organized sentences are not Ciceronian: they do not rise then fall to a close, but rise and expand with the thought to the end; they are not always, grammatically speaking, complete or distinct sentences: sometimes no main verb is provided; sometimes a string of such incomplete sentences succeeds for many lines with no preceding or final co-ordinating clause. They exemplify the fusion of two seventeenth-century anti-Ciceronian styles: the curt, favoured by Bacon ('While it is in aphorisms, it is in growth'); and the loose, which lets the mass and movement of thought have its way, helped on only by slight conjunctions, well characterized by Croll as 'frail and small hinges for the weights that turn on them; ... the period abounds and expands in nonchalant disregard of their tight, frail logic'.[2] This combined style enables Browne both to deliver his conclusions as decisive maxims or intense images, and to let his curiosity freely explore the doubts and paradoxes surrounding his subject. D. C. Allen has plausibly singled out as an influence on Browne the style of his favourite early Christian writers, 'of which Milton ... complained when he wrote about "the knotty Africanisms, the pampered metaphors, the intricate and involved sentences of the fathers"'.[3]

The intimate tone of *Religio Medici* lends plausibility to Browne's claim in his preface to the 1643 edition that he had, some seven years previously, composed the work for his 'private exercise and satisfaction', and that the two anonymous editions of 1642 had been printed without his knowledge from a corrupt text. Certainly these editions contain many evident defects (not all of which were remedied in 1643). There were, moreover, certain passages which Browne seems to have regarded as undesirably revealing in a published

---

[1] M. W. Croll, '"Attic Prose" in the Seventeenth Century', *Studies in Philology*, 18 (1921), 123.

[2] M. W. Croll, 'The Baroque Style in Prose', in *Studies in Honor of Frederick Klaeber* (Minneapolis, Minn., 1929), pp. 445–46.

[3] Don Cameron Allen, 'Style and Certitude', *Journal of English Literary History*, 15 (1948), 174.

work. A doctor would not wish to advise the public at large, as he
originally did in i.42, that 'Cold, I cure not myself by heat; when
sick, not by physic.' It could also have been professional caution that
led him to modify the confession in ii.9 that where he did a patient no
good his fee seemed 'no honest gain' to 'scarce honest gain'. He
acknowledges the contemporary Christian taboo on suicide by
deleting from ii.7 the assertion 'I detest my own nature, and in my
retired imaginations cannot withhold my hands from violence on
myself.' Beseeming modesty overcame spontaneous frankness in the
removal from ii.11 of 'I am the happiest man alive: I have that in me
can convert poverty into riches, transform adversity into prosperity;
I am more invulnerable than Achilles—fortune hath not one place to
hit me.' Likewise, in ii.13, he moderated the claim 'I can justly boast
I am as charitable as some who have built hospitals or erected
cathedrals' to 'Surely poor men may also build hospitals, and the
rich alone have not erected cathedrals.'

Even by taking such pains Browne could not avoid all criticism.
First in the field was a Roman Catholic aristocrat, Sir Kenelm Digby.
His *Observations* (whose reliance on the unrevised text of 1642 pro-
voked the correspondence with Browne appended to *Religio Medici*)
express disagreement on various points of theology, and his compli-
ments are accordingly qualified:

Assuredly, he is owner of a solid head, and of a strong, generous heart.
Where he employeth his thoughts upon such things as resort to no higher
or more abstruse principles than such as occur in ordinary conversation
with the world, or in the common track of study or learning, I know no
man would say better. . . . Most assuredly, his wit and smartness in this
discourse is of the finest standard; and his insight into severer learning
will appear as piercing unto such as use not strictly the touchstone and the
test to examine every piece of the glittering coin he payeth his reader with.[1]

While his cautions against swallowing wholesale Browne's religious
assertions are unobjectionable, the modern peruser of Digby's
Observations may agree with Coleridge that they are 'those of a
pedant in his own system and opinion'.[2] A less intellectually re-
doubtable, if livelier, critic was Alexander Ross, who, in his *Medicus
Medicatus: or the physician's religion cured by a lenitive or gentle*

[1] Sir Kenelm Digby, *Observations upon Religio Medici* (London, 1643), pp. 75,
77.
[2] S. T. Coleridge, *Literary Remains* (London, 1836), i.242.

potion (1645), after claiming that he wrote 'with as great modesty and gentleness as I could', launches into pugnacious doctrinal argument with a wrong-headed vivacity which would be amusing if not sustained for so long. His scepticism regarding Browne's belief (i.46) in the resurrection of a plant from its ashes shows a common sense rare in this farrago of abuse and Puritan dogma. The achievement of the frantic schoolmaster from Southampton has been well summed up by a recent writer: 'His diatribes against Bacon, Hobbes, Galileo, and William Harvey, to name only his most notable targets, have won him a place in English thought and letters that most men would gladly exchange for oblivion.'[1]

From Browne's assertions in i.41 and ii.11 that he was about thirty years old at the time of writing, we may assume that *Religio Medici* was substantially completed in 1635. In 1637 he moved from a place in the country, perhaps in Oxfordshire or Yorkshire, to Norwich, where he settled for the rest of his life. Here he built up a busy and prosperous practice, numbering among his patients many of the gentry of the surrounding county. In 1641 he married into one such family, the Milehams of Burlingham. His affluence and established residence (the transport of a collection containing many folio volumes is not lightly to be undertaken) enabled him to build up in ten years or so the substantial scholarly library which provided the materials for his longest work, *Pseudodoxia Epidemica or Enquiries into very many Received Tenents and Commonly Presumed Truths*. First published in 1646, it was revised and expanded in successive editions up to the sixth in 1672. In it Browne took up a suggestion by Bacon in his *Advancement of Learning* that there should be compiled a list of the erroneous beliefs held at that time in the fields of the natural sciences and general knowledge. Browne went further, and, by combining in his disquisition on each topic the testimonies of authority, reason, and experiment, endeavoured to dispose once for all of some hundreds of fallacies. The work, executed with wide learning, wit, and characteristic style, immediately established his reputation as a savant, remaining popular at home and abroad for at least a century. It has been a matter for remark that, for all his renown among such men as Evelyn and Boyle, Browne was never elected to a Fellowship of the Royal Society, although he corresponded with it. The reason is probably to be found in his living and working in Norwich: regular attendance at its meetings in London was at that time a condition of membership.

[1] L. I. Nathanson, *The Strategy of Truth* (Chicago, Ill., 1967), p. 75.

Though the attacks on *Religio Medici* by extremists did not deter
Browne from his vocation as an author, in his preface to *Pseudodoxia*
he disclaims controversy for its own sake. His next publication, in
1658, was far less controversial than an attack on ubiquitous error,
or a plea for religious tolerance. Dedicated to two of his friends
among the Norfolk gentry, *Hydriotaphia* is the leisurely excursion of
a scholarly mind into the burial customs of past nations, and *The
Garden of Cyrus* a pursuit of number and form through art, nature,
and philosophy. The two pieces are not devoid of deeper meaning,
nor are they presented together by chance: the first is predominantly
a meditation on death, the second on life. As in *The Winter's Tale*,
there are things dying and things new-born, with the emphasis—by
positioning—on the hope to be vested in the latter against the
former's heavy message.

Hydriotaphia has been considered by George Williamson as a
dissertation on human identity and the quest for its immortal reten-
tion. Its sections develop from the initial ease of identifying the
purpose of the relics discussed, through a consideration of their
failure to achieve this purpose—in that it is difficult to date such
relics, let alone put a name to them—to the orthodox Christian con-
solation of expected resurrection, and the vanity by contrast of all
earthly monuments.[1]

The movement of thought in *The Garden of Cyrus* is not so simply
charted: the title-page promises a systematic treatise, that the
quincunx is to be 'artificially, naturally, mystically considered', but
within the broad classes of artefacts, plants and animals, and philo-
sophical ideas, Browne intertwines many heterogeneous observations. The general progression, however, as in *Hydriotaphia*, is from
the concrete to the abstract, the last section, as it draws to a close,
proliferating in abstruse queries which express the boundlessly
questing life of Browne's mind, while acknowledging at the end the
limiting humanity of his body, oppressed by the call of sleep.

Far more than *Religio Medici*, these two works show us Browne
the scholar, working up notes from his library and from his walks
in Norfolk. Some of his former favourites among the classics—
Tacitus, Suetonius, Cicero, Horace, Lucian and Josephus—reappear
noticeably in *Hydriotaphia*, while others, such as Homer, Plutarch,
Pliny and Plato, are much more prominent than before. As befits the
subject Browne draws on additional historians, such as Dio Cassius,
Caesar and the *Augustan History*. Amongst modern writers, Dante

[1] G. Williamson, *Milton and Others* (London, 1965), pp. 180–91.

enriches Browne's theme, while factual materials (and many classical citations) derive from such antiquaries as Kirchmann on the Continent and Camden at home. Homer, Plutarch and Plato appear often in *The Garden of Cyrus* too; here Browne draws for specialist information on the writings on medicine, botany, horticulture and mathematics of Hippocrates, Theophrastus and Varro, among the ancients, and the moderns Curtius, J. C. Scaliger, Blancanus and J. Bauhin.

Nevertheless, these two long essays are not now read (if they ever were) as learned treatises. Rather, as Sir Edmund Gosse says, the writer of *Hydriotaphia* is for us 'the laureate of the forgotten dead', with whom 'we may take refuge from the sad pressure of infinity in speculation'.[1] His achievement is thus characterized by E. S. Merton:

The art of the *Urn Burial* is a variation on the themes of his learning and science. Here we are enveloped in the atmosphere of a Pharaoh's tomb, rather than that of a morgue; the *Urn Burial* cherishes fossils and retails the post mortem of mummies. Death reverberates in the corridors of history and eternity. The temporal themes of human living and dying are magnified in the grander themes of geological and ancient history, of the world's decay and reincarnation. The subject of the *Urn Burial* is death, its dimension is time, and its articulation is music.[2]

Likewise, *The Garden of Cyrus* is no horticultural handbook: rather, its pentatonic groves and thickets are a musical score transposed into verbal imagery, a reading of 'that universal and public manuscript' of the great Platonic Idea, of 'that harmony which intellectually sounds in the ears of God'.

It is the medium as much as the message that we enjoy now in these two works. The style has changed from that of *Religio Medici*: the meditative voice of a private study is succeeded by the rhetoric of a lecture in a great library. It is still far, however, from being the oratory of the platform. The observation that 'Man is a noble animal, splendid in ashes and pompous in the grave', is more thoughtful in tone as well as in content than Raleigh's dramatic apostrophe in the preface to his *History of the World*, 'O eloquent, just, and mighty Death!' The rhythms of Browne's prose are always those rather of the Bible than of the pulpit. His diction, for all its adoptions and adaptations from Latin and French, is substantially everyday language, heightened to a rich strangeness by the juxtaposition of

[1] Sir Edmund Gosse, *Sir Thomas Browne* (London, 1905), pp. 205–6.
[2] E. S. Merton, *Science and Imagination in Sir Thomas Browne* (New York, 1949), pp. 129–30.

choice coinages and learned polysyllables. Rhythm and diction together express unforgettably the personality of an especially learned, sensitive and musical writer in a magnificent era of English prose.

Browne's other considerable works were all published posthumously. They include his *Miscellany Tracts* (1683), on biblical, scientific, archaeological, historical and classical topics; *A Letter to a Friend upon Occasion of the Death of his Intimate Friend* (1690); and *Christian Morals* (1716). The *Letter* shows something of Browne's characteristic inventiveness and harmony. *Christian Morals* is frankly didactic, recalling in substance and mode the Book of Proverbs. It was edited in 1756 with a biography of Browne by Dr. Johnson, perhaps the most distinguished member of that company of Browne's admirers whose list runs from John Evelyn and Robert Boyle in the seventeenth century through Lamb and Coleridge, Hazlitt and Southey, Pater and Lytton Strachey, to innumerable scholars and common readers today.

Chronological Table

1605 Born the son of a gentleman mercer in the parish of St. Michael in Cheapside, in London, on 19 October.

1616 Scholar of Winchester College.

1623 Entered Broadgates Hall (Pembroke College), Oxford.

1626 Bachelor of Arts, Oxford.

1629 Master of Arts, Oxford.

1633 Doctor of Medicine, Leiden, after studying also at Montpellier and Padua.

1637 Doctor of Medicine, Oxford. Settled at Norwich.

1641 Married Dorothy Mileham.

1642 Two unauthorized editions of *Religio Medici*.

1643 First authorized edition of *Religio Medici*.

1646 First edition of *Pseudodoxia Epidemica* (revised editions in 1650, 1658, 1672).

1658 *Hydriotaphia* and *The Garden of Cyrus*.

1664 Honorary Fellow of the Royal College of Physicians.

1671 Knighted by Charles II in Norwich.

1682 Died on 19 October.

Note on the Text

This edition follows the text given by Professor L. C. Martin (Oxford, 1964). For *Religio Medici* he used the authorized edition of 1643, emended from the editions of 1642 and from the eight surviving manuscripts listed by him on p. xii; the present editor has adopted from the manuscripts and from editions before and after 1643 a further twenty-three readings (as given in Professor Martin's textual notes, and in the apparatuses of the editions by J.-J. Denonain and Vittoria Sanna) which give clearer grammar, logic, or meaning. Professor Martin's text of *Hydriotaphia* and *The Garden of Cyrus* follows that of the first edition of 1658, incorporating the authorial corrections found in some copies by Mr. John Carter. A few errors of transcription from the texts of 1643 and 1658 have here been corrected. All substantive departures from Professor Martin's text are recorded in the textual notes below, p. 196.

Most of Browne's own sidenotes are reproduced among the footnotes of the present edition, distinguished by the initial B. Where they have been adapted or expanded this is italicized thus: *B.*

The modernization of the spelling has stopped short (where practicable) of affecting the sound of the prose by reducing syllables or altering vowels. The punctuation attempts to facilitate fluent reading, and to elucidate Browne's sometimes densely or tortuously expressed meaning.

Reading List

1. *Early Editions:*

Religio Medici. London, 1642 (twice), 1643, 1645 (twice), 1656, 1659 (twice), 1669, 1672, 1678, 1682.

Hydriotaphia and *The Garden of Cyrus.* London, 1658 (twice), 1659, 1669.

The Works of the Learned Sir Thomas Brown. London, 1685–6.

2. *Major Modern Editions:*

Sir Thomas Browne's Works, ed. Simon Wilkin. London and Norwich, 1835–6.

Religio Medici, A Letter to a Friend, and *Christian Morals,* ed. W. A. Greenhill. London, 1881.

Religio Medici, ed. from the manuscript copies and early editions by J.-J. Denonain. Cambridge, 1953.

Religio Medici, ed. Vittoria Sanna. Cagliari, 1958.

Une Version primitive de Religio Medici, ed. J.-J. Denonain. Algiers, 1958.

Hydriotaphia and *The Garden of Cyrus,* ed. W. A. Greenhill. London, 1896.

Urne Buriall and *The Garden of Cyrus,* ed. John Carter. London, 1932; revised ed. Cambridge, 1958.

The Works of Sir Thomas Browne, ed. Geoffrey Keynes. 2nd ed. London, 1964.

Religio Medici and Other Works, ed. L. C. Martin. Oxford, 1964.

3. *Important Books:*

JOHNSON, SAMUEL, *Life of Sir Thomas Browne,* with Wilkin's 'Supplementary Memoir', in Browne's *Works,* ed. Wilkin (1836), I.xvii–cx.

BAKER, HERSCHEL, *The Wars of Truth.* Cambridge, Mass., 1952.

BENNETT, JOAN, *Sir Thomas Browne.* Cambridge, 1962.

BREDVOLD, LOUIS I., *The Intellectual Milieu of John Dryden.* Ann Arbor, Mich., 1934.

GOSSE, EDMUND, *Sir Thomas Browne.* London, 1905.

KEYNES, GEOFFREY, *A Bibliography of Sir Thomas Browne.* 2nd ed. Oxford, 1968.

LEROY, OLIVIER, *Le Chevalier Thomas Browne.* Paris, 1931.

MERTON, E. S., *Science and Imagination in Sir Thomas Browne.* New York, 1949.

NATHANSON, L. I., *The Strategy of Truth.* Chicago, Ill., 1967.

WILEY, MARGARET L., *The Subtle Knot.* London, 1952.

WILLIAMSON, GEORGE, *The Senecan Amble.* London, 1951.

—— *Seventeenth Century Contexts.* London, 1960.

WILSON, F. P., *Seventeenth Century Prose.* Cambridge, 1960.

4. *Important Articles:*

BENNETT, JOAN, '*Religio Medici* and some of its Critics', *Studies in the Renaissance,* 3 (1956), 175–84.

CROLL, MORRIS W., '"Attic Prose" in the Seventeenth Century', *SP*, 18 (1921), 79–128.

—— 'The Baroque Style in Prose', in *Studies in Honor of Frederick Klaeber*. Minneapolis, Minn., 1929, pp. 427 ff.

ENDICOTT, N. J., 'Some Aspects of Self-Revelation', in *Essays Presented to A. S. P. Woodhouse*. Toronto, 1964, pp. 85–102.

HOWELL, A. C., 'Sir Thomas Browne as Wit and Humorist', *SP*, 42 (1945), 564–77.

MERTON, E. S., 'The Botany of Sir Thomas Browne', *Isis*, 47 (1956), 161–71.

MORGAN, EDWIN, 'Reflections on the Prose of Browne and Johnson', *Cambridge Journal*, 4 (1951), 481–91.

WHALLON, WILLIAM, 'Hebraic Synonymy in Sir Thomas Browne', *ELH*, 28 (1961), 335–52.

Religio Medici

To the Reader

Certainly that man were greedy of life who should desire to live when all the world were at an end, and he must needs be very impatient who would repine at death in the society of all things that suffer under it. Had not almost every man suffered by the press, or were not the tyranny thereof become universal, I had not wanted reason for complaint; but in times wherein I have lived to behold the highest perversion of that excellent invention—the name of His Majesty defamed; the honour of Parliament depraved; the writings of both depravedly, anticipatively, counterfeitly imprinted[n]—complaints may seem ridiculous in private persons, and men of my condition may be as incapable of affronts as hopeless of their reparations. And truly, had not the duty I owe unto the importunity of friends and the allegiance I must ever acknowledge unto truth prevailed with me, the inactivity of my disposition might have made these sufferings continual; and time, that brings other things to light, should have satisfied me in the remedy of its oblivion. But because things evidently false are not only printed, but many things of truth most falsely set forth, in this latter I could not but think myself engaged; for though we have no power to redress the former, yet in the other, the reparation being within ourselves, I have at present represented unto the world a full and intended copy of that piece which was most imperfectly and surreptitiously published before.

This I confess, about seven years past, with some others of affinity thereto, for my private exercise and satisfaction I had at leisurable hours composed; which being communicated unto one, it became common unto many, and was by transcription successively corrupted until it arrived in a most depraved copy at the press. He that shall peruse that work, and shall take notice of sundry particularities and personal expressions therein, will easily discern the intention was not public; and being a private exercise directed to myself, what is delivered therein was rather a memorial unto me than an example or rule unto any other: and therefore if there be any singularity therein correspondent unto the private conceptions of any man, it doth not

that man were greedy: Seneca, *Thyestes*, 883–4.
leisurable hours: leisure time.

throws them. It was penned in such a place, and with such disadvantage, that, I protest, from the first setting of pen unto paper, I had
not the assistance of any good book whereby to promote my invention or relieve my memory; and therefore there might be many
real lapses therein which others might take notice of, and more that I
suspected myself. It was set down many years past, and was the sense
of my conceptions at that time, not an immutable law unto my ad-
vancing judgement at all times; and therefore there might be many
things therein plausible unto my past apprehension which are not
agreeable unto my present self. There are many things delivered
rhetorically, many expressions therein merely tropical and as they
best illustrate my intention; and therefore, also, there are many
things to be taken in a soft and flexible sense, and not to be called
unto the rigid test of reason. Lastly, all that is contained therein is in
submission unto maturer discernments, and, as I have declared, shall
no further father them than the best and learned judgements shall
authorize them; under favour of which considerations I have made
its secrecy public, and committed the truth thereof to every ingenuous
reader.

THOMAS BROWNE

dissentaneous: contrary.   *discernments*: minds.
ingenuous: generous, liberal.

The First Part

SECT. 1

For my religion, though there be several circumstances that might persuade the world I have none at all, as the general scandal of my profession, the natural course of my studies, the indifference of my behaviour and discourse in matters of religion (neither violently defending one, nor, with that common ardour and contention, opposing another); yet, in despite hereof, I dare without usurpation assume the honourable style of a Christian. Not that I merely owe this title to the font, my education, or clime wherein I was born, as being bred up either to confirm those principles my parents instilled into my unwary understanding, or by a general consent proceed in the religion of my country; but having, in my riper years and confirmed judgement, seen and examined all, I find myself obliged by the principles of grace and the law of mine own reason to embrace no other name but this. Neither doth herein my zeal so far make me forget the general charity I owe unto humanity as rather to hate than pity Turks, infidels, and (what is worse) Jews; rather contenting myself to enjoy that happy style than maligning those who refuse so glorious a title.

SECT. 2

But because the name of a Christian is become too general to express our faith—there being a geography of religions as well as lands, and every clime distinguished not only by their laws and limits, but circumscribed by their doctrines and rules of faith—to be particular, I am of that reformed, new-cast religion wherein I dislike nothing but the name: of the same belief our Saviour taught, the Apostles disseminated, the Fathers authorized, and the Martyrs confirmed; but by the sinister ends of princes, the ambition and avarice of prelates, and the fatal corruption of times, so decayed, impaired, and fallen from its native beauty, that it required the careful and charitable hand of these times to restore it to its primitive integrity. Now the accidental occasion whereon, the slender means whereby, the low and abject condition of the person by whom so good a work was

scandal of my profession: It was a vulgar proverb that two out of three physicians were atheists.
natural: scientific.   *indifferency*: impartiality.
the name: Protestant.   *abject condition*: Luther was a miner's son.

set on foot, which in our adversaries begets contempt and scorn, fills
me with wonder, and is the very same objection the insolent pagans
first cast at Christ and his disciples.

SECT. 3

Yet have I not so shaken hands with those desperate resolutions
who had rather venture at large their decayed bottom than bring her in
to be new trimmed in the dock—who had rather promiscuously retain
all than abridge any, and obstinately be what they are than what they
have been—as to stand in diameter and sword's-point with them: we
have reformed from them, not against them; for, omitting those improperations and terms of scurrility betwixt us—which only difference
our affections, and not our cause—there is between us one common
name and appellation, one faith and necessary body of principles
common to us both; and therefore I am not scrupulous to converse
and live with them, to enter their churches in defect of ours, and
either pray with them, or for them. I could never perceive any
rational consequence from those many texts which prohibit the
children of Israel to pollute themselves with the temples of the
heathens, we being all Christians, and not divided by such detested
impieties as might profane our prayers, or the place wherein we
make them; or that a resolved conscience may not adore her Creator
anywhere—especially in places devoted to his service, where, if their
devotions offend him, mine may please him; if theirs profane it, mine
may hallow it: holy water and crucifix (dangerous to the common
people) deceive not my judgement, nor abuse my devotion at all.

I am, I confess, naturally inclined to that which misguided zeal
terms superstition: my common conversation I do acknowledge
austere, my behaviour full of rigour, sometimes not without morosity;
yet at my devotion I love to use the civility of my knee, my hat, and
hand, with all those outward and sensible motions which may express
or promote my invisible devotion. I should violate my own arm
rather than a church window, nor willingly deface the memory of
saint or martyr. At the sight of a cross or crucifix I can dispense
with my hat, but scarce with the thought or memory of my Saviour. I
cannot laugh at, but rather pity the fruitless journeys of pilgrims; or
contemn the miserable condition of friars: for, though misplaced in
circumstance, there is something in it of devotion. I could never hear

resolutions: resolute people.
improperations: taunts.
memory: memorial.

the Ave Mary bell without an elevation; or think it a sufficient
warrant, because they erred in one circumstance, for me to err in all—
that is, in silence and dumb contempt: whilst, therefore, they directed
their devotions to her, I offered mine to God, and rectified the errors
of their prayers by rightly ordering mine own. At a solemn procession
I have wept abundantly while my consorts, blind with opposition and
prejudice, have fallen into an access of scorn and laughter. There are,
questionless, both in Greek, Roman, and African Churches, solemnities and ceremonies whereof the wiser zeals do make a Christian use;
and stand condemned by us, not as evil in themselves, but as allure-
ments and baits of superstition to those vulgar heads that look a-
squint on the face of truth, and those unstable judgements that cannot consist in the narrow point and centre of virtue without a reel
or stagger to the circumference.

SECT. 4

As there were many reformers, so likewise many reformations, every
country proceeding in a particular way and method, according as
their national interest, together with their constitution and clime,
inclined them: some angrily and with extremity; others calmly and
with mediocrity, not rending, but easily dividing the community, and
leaving an honest possibility of a reconciliation—which though
peaceable spirits do desire, and may conceive that revolution of
time, and the mercies of God may effect; yet that judgement that
shall consider the present antipathies between the two extremes,
their contrarieties in condition, affection and opinion, may with the
same hopes expect an union in the poles of heaven.

SECT. 5

But to difference myself nearer, and draw into a lesser circle: there
is no Church whose every part so squares unto my conscience,
whose articles, constitutions, and customs seem so consonant unto
reason, and as it were framed to my particular devotion, as this
whereof I hold my belief, the Church of England; to whose faith I am
a sworn subject, and therefore in a double obligation subscribe unto
her Articles, and endeavour to observe her constitutions. Whatsoever
is beyond, as points indifferent, I observe according to the rules of
my private reason, or the humour and fashion of my devotion—

Ave Mary bell: a church bell that tolls every day at six and twelve of the clock, at
    the hearing whereof everyone, in what place soever either of house or street,
    betakes him to his prayer, which is commonly directed to the Virgin.—B.
elevation: of the host.

neither believing this, because Luther affirmed it, or disproving that, because Calvin hath disavouched it; I condemn not all things in the Council of Trent, nor approve all in the Synod of Dort. In brief, where the Scripture is silent, the Church is my text; where that speaks, 'tis but my comment; where there is a joint silence of both, I borrow not the rules of my religion from Rome or Geneva, but the dictates of my own reason.

It is an unjust scandal of our adversaries, and a gross error in ourselves, to compute the nativity of our religion from Henry the Eighth; who, though he rejected the Pope, refused not the faith of Rome, and effected no more than what his own predecessors desired and assayed in ages past, and was conceived the State of Venice would have attempted in our days. It is as uncharitable a point in us to fall upon those popular scurrilities and opprobrious scoffs of the Bishop of Rome, to whom, as a temporal prince, we owe the duty of good language. I confess there is cause of passion between us—by his sentence I stand excommunicated; heretic is the best language he affords me—yet can no ear witness I ever returned to him the name of Antichrist, Man of Sin, or Whore of Babylon: it is the method of charity to suffer without reaction. Those usual satires and invectives of the pulpit may, perchance, produce a good effect on the vulgar, whose ears are opener to rhetoric than logic; yet do they in no wise confirm the faith of wiser believers, who know that a good cause needs not to be patroned by a passion, but can sustain itself upon a temperate dispute.

SECT. 6

I could never divide myself from any man upon the difference of an opinion, or be angry with his judgement for not agreeing with me in that from which, perhaps, within a few days, I should dissent myself. I have no genius to disputes in religion, and have often thought it wisdom to decline them—especially upon a disadvantage, or when the cause of truth might suffer in the weakness of my patronage. Where we desire to be informed, 'tis good to contest with men above ourselves; but to confirm and establish our opinions, 'tis best to argue with judgements below our own, that the frequent spoils and vic-

---

disproving: disapproving of.
disavouched: disavowed, repudiated.
Council of Trent: which, between 1545 and 1563, defined the doctrines of the
   Counter-Reformation.
Synod of Dort: a Calvinist counterpart (1618–19) of the above.
State of Venice: In 1606 Pope Paul V excommunicated the entire Venetian Re-
   public for its repudiation of papal authority.

tories over their reasons may settle in ourselves an esteem and confirmed opinion of our own. Every man is not a proper champion for truth, nor fit to take up the gauntlet in the cause of verity. Many, from the ignorance of these maxims, and an inconsiderate zeal unto truth, have too rashly charged the troops of error, and remain as trophies unto the enemies of truth. A man may be in as just possession of truth as of a city, and yet be forced to surrender; 'tis therefore far better to enjoy her with peace than to hazard her on a battle. If, therefore, there rise any doubts in my way, I do forget them, or at least defer them till my better settled judgement and more manly reason be able to resolve them; for I perceive every man's own reason is his best Oedipus, and will, upon a reasonable truce, find a way to loose those bonds wherewith the subtleties of error have enchained our more flexible and tender judgements.

In philosophy, where truth seems double-faced, there is no man more paradoxical than myself; but in divinity I love to keep the road, and though not in an implicit, yet an humble faith follow the great wheel of the Church, by which I move, not reserving any proper poles or motion from the epicycle of my own brain. By this means I leave no gap for heresies, schisms, or errors, of which at present (I hope I shall not injure truth to say), I have no taint or tincture. I must confess, my greener studies have been polluted with two or three—not any begotten in the latter centuries, but old and obsolete, such as could never have been revived but by such extravagant and irregular heads as mine. For, indeed, heresies perish not with their authors, but, like the River Arethusa, though they lose their currents in one place, they rise up again in another. One general council is not able to extirpate one single heresy: it may be cancelled for the present; but revolution of time, and the like aspects from heaven, will restore it; when it will flourish till it be condemned again. For as though there were a metempsychosis, and the soul of one man passed into another, opinions do find, after certain revolutions, men and minds like those that first begat them. To see ourselves again, we need not look for Plato's year; every man is not only himself; there have been many Diogenes, and as many Timons, though but few of that name; men

---

Oedipus: who saved the Thebans from the devouring Sphinx by solving its riddle.
extravagant: wandering.
Arethusa: a mythical river which passed from Arcadia under the Adriatic to rise again in Sicily. (Ovid, *Metamorphoses*, 5.639–40.)
Plato's year: a revolution of certain thousand years when all things should return unto their former estate, and he be teaching again in his school as when he delivered this opinion (*Timaeus*, 39).—*B*.
Diogenes: cynics.   *Timons*: misanthropists.

are lived over again; the world is now as it was in ages past—there was none then, but there hath been someone since that parallels him, and is, as it were, his revived self.

SECT. 7

Now the first of mine was that of the Arabians, that the souls of men perished with their bodies, but should yet be raised again at the last day; not that I did absolutely conceive a mortality of the soul, but if that were which faith, not philosophy, hath yet thoroughly disproved, and that both entered the grave together, yet I held the same conceit thereof that we all do of the body, that it should rise again. Surely it is but the merits of our unworthy natures if we sleep in darkness until the last alarum: a serious reflex upon my own unworthiness did make me backward from challenging this prerogative of my soul; so I might enjoy my Saviour at the last, I could with patience be nothing almost unto eternity. The second was that of Origen, that God would not persist in his vengeance for ever, but after a definite time of his wrath he would release the damned souls from torture; which error I fell into upon a serious contemplation of the great attribute of God his mercy; and did a little cherish it in myself, because I found therein no malice, and a ready weight to sway me from the other extreme of despair, whereunto melancholy and contemplative natures are too easily disposed. A third there is which I did never positively maintain or practise, but have often wished it had been consonant to truth, and not offensive to my religion, and that is the prayer for the dead; whereunto I was inclined from some charitable inducements, whereby I could scarce contain my prayers for a friend at the ringing of a bell, or behold his corpse without an orison for his soul. 'Twas a good way, methought, to be remembered by posterity, and far more noble than an history.

These opinions I never maintained with pertinacity, or endeavoured to inveigle any man's belief unto mine; nor so much as ever revealed or disputed them with my dearest friends; by which means I neither propagated them in others, nor confirmed them in myself, but suffering them to flame upon their own substance, without addition of new fuel, they went out insensibly of themselves. Therefore, these opinions, though condemned by lawful councils, were not heresies in me, but bare errors and single lapses of my understanding, without a joint depravity of my will. Those have not only depraved understandings but diseased affections, which cannot enjoy a singularity without

Origen: Alexandrian religious writer of the third century A.D.

a heresy, or be the author of an opinion without they be of a sect also: this was the villainy of the first schism of Lucifer, who was not content to err alone, but drew into his faction many legions of spirits; and upon this experience he tempted only Eve, as well understanding the communicable nature of sin, and that to deceive but one, was tacitly and upon consequence to delude them both.

SECT. 8

That heresies should arise, we have the prophecy of Christ; but that old ones should be abolished, we hold no prediction. That there must be heresies is true, not only in our Church, but also in any other: even in doctrines heretical there will be superheresies, and Arians not only divided from their Church, but also among themselves; for heads that are disposed unto schism, and complexionally propense to innovation, are naturally indisposed for a community, nor will ever be confined unto the order or economy of one body; and therefore, when they separate from others, they knit but loosely among themselves; nor contented with a general breach or dichotomy with their Church, do subdivide and mince themselves almost into atoms. 'Tis true that men of singular parts and humours have not been free from singular opinions and conceits in all ages, retaining something not only beside the opinion of his own Church or any other, but also any particular author; which, notwithstanding, a sober judgement may do without offence or heresy, for there is yet, after all the decrees of councils and the niceties of the schools, many things untouched, unimagined, wherein the liberty of an honest reason may play and expatiate with security and far without the circle of an heresy.

SECT. 9

As for those wingy mysteries in divinity, and airy subtleties in religion, which have unhinged the brains of better heads, they never stretched the pia mater of mine. Methinks there be not impossibilities enough in religion for an active faith; the deepest mysteries ours contains have not only been illustrated, but maintained by syllogism and the rule of reason: I love to lose myself in a mystery, to pursue my reason to an *O altitudo*. 'Tis my solitary recreation to pose my apprehension with

---

prophecy of Christ: Matt. 24:11.   *superheresies*: further heresies.
Arians: who, denying the divinity of Christ, split into three principal factions.
complexionally propense: naturally inclined.   *wingy*: soaring.
O altitudo: Rom. 11:33: O the depth of the riches both of the wisdom and the knowledge of God! how unsearchable are his judgements, and his ways past tracing out.

those involved enigmas and riddles of the Trinity, with Incarnation
and Resurrection. I can answer all the objections of Satan and my
rebellious reason with that odd resolution I learned of Tertullian:
Certum est quia impossibile est. I desire to exercise my faith in the
difficultest points, for to credit ordinary and visible objects is not
faith, but persuasion. Some believe the better for seeing Christ his
sepulchre; and when they have seen the Red Sea, doubt not of the
miracle. Now, contrarily, I bless myself and am thankful that I lived
not in the days of miracles; that I never saw Christ, nor his disciples.
I would not have been one of those Israelites that passed the Red
Sea, nor one of Christ's patients on whom he wrought his wonders:
then had my faith been thrust upon me, nor should I enjoy that greater
blessing pronounced to all that believe and saw not. 'Tis an easy and
necessary belief, to credit what our eye and sense hath examined: I
believe he was dead, and buried, and rose again; and desire to see
him in his glory, rather than to contemplate him in his cenotaph or
sepulchre. Nor is this much to believe, as we have reason; we owe
this faith unto history: they only had the advantage of a bold and
noble faith who lived before his coming; who upon obscure prophecies and mystical types could raise a belief, and expect apparent impossibilities.

SECT. 10

'Tis true, there is an edge in all firm belief, and with an easy metaphor
we may say 'the sword of faith'; but in these obscurities I rather use
it in the adjunct the Apostle gives it—a buckler—under which I perceive a wary combatant may lie invulnerable. Since I was of understanding to know we knew nothing, my reason hath been more
pliable to the will of faith: I am now content to understand a mystery
without a rigid definition, in an easy and Platonic description. That
allegorical description of Hermes pleaseth me beyond all the metaphysical definitions of divines. Where I cannot satisfy my reason, I
love to humour my fancy: I had as leif you tell me that *anima est*

Tertullian: *De Carne Christi*, 5: It is certain because impossible.
miracle: Exod. 14:15–29.
believe and saw not: John 20:29.
buckler: Eph. 6:16. The shield of faith.
Platonic: here implying generalized mystical abstraction.
allegorical description: a sphere whose centre is everywhere, circumference nowhere.—*B.*
Hermes: reputed Egyptian author of several mystical writings of varying antiquity.
anima: The soul is the angel of man, is the body of God.

angelus hominis, est corpus Dei, as *entelechia; lux est umbra Dei,* as
actus perspicui.[n] Where there is an obscurity too deep for our reason,
'tis good to sit down with a description, periphrasis, or adumbration;
for by acquainting our reason how unable it is to display the visible
and obvious effects of nature, it becomes more humble and sub-
missive unto the subtleties of faith: and thus I teach my haggard and
unreclaimed reason to stoop unto the lure of faith. I believe there was
already a tree whose fruit our unhappy parents tasted, though, in the
same chapter where God forbids it, 'tis positively said the plants of
the field were not yet grown, for God had not caused it to rain upon
the earth. I believe that the Serpent (if we shall literally understand
it), from his proper form and figure, made his motion on his belly
before the curse. I find the trial of the pucelage and virginity of
women which God ordained the Jews is very fallible. Experience
(and history) informs me that not only many particular women, but
likewise whole nations have escaped the curse of childbirth which
God seems to pronounce upon the whole sex; yet do I believe that
all this is true which, indeed, my reason would persuade me to be
false. And this, I think, is no vulgar part of faith: to believe a thing
not only above, but contrary to reason, and against the arguments of
our proper senses.

SECT. 11

In my solitary and retired imaginations—*Neque enim cum porticus
aut me lectulus accepit, desum mihi*—I remember I am not alone, and
therefore forget not to contemplate him and his attributes who is ever
with me; especially those two mighty ones, his wisdom and eternity.
With the one I recreate, with the other I confound my understanding;
for who can speak of eternity without a solecism, or think thereof
without an ecstasy? Time we may comprehend—'tis but five days
elder than ourselves, and hath the same horoscope with the world—
but to retire so far back as to apprehend a beginning, to give such an
infinite start forward as to conceive an end, in an essence that we

---

entelechia: essence.　　*lux*: Light is the shadow of God.
actus: actual transparency.
plants of the field: Gen. 2:5, 17. Verse 6 removes the difficulty.
Serpent: Gen. 3:14 had sometimes been taken to imply that the Serpent had
　　previously moved with its head and most of its body off the ground.
pucelage: virginity.
God ordained the Jews: Deut. 22:13–21.
curse of childbirth: Gen. 3:16.
Neque enim: Horace, *Satires*, 1.4.133–4: For when the colonnade or my couch
　　entertains me, I do not fail myself.

affirm hath neither the one nor the other—it puts my reason to Saint
Paul's sanctuary. My philosophy dares not say the angels can do it:
God hath not made a creature that can comprehend him—'tis the
privilege of his own nature. 'I am that I am,' was his own definition
unto Moses; and 'twas a short one, to confound mortality that durst
question God, or ask him what he was; indeed, he only is: all others
have and shall be. But in eternity there is no distinction of tenses, and
therefore that terrible term 'predestination'—which hath troubled so
many weak heads to conceive, and the wisest to explain—is, in respect
to God, no prescious determination of our estates to come, but a
definitive blast of his will already fulfilled, and at the instant that he
first decreed it; for to his eternity, which is indivisible and altogether,
the last trump is already sounded, the reprobates in the flame, and the
blessed in Abraham's bosom. Saint Peter speaks modestly when he
saith a thousand years to God are but as one day; for (to speak like a
philosopher) those continued instances of time which flow into
thousand years make not to him one moment; what to us is to come,
to his eternity is present, his whole duration being but one permanent
point, without succession, parts, flux, or division.

SECT. 12

There is no attribute that adds more difficulty to the mystery of the
Trinity, where (though in a relative way of father and son) we must
deny a priority. I wonder how Aristotle could conceive the world
eternal, or how he could make good two eternities. His similitude of a
triangle comprehended in a square doth somewhat illustrate the
trinity of our souls; and that, the triple unity of God: for there is in us
not three, but a trinity of souls, because there is in us, if not three
distinct souls, yet differing faculties, that can and do subsist apart in
different subjects, and yet in us are so united as to make but one soul
and substance. If one soul were so perfect as to inform three distinct
bodies, that were a petty trinity: conceive the distinct number of
three, not divided, nor separated by the intellect, but actually comprehended in its unity, and that is a perfect trinity.

Saint Paul's sanctuary: Rom. 11:33.   *Moses*: Exod. 3:14.
prescious: foreknowing.
blast: mighty creative breath: 2 Sam. 22:16; Ps. 18:15.
Abraham's bosom: heaven: Luke 16:22.
Saint Peter: 2 Pet. 3:8.   *instances*: instants.
Aristotle: *De Caelo*, 1.10–12.
two eternities: the visible world as well as the invisible.
his similitude: *De Anima*, 2.3. Just as the more complex figure of a square implies
   the existence of the simpler triangle, so the sensitive soul implies the vegetative.
trinity: vegetative, sensitive, rational.   *inform*: dwell in.

I have often admired the mystical way of Pythagoras,[n] and the secret magic of numbers: 'Beware of philosophy' is a precept not to be received in too large a sense, for in this mass of nature there is a set of things that carry in their front—though not in capital letters, yet in stenography and short characters[n]—something of divinity, which to wiser reasons serve as luminaries in the abyss of knowledge, and to judicious beliefs as scales and roundles to mount the pinnacles and highest pieces of divinity. The severe schools shall never laugh me out of the philosophy of Hermes that this visible world is but a picture of the invisible, wherein, as in a portrait, things are not truly, but in equivocal shapes, and as they counterfeit some more real substance in that invisible fabric.[n]

SECT. 13

That other attribute wherewith I recreate my devotion is his wisdom, in which I am happy, and for the contemplation of this only, do not repent me that I was bred in the way of study. The advantage I have of the vulgar, with the content and happiness I conceive therein, is an ample recompense for all my endeavours in what part of knowledge soever. Wisdom is his most beauteous attribute; no man can attain unto it, yet Solomon pleased God when he desired it. He is wise because he knows all things, and he knoweth all things because he made them all; but his greatest knowledge is in comprehending that he made not, that is, himself. And this is also the greatest knowledge in man. For this do I honour my own profession, and embrace the counsel even of the Devil himself; had he read such a lecture in paradise as he did at Delphos, we had better known ourselves; nor had we stood in fear to know him.

I know he is wise in all, wonderful in what we conceive, but far more in what we comprehend not, for we behold him but asquint upon reflex or shadow; our understanding is dimmer than Moses' eye —we are ignorant of the backparts, or lower side of his divinity. Therefore, to pry into the maze of his counsels is not only folly in man, but presumption even in angels; like us, they are his servants, not his senators: he holds no council but that mystical one of the Trinity; wherein, though there be three persons, there is but one mind that decrees, without contradiction. Nor needs he any: his actions are not begot with deliberation; his wisdom naturally knows

'*Beware of philosophy*': Col. 2:8.   *scales*: ladders.
roundles: rungs.   *Solomon*: 1 Kings 3:9–10.
Delphos: The motto γνῶθι σεαυτὸν (Know thyself) was inscribed on the temple of the oracle at Delphi.—*B.*
Moses: Exod. 33:23.

what's best; his intellect stands ready-fraught with the superlative and purest ideas of goodness. Consultation and election, which are two motions in us, make but one in him, his actions springing from his power at the first touch of his will.

These are contemplations metaphysical; my humble speculations have another method, and are content to trace and discover those expressions he hath left in his creatures and the obvious effects of nature. There is no danger to profound these mysteries, no *sanctum sanctorum* in philosophy. The world was made to be inhabited by beasts, but studied and contemplated by man: 'tis the debt of our reason we owe unto God, and the homage we pay for not being beasts. Without this, the world is still as though it had not been, or as it was before the sixth day, when as yet there was not a creature that could conceive or say there was a world. The wisdom of God receives small honour from those vulgar heads that rudely stare about, and with a gross rusticity admire his works: those highly magnify him whose judicious enquiry into his acts, and deliberate research into his creatures, return the duty of a devout and learned admiration. Therefore,

> Search while thou wilt, and let thy reason go,
> To ransom truth, even to the abyss below.
> Rally the scattered causes, and that line
> Which nature twists be able to untwine.
> It is thy Maker's will, for unto none
> But unto reason can he e'er be known.
> The devils do know thee, but those damned meteors
> Build not thy glory, but confound thy creatures.
> Teach my endeavours so thy works to read
> That, learning them, in thee I may proceed.
> Give thou my reason that instructive flight
> Whose weary wings may on thy hands still light.
> Teach me to soar aloft, yet ever so,
> When near the sun, to stoop again below.
> Thus shall my humble feathers safely hover,
> And, though near earth, more than the heavens discover.
> And then at last, when homeward I shall drive,
> Rich with the spoils of nature, to my hive,
> There will I sit, like that industrious fly,

sanctum sanctorum: holy of holies. Exod. 26:33–4 (Vulgate version).
owe unto God: Study and contemplation are our duty to God in return for the gift of reason.
near the sun: alluding to the Greek myth of Icarus, who flew so near the sun that it melted the wax which held the feathers of his wings in place.

> Buzzing thy praises, which shall never die
> Till death abrupts them, and succeeding glory
> Bid me go on in a more lasting story.

And this is almost all wherein an humble creature may endeavour to requite and someway to retribute unto his Creator; for if not he that saith Lord, Lord, but he that doth the will of the Father shall be saved—certainly our wills must be our performances, and our intents make out our actions; otherwise our pious labours shall find anxiety in their graves, and our best endeavours not hope but fear a resurrection.

SECT. 14

There is but one first cause and four second causes of all things; some are without efficient, as God; others without matter, as angels; some without form, as the first matter; but every essence, created or uncreated, hath its final cause, and some positive end both of its essence and operation. This is the cause I grope after in the works of nature; on this hangs the providence of God: to raise so beauteous a structure as the world and the creatures thereof was but his art; but their sundry and divided operations, with their predestinated ends, are from the treasury of his wisdom. In the causes, nature, and affections of the eclipse of sun and moon there is most excellent speculation; but to profound farther, and to contemplate a reason why his providence hath so disposed and ordered their motions in that vast circle as to conjoin and obscure each other, is a sweeter piece of reason, and a diviner point of philosophy: therefore—sometimes and in some things—there appears to me as much divinity in Galen his books *De Usu Partium*, as in Suarez' *Metaphysics*. Had Aristotle been as curious in the enquiry of this cause as he was of the other, he had not left behind him an imperfect piece of philosophy, but an absolute tract of divinity.

abrupts them: breaks them off.   *retribute unto*: repay.
Lord, Lord, : Matt. 7:21.
one first cause: contradicting the Manichaean assertion of two, a good and an
   evil.
causes: efficient—the producing agency; formal—the form; material—the substance; final—the purpose.
affections: effects.   *profound*: investigate deeply.
De Usu Partium: C. Galen (129–99), *On the Use of the Parts of the Human Body*.
Suarez' Metaphysics: F. Suarez, *Metaphysicae Disputationes* (1600, etc.), treated
   of a universal natural theology, and of various questions arising out of the
   works of Aristotle.
this cause: the final cause or purpose.
the other: Aristotle's *Metaphysica* very thoroughly discusses first causes.
imperfect: because pre-Christian.

SECT. 15

Natura nihil agit frustra is the only indisputable axiom in philosophy: there are no grotesques in nature, nor any thing framed to fill up empty cantons and unnecessary spaces. In the most imperfect creatures and such as were not preserved in the Ark but, having their seeds and principles in the womb of nature, are everywhere where the power of the sun is—in these is the wisdom of his hand discovered. Out of this rank Solomon chose the object of his admiration— indeed, what reason may not go to school to the wisdom of bees, ants, and spiders? What wise hand teacheth them to do what reason cannot teach us? Ruder heads stand amazed at those prodigious pieces of nature, whales, elephants, dromedaries, and camels;[n] these, I confess, are the colossus and majestic pieces of her hand; but in these narrow engines there is more curious mathematics, and the civility of these little citizens more neatly sets forth the wisdom of their Maker. Who admires not Regiomontanus his fly beyond his eagle, or wonders not more at the operation of two souls[n] in those little bodies, than but one in the trunk of a cedar?

I could never content my contemplation with those general pieces of wonders, the flux and reflux of the sea, the increase of Nile, the conversion of the needle to the north; and have studied to match and parallel those in the more obvious and neglected pieces of nature, which without further travel I can do in the cosmography of myself: we carry with us the wonders we seek without us; there is all Africa and her prodigies in us. We are that bold and adventurous piece of nature which he that studies wisely learns in a compendium what others labour at in a divided piece and endless volume.

SECT. 16

Thus there are two books from whence I collect my divinity: besides that written one of God, another of his servant Nature—that universal and public manuscript that lies expansed unto the eyes of

---

Natura: Aristotle, *Parts of Animals*, 3.1, etc. Nature does nothing in vain.

cantons: corners, portions of space.

power of the sun: referring to the supposed spontaneous generation of insects in decaying matter.

Solomon: Proverbs 6:6–8 (ants; Septuagint adds bees), 30:24–5 (ants), 30:28 (spiders in A.V.).   *civility*: social organization.

Regiomontanus: Johann Müller of Königsberg (1436–76) constructed flying models of a fly in iron and an eagle in wood.

flux and reflux: tides.

increase of Nile: The flood was widely held to occur on precisely the same date each year. See *Pseudodoxia Epidemica*, 6.8.

conversion: turning.   *needle*: in the magnetic compass.

expansed: spread out.

all.[n] Those that never saw him in the one have discovered him in the other: this was the scripture and theology of the heathens. The natural motion of the sun made them more admire him, than its supernatural station did the Children of Israel; the ordinary effects of nature wrought more admiration in them, than in the other all his miracles. Surely the heathens knew better how to join and read these mystical letters than we Christians, who cast a more careless eye on these common hieroglyphics, and disdain to suck divinity from the flowers of nature.

Nor do I so forget God as to adore the name of nature, which I define not with the schools, the principle of motion and rest, but that straight and regular line, that settled and constant course the wisdom of God hath ordained the actions of his creatures, according to their several kinds. To make a revolution every day is the nature of the sun because that necessary course which God hath ordained it, from which it cannot swerve but by a faculty from that voice which first did give it motion.

Now this course of nature God seldom alters or perverts, but, like an excellent artist, hath so contrived his work that with the selfsame instrument, without a new creation, he may effect his obscurest designs. Thus he sweetened the water with a wood; preserved the creatures in the Ark, which the blast of his mouth might have as easily created: for God is like a skilful geometrician, who, when more easily, and with one stroke of his compass, he might describe or divide a right line, had yet rather do this in a circle or longer way, according to the constituted and forelaid principles of his art—yet this rule of his he doth sometimes pervert, to acquaint the world with his prerogative, lest the arrogancy of our reason should question his power, and conclude he could not. And thus I call the effects of nature the works of God, whose hand and instrument she only is; and therefore to ascribe his actions unto her, is to devolve the honour of the principal agent upon the instrument; which if with reason we may do, then let our hammers rise up and boast they have built our houses, and our pens receive the honour of our writings.

I hold there is a general beauty in the works of God, and therefore no deformity in any kind of species or creature whatsoever: I cannot tell by what logic we call a toad, a bear, or an elephant, ugly, they

---

Children of Israel: Josh. 10:12–13.
motion and rest: Aristotle, *Physics*, 2.1.   *wood*: Exod. 15:25.
geometrician: attributed to Plato by Plutarch, *Symposiacs*, 8.2.
forelaid: laid down beforehand.

being created in those outward shapes and figures which best express the actions of their inward forms,[n] and having passed that general visitation of God, who saw that all that he had made was good—that is, conformable to his will, which abhors deformity, and is the rule of order and beauty. There is no deformity but in monstrosity; wherein, notwithstanding, there is a kind of beauty, nature so ingeniously contriving the irregular parts as they become sometimes more remarkable than the principal fabric. To speak yet more narrowly, there was never anything ugly or mis-shapen but the Chaos; wherein, notwithstanding, to speak strictly, there was no deformity, because no form, nor was it yet impregnate by the voice of God. Now nature is not at variance with art, nor art with nature, they being both the servants of his providence. Art is the perfection of nature: were the world now as it was the sixth day, there were yet a Chaos: nature hath made one world, and art another. In brief, all things are artificial, for nature is the art of God.[n]

SECT. 17

This is the ordinary and open way of his providence, which art and industry have in a good part discovered, whose effects we may foretell without an oracle—to foreshow these is not prophecy but prognostication. There is another way, full of meanders and labyrinths, whereof the Devil and spirits have no exact ephemerides; and that is a more particular and obscure method of his providence, directing the operations of individuals and single essences: this we call fortune, that serpentine and crooked line whereby he draws those actions his wisdom intends in a more unknown and secret way.

This cryptic and involved method of his providence have I ever admired; nor can I relate the history of my life, the occurrences of my days, the escapes of dangers, and hits of chance, with a *bezo las manos* to Fortune, or a bare gramercy to my good stars. Abraham might have thought the ram in the thicket came thither by accident; human reason would have said that mere chance conveyed Moses in the Ark to the sight of Pharaoh's daughter; what a labyrinth is there in the story of Joseph, able to convert a Stoic. Surely there are in every man's life certain rubs, doublings and wrenches which pass awhile under the effects of chance, but at the last, well examined, prove the mere hand of God.

---

bezo las manos: salute (lit. I kiss the hands).   *Abraham*: Gen. 22:13.
human: secular.   *Moses*: Exod. 2:5.   *Joseph*: Gen. 37:2–50:26.
convert a Stoic: by showing that inevitable necessity, which must be endured, derives not from blind fate but from God's considered will.

'Twas not dumb chance that, to discover the Fougade or Powder Plot, contrived a miscarriage in the letter. I like the victory of '88 the better for that one occurrence which our enemies imputed to our dishonour and the partiality of fortune, to wit, the tempests and contrariety of winds: King Philip did not detract from the nation when he said he sent his Armada to fight with men, and not to combat with the winds. Where there is a manifest disproportion between the powers and forces of two several agents, upon a maxim of reason we may promise the victory to the superior; but when unexpected accidents slip in, and unthought of occurrences intervene, these must proceed from a power that owes no obedience to those axioms —where, as in the writing upon the wall, we behold the hand, but see not the spring that moves it. The success of that petty province of Holland (of which the Grand Seigneur proudly said that if they should trouble him as they did the Spaniard, he would send his men with shovels and pickaxes, and throw it into the sea) I cannot altogether ascribe to the ingenuity and industry of the people, but to the mercy of God, that hath disposed them to such a thriving genius; and to the will of his providence, that dispenseth her favour to each country in their preordinate season. All cannot be happy at once, for, because the glory of one state depends upon the ruin of another, there is a revolution and vicissitude of their greatness, and they must obey the swing of that wheel, not moved by intelligences,[n] but by the hand of God; whereby all estates arise to their zenith and vertical points, according to their predestinated periods. For the lives, not only of men, but of commonweals and the whole world, run not upon an helix that still enlargeth, but on a circle; where, arriving to their meridian, they decline in obscurity, and fall under the horizon again.

SECT. 18

These must not therefore be named the effects of fortune but in a relative way, and as we term the works of nature. It was the ignorance of man's reason that begat this very name, and by a careless term miscalled the providence of God: for there is no liberty for causes to operate in a loose and straggling way, nor any effect whatsoever but hath its warrant from some universal or superior cause.

Fougade: subterranean charge of gunpowder.
miscarriage: of the plot, not the letter, which was an anonymous warning to Lord Monteagle.   *victory of '88*: defeat of the Spanish Armada.
writing upon the wall: Dan. 5:5, 24.
Holland: After half a century's struggle against Spain, the Netherlands won independence in 1609, though war was renewed in 1622.
Grand Seigneur: Sultan of Turkey.   *preordinate*: foreordained.

'Tis not a ridiculous devotion to say a prayer before a game at tables, for even in sortileges and matters of greatest uncertainty there is a settled and preordered course of effects. 'Tis we that are blind, not Fortune: because our eye is too dim to discover the mystery of her effects, we foolishly paint her blind, and hoodwink the providence of the Almighty.

I cannot justify that contemptible proverb that 'Fools only are fortunate', or that insolent paradox that 'A wise man is out of the reach of fortune'; much less those opprobrious epithets of poets— whore, bawd, and strumpet. 'Tis, I confess, the common fate of men of singular gifts of mind to be destitute of those of fortune; which doth not any way deject the spirit of wiser judgements, who thoroughly understand the justice of this proceeding; and, being enriched with higher donatives, cast a more careless eye on these vulgar parts of felicity. 'Tis a most unjust ambition to desire to engross the mercies of the Almighty, nor to be content with the goods of mind without a possession of those of body or fortune; and 'tis an error worse than heresy to adore these complemental and circumstantial pieces of felicity, and undervalue those perfections and essential points of happiness wherein we resemble our Maker. To wiser desires 'tis satisfaction enough to deserve, though not to enjoy, the favours of fortune; let providence provide for fools. 'Tis not partiality but equity in God, who deals with us but as our natural parents: those that are able of body and mind, he leaves to their deserts; to those of weaker merits he imparts a larger portion, and pieces out the defect of one by the excess of the other. Thus have we no just quarrel with nature for leaving us naked, or to envy the horns, hooves, skins, and furs of other creatures, being provided with reason that can supply them all.

We need not labour with so many arguments to confute judicial astrology, for if there be a truth therein, it doth not injure divinity: if to be born under Mercury disposeth us to be witty, under Jupiter to be wealthy, I do not owe a knee unto these, but unto that merciful hand that hath ordered my indifferent and uncertain nativity unto such benevolous aspects. Those that held that all things were governed by fortune had not erred, had they not persisted there. The Romans that erected a temple to Fortune acknowledged therein—though in a

---

preordered: already arranged.   *judicial*: that estimates the future.
under Mercury: when Mercury, the planet supposed to govern mental activity, is the planet nearest the zenith.
Jupiter: supposed to confer success on merchants and wealth on the poor.
benevolous: auspicious.

blinder way—somewhat of divinity; for in a wise supputation all things begin and end in the Almighty. There is a nearer way to heaven than Homer's chain; an easy logic may conjoin heaven and earth in one argument, and with less than a sorites resolve all things unto God. For though we christen effects by their most sensible and nearest causes, yet is God the true and infallible cause of all; whose concourse, though it be general, yet doth it subdivide itself into the particular actions of everything, and is that spirit by which each singular essence not only subsists, but performs its operations.

SECT. 19

The bad construction and perverse comment on these pair of second causes, or visible hands of God, have perverted the devotion of many unto atheism; who, forgetting the honest advisoes of faith, have listened unto the conspiracy of passion and reason. I have therefore always endeavoured to compose those feuds and angry dissensions between affection, faith, and reason: for there is in our soul a kind of triumvirate, or triple government of three competitors, which distract the peace of this our commonwealth no less than did that other the state of Rome.

As reason is a rebel unto faith, so passion unto reason: as the propositions of faith seem absurd unto reason, so the theorems of reason unto passion, and both unto faith; yet a moderate and peaceable discretion may so state and order the matter that they may be all kings, and yet make but one monarchy—every one exercising his sovereignty and prerogative in a due time and place, according to the restraint and limit of circumstance.

There is, as in philosophy, so in divinity, sturdy doubts and boisterous objections, wherewith the unhappiness of our knowledge too nearly acquainteth us. More of these no man hath known than myself, which I confess I conquered, not in a martial posture, but on my knees. For our endeavours are not only to combat with doubts, but always to dispute with the Devil: the villainy of that spirit takes a hint of infidelity from our studies, and, by demonstrating a naturality in one way, makes us mistrust a miracle in another. Thus, having perused the *Archidoxis*, and read the secret sympathies of things, he would

---

supputation: estimation.
Homer's chain: *Iliad*, 8.18–26. By his golden chain Zeus could hoist all earth and sea, gods and goddesses.   *advisoes*: suggestions.
triumvirate: referring to Octavian, Mark Antony, and Lepidus.
naturality: conformity with natural processes.
Archidoxis: Paracelsus, *Archidoxis Magica*, teaches the making of amulets and signs to cure specific diseases by occult sympathy.

dissuade my belief from the miracle of the brazen serpent; make me
conceit that image worked by sympathy, and was but an Egyptian
trick to cure their diseases without a miracle. Again, having seen
some experiments of bitumen, and having read far more of naphtha,
he whispered to my curiosity the fire of the altar might be natural;
and bid me mistrust a miracle in Elias when he entrenched the altar
round with water: for that inflammable substance yields not easily
unto water, but flames in the arms of its antagonist. And thus would
he inveigle my belief to think the combustion of Sodom might be
natural, and that there was an asphaltic and bituminous nature in
that lake before the fire of Gomorrah. I know that manna is now
plentifully gathered in Calabria, and Josephus tells me in his days
'twas as plentiful in Arabia: the Devil therefore made the query,
'Where was then the miracle in the days of Moses? The Israelites saw
but that in his time, the natives of those countries behold in ours.'
Thus the Devil played at chess with me, and yielding a pawn,
thought to gain a queen of me, taking advantage of my honest endeavours; and whilst I laboured to raise the structure of my reason,
he strived to undermine the edifice of my·faith.

SECT. 20

Neither had these or any other ever such advantage of me as to incline me to any point of infidelity or desperate positions of atheism,
for I have been, these many years, of opinion there was never any.
Those that held religion was the difference of man from beasts have
spoken probably, and proceed upon a principle as inductive as the
other. That doctrine of Epicurus that denied the providence of God[n]
was no atheism, but a magnificent and high-strained conceit of his
majesty, which he deemed too sublime to mind the trivial actions of
those inferior creatures. That fatal necessity of the Stoics is nothing
but the immutable law of his will. Those that heretofore denied the
divinity of the Holy Ghost have been condemned but as heretics, and
those that now deny our Saviour, though more than heretics, are not
so much as atheists; for though they deny two persons in the Trinity,
they hold as we do there is but one God.

brazen serpent: Num. 21:9.   fire of the altar: Lev. 6:13; 2 Macc. 1:19–36.
Elias: Elijah—1 Kgs. 18:35–8.   Gomorrah: Gen. 19:24.
Calabria: The flowering or manna ash tree was established in S. Italy in the six-
    teenth century.
Josephus: Jewish Antiquities, 3.1.6(31).   inductive: persuasive.
Holy Ghost: The fourth-century sect of Pneumatomachians or Macedonians re-
    garded it as merely a superior ministering angel.
deny our Saviour: i.e. the unitarian Socinians.

That villain and secretary of hell that composed that miscreant piece of the three impostors, though divided from all religions and was neither Jew, Turk, nor Christian, was not a positive atheist. I confess every country hath its Machiavel, every age its Lucian, whereof common heads must not hear, nor more advanced judgements too rashly venture on: 'tis the rhetoric of Satan, and may pervert a loose or prejudicate belief.

SECT. 21

I confess I have perused them all, and can discover nothing that may startle a discreet belief; yet are there heads carried off with the wind and breath of such motives. I remember a Doctor in Physic of Italy who could not perfectly believe the immortality of the soul, because Galen seemed to make a doubt thereof. With another I was familiarly acquainted in France, a divine and man of singular parts, that on the same point was so plunged and gravelled with three lines of Seneca that all our antidotes—drawn from both scripture and philosophy—could not expel the poison of his error.

There are a set of heads that can credit the relations of mariners yet question the testimonies of Saint Paul; and peremptorily maintain the traditions of Aelian or Pliny, yet in histories of Scripture raise queries and objections, believing no more than they can parallel in humane authors. I confess there are in Scripture stories that do exceed the fables of poets, and to a captious reader sound like *Gargantua* or *Bevis*—search all the legends of times past and the fabulous conceits of these present, and 'twill be hard to find one that deserves to carry the buckler unto Samson—yet is all this of an easy possibility if we conceive a divine concourse, or an influence but from the little finger of the Almighty.

three impostors: an apparently non-existent work allegedly unmasking Moses, Jesus, and Mohammed.
Machiavel: Machiavelli, famous expounder of political expediency in *The Prince*.
Lucian: Greek satirist (*c*. A.D. 115–*c*. 200) who was sceptical about the existence of deities.
prejudicate: premature, shallowly founded.
Galen: *Quod Animi Mores Temperamenta Sequantur*, 3.
Seneca: *Troades*, 397—After death there is nothing, and death itself is nothing; 401–2—Death is indivisible, destructive of the body, and unsparing of the soul; 378–9—We die completely and no part of us remains.—*B*.
Aelian or Pliny: writers of partly fabulous natural histories.
humane: classical.
Gargantua: the first book of Rabelais's satirical fantasy.
Bevis: *Sir Bevis of Hampton*, a popular medieval romance.
carry the buckler unto: to follow, i.e. resemble closely.
Samson: Judg. 14:5—16:30.

It is impossible that, either in the discourse of man or in the infallible voice of God, to the weakness of our apprehensions there should not appear irregularities, contradictions, and antinomies. Myself could show a catalogue of doubts, never yet imagined nor questioned, as I know, which are not resolved at the first hearing— nor fantastic queries or objections of air. For I cannot hear of atoms in divinity. I can read the history of the pigeon that was sent out of the Ark and returned no more, yet not question how she found out her mate that was left behind. That Lazarus was raised from the dead, yet not demand where in the interim his soul awaited; or raise a law-case whether his heir might lawfully detain his inheritance bequeathed unto him by his death; and he, though restored to life, have no plea or title unto his former possessions. Whether Eve was framed out of the left side of Adam I dispute not, because I stand not yet assured which is the right side of a man, or whether there be any such distinction in nature;[n] that she was edified out of the rib of Adam I believe, yet raise no question who shall arise with that rib at the Resurrection. Whether Adam was an hermaphrodite—as the Rabbins contend upon the letter of the text—because it is contrary to reason there should be an hermaphrodite before there was a woman, or a composition of two natures before there was a second composed. Likewise, whether the world was created in autumn, summer, or the spring; because it was created in them all: for whatsoever sign the sun possesseth, those four seasons are actually existent; it is the nature of this luminary to distinguish the several seasons of the year, all which it makes at one time in the whole earth, and successive in any part thereof.[n] There are a bundle of curiosities, not only in philosophy but in divinity, proposed and discussed by men of most supposed abilities, which indeed are not worthy our vacant hours, much less our serious studies: pieces only fit to be placed in Pantagruel's library, or bound up with Tartaretus *De Modo Cacandi*.

SECT. 22

These are niceties that become not those that peruse so serious a mystery. There are others more generally questioned and called to the bar, yet methinks of an easy and possible truth. 'Tis ridiculous to

history of the pigeon: Gen. 8:12.   *Lazarus*: John 11:44.
side of Adam: Gen. 2:21–2.
letter of the text: Gen. 1:27: Male and female created he them. See *Pseudodoxia Epidemica*, 3.17.
sign: of the zodiac.   *Pantagruel's library*: Rabelais, 2.7.—*B*.
De Modo Cacandi: Rabelais humorously attributes such a treatise, *Of the Way to Shit*, to the fifteenth-century logician and theologian, Pierre Tartaret.

put off or drown the general flood of Noah in that particular inundation of Deucalion: that there was a deluge once seems not to
me so great a miracle as that there is not one always.[n] How all the
kinds of creatures, not only in their own bulks, but with a competency
of food and sustenance, might be preserved in one Ark and within
the extent of three hundred cubits, to a reason that rightly examines
it, will appear very feasible. There is another secret, not contained in
the Scripture, which is more hard to comprehend, and put the
honest Father to the refuge of a miracle; and that is, not only how
the distinct pieces of the world and divided islands should be first
planted by men, but inhabited by tigers, panthers, and bears. How
America abounded with beasts of prey and noxious animals, yet contained not in it that necessary creature a horse, is very strange. By
what passage those, not only birds, but dangerous and unwelcome
beasts came over; how there be creatures there which are not found
in this triple continent—all which must needs be strange unto us that
hold but one Ark, and that the creatures began their progress from the
mountains of Ararat. They who, to salve this, would make the Deluge
particular, proceed upon a principle that I can no way grant; not
only upon the negative of Holy Scriptures, but of mine own reason,
whereby I can make it probable that the world was as well peopled in
the time of Noah as in ours, and fifteen hundred years to people the
world[n] as full a time for them as four thousand years since have been
to us.

   There are other assertions and common tenets drawn from Scripture—and generally believed as Scripture—whereunto, notwithstanding, I would never betray the liberty of my reason. 'Tis a
postulate to me that Methusalem was the longest lived of all the
children of Adam, and no man will be able to prove it, when from
the process of the text I can manifest it may be otherwise.[n] That
Judas perished by hanging himself there is no certainty in Scripture:
though in one place it seems to affirm it, and by a doubtful word hath
given occasion so to translate it, yet in another place, in a more
punctual description, it makes it improbable and seems to overthrow
it.[n] That our fathers, after the Flood, erected the Tower of Babel[n] to

---

inundation of Deucalion: the Greek version of the Mesopotamian myth, parallel in
   derivation to the Hebrew.
three hundred cubits: Gen. 6:14–22.
honest Father: Augustine, *City of God*, 16.7, opined that these transmarine
   migrations of animals might have been effected by angels.
triple continent: Europe, Asia, and Africa.
Ararat: Gen. 8:4.   *Scriptures*: Gen. 7:19–20.
Methusalem: Gen. 5:27.   *Judas*: Matt. 27:5, Acts 1:18.

preserve themselves against a second Deluge, is generally opinioned and believed; yet is there another intention of theirs expressed in Scripture—besides, it is improbable from the circumstance of the place, that is, a plain in the land of Shinar.

These are no points of faith, and therefore may admit a free dispute. There are yet others, and those familiarly concluded from the text, wherein (under favour) I see no consequence. The Church of Rome confidently proves the opinion of tutelary angels from that answer when Peter knocked at the door: "'Tis not he but his angel'—that is, might some say, his messenger, or somebody from him; for so the original signifies, and is as likely to be the doubtful family's meaning. This exposition I once suggested to a young divine that answered upon this point, to which, I remember, the Franciscan opponent replied no more but that it was a new and no authentic interpretation.

SECT. 23

These are but the conclusions and fallible discourses of man upon the word of God; for such I do believe the Holy Scriptures—yet were it of man, I could not choose but say it was the singularest and superlative piece that hath been extant since the Creation. Were I a pagan, I should not refrain the lecture of it; and cannot but commend the judgement of Ptolemy, that thought not his library complete without it.[n] The Alcoran of the Turks (I speak without prejudice) is an ill-composed piece, containing in it vain and ridiculous errors in philosophy—impossibilities, fictions, and vanities beyond laughter,[n] maintained by evident and open sophisms, the policy of ignorance, deposition of universities, and banishment of learning. That hath gotten foot by arms and violence: this without a blow hath disseminated itself through the whole earth.

It is not unremarkable what Philo first observed, that the Law of Moses continued two thousand years without the least alteration; whereas we see the laws of other commonweals do alter with occasions, and even those that pretended their original from some divinity, to have vanished without trace or memory. I believe, besides Zoroaster, there were divers that writ before Moses who, notwith-

opinioned and believed: Josephus, *Jewish Antiquities*, 1.4.2(114).
another intention: Gen. 11:4.
Peter: Acts 12:15.   *family's*: congregation's.
answered: was replying in a formal disputation.
Philo: Philo Judaeus, *Life of Moses*, 2.3(14).
Zoroaster: the Persian magus whom Plutarch, *Isis and Osiris*, notes as reputed to have lived five thousand years before the Trojan War.
before Moses: Augustine, *City of God*, 15.23 mentions the writings dubiously ascribed to Enoch.

standing, have suffered the common fate of time. Men's works have an age like themselves; and though they outlive their authors, yet have they a stint and period to their duration. This only is a work too hard for the teeth of time; and cannot perish but in the general flames, when all things shall confess their ashes.

SECT. 24

I have heard some with deep sighs lament the lost lines of Cicero;[n] others with as many groans deplore the combustion of the Library of Alexandria:[n] for my own part, I think there be too many in the world, and could with patience behold the urn and ashes of the Vatican, could I, with a few others, recover the perished leaves of Solomon. I would not omit a copy of Enoch's pillars, had they many nearer authors than Josephus, or did not relish somewhat of the fable.

Some men have written more than others have spoken: Pineda quotes more authors in one work than are necessary in a whole world. Of those three great inventions in Germany, there are two which are not without their incommodities; and 'tis disputable whether they exceed not their use and commodities. 'Tis not a melancholy *utinam* of mine own, but the desire of better heads, that there were a general synod—not to unite the incompatible differences of religion, but for the benefit of learning: to reduce it as it lay at first, in a few and solid authors; and to condemn to the fire those swarms and millions of rhapsodies begotten only to distract and abuse the weaker judgements of scholars, and to maintain the trade and mystery of typographers.

SECT. 25

I cannot but wonder with what exceptions the Samaritans could confine their belief to the Pentateuch or five books of Moses.[n] I am ashamed at the rabbinical interpretations of the Jews upon the Old Testament, as much as their defection from the New: and truly it is beyond wonder how that contemptible and degenerate issue of Jacob, once so devoted to ethnic superstition, and so easily seduced to the idolatry of their neighbours, should now in such an obstinate and

---

leaves of Solomon: 1 Kgs. 4:32–3; Josephus, *Jewish Antiquities*, 8.2.5(44).
Enoch's pillars: on which the inscriptions were intended to be a disaster-proof record of all inventions up to that time. Josephus, 1.2.3(70–71).
Pineda: J. de Pineda in his *Monarchia Ecclesiastica* quotes one thousand and forty authors.—B.
three great inventions: guns, printing, and the mariner's compass.
utinam: wish.   *rhapsodies*: miscellaneous compilations.
rabbinical interpretations: e.g. the Talmud.   *ethnic*: heathen.

peremptory belief adhere unto their own doctrine, expect impossibilities, and, in the face and eye of the Church, persist without the
least hope of conversion. This is a vice in them that were a virtue in
us, for obstinacy in a bad cause is but constancy in a good. And herein I must accuse those of my own religion, for there is not any of such
a fugitive faith, such an unstable belief, as a Christian; none that do
so oft transform themselves, not unto several shapes of Christianity
and of the same species, but unto more unnatural and contrary
forms of Jew and Mahometan; that from the name of Saviour can
descend to the bare term of prophet; and from an old belief that he is
come, fall to a new expectation of his coming.

It is the promise of Christ to make us all one flock; but how and
when this union shall be, is as obscure to me as the last day. Of those
four members of religion we hold a slender proportion; there are I
confess some new additions, yet small to those which accrue to our
adversaries, and those only drawn from the revolt of pagans—men
but of negative impieties, and such as deny Christ but because they
never heard of him. But the religion of the Jew is expressly against
the Christian, and the Mahometan against both. For the Turk, in the
bulk he now stands he is beyond all hope of conversion; if he fall
asunder there may be conceived hopes, but not without strong im-
probabilities. The Jew is obstinate in all fortunes; the persecution of
fifteen hundred years hath but confirmed them in their error: they
have already endured whatsoever may be inflicted, and have suffered,
in a bad cause, even to the condemnation of their enemies.

Persecution is a bad and indirect way to plant religion: it hath been
the unhappy method of angry devotions not only to confirm honest
religion, but wicked heresies and extravagant opinions. It was the
first stone and basis of our faith: none can more justly boast of
persecutions, and glory in the number and valour of martyrs. For, to
speak properly, those are true and almost only examples of fortitude:
those that are fetched from the field or drawn from the actions of the
camp are not oft-times so truly precedents of valour as audacity, and
at the best attain but to some bastard piece of fortitude. If we shall
strictly examine the circumstances and requisites which Aristotle
requires to true and perfect valour, we shall find the name only in his
master Alexander, and as little in that Roman worthy, Julius Caesar;

promise of Christ: John 10:16.
four members: Pagan, Jewish, Islamic, and Christian.
to the condemnation of: to such an extent as to discredit the cruelty of.
devotions: devotees.   *Aristotle*: *Nicomachean Ethics*, 3.6–9, 2.7.2.
the name only: only the name.

and if any in that easy and active way have done so nobly as to deserve that name, yet in the passive and more terrible piece these have surpassed, and in a more heroical way may claim the honour of that title. 'Tis not in the power of every honest faith to proceed thus far, or pass to heaven through the flames; everyone hath it not in that full measure, nor in so audacious and resolute a temper, as to endure those terrible tests and trials; who, notwithstanding, in a peaceable way do truly adore their Saviour, and have, no doubt, a faith acceptable in the eyes of God.

SECT. 26

Now, as all that die in war are not termed soldiers, so neither can I properly term all those that suffer in matters of religion martyrs. The Council of Constance condemns John Huss for an heretic; the stories of his own party style him a martyr: he must needs offend the divinity of both that says he was neither the one nor the other. There are many, questionless, canonized on earth, that shall never be saints in heaven; and have their names in histories and martyrologies, who in the eyes of God are not so perfect martyrs as was that wise heathen, Socrates, that suffered on a fundamental point of religion —the unity of God.[n] I have often pitied the miserable bishop that suffered in the cause of antipodes, yet cannot choose but accuse him of as much madness—for exposing his living on such a trifle—as those of ignorance and folly that condemned him.[n] I think my conscience will not give me the lie if I say there are not many extant that in a noble way fear the face of death less than myself; yet, from the moral duty I owe to the commandment of God, and the natural respect that I tender unto the conservation of my essence and being, I would not perish upon a ceremony, politic point, or indifferency: nor is my belief of that untractable temper as not to bow at their obstacles, or connive at matters wherein there are not manifest impieties. The leaven, therefore, and ferment of all—not only civil but religious—actions, is wisdom; without which to commit ourselves to the flames is homicide, and, I fear, but to pass through one fire into another.

SECT. 27

That miracles are ceased I can neither prove nor absolutely deny, much less define the time and period of their cessation. That they survived Christ is manifest upon record of Scripture; that they

these have surpassed: i.e. the Christian martyrs.
John Huss: the Bohemian reformer, burnt in 1415.

outlived the Apostles also, and were revived at the conversion of
nations many years after, we cannot deny if we shall not question
those writers whose testimonies we do not controvert in points that
make for our own opinions. Therefore, that may have some truth in it
that is reported by the Jesuits of their miracles in the Indies. I could
wish it were true, or had any other testimony than their own pens:
they may easily believe those miracles abroad who daily conceive a
greater at home—the transmutation of those visible elements into the
body and blood of our Saviour. For the conversion of water into
wine which he wrought in Cana, or, what the Devil would have had
him do in the wilderness, of stones into bread, compared to this,
will scarce deserve the name of a miracle; though, indeed, to speak
properly, there is not one miracle greater than another, they being
the extraordinary effects of the hand of God, to which all things are
of an equal facility, and to create the world as easy as one single
creature. For this is also a miracle, not only to produce effects against
or above nature, but before nature; and to create nature as great a
miracle as to contradict or transcend her.[n]

We do too narrowly define the power of God, restraining it to our
capacities. I hold that God can do all things; how he should work
contradictions I do not understand, yet dare not therefore deny. I
cannot see why the angel of God should question Esdras to recall the
time past if it were beyond his own power; or that God should pose
mortality in that which he was not able to perform himself. I will not
say God cannot, but he will not perform many things which we
plainly affirm he cannot. This, I am sure, is the mannerliest proposition, wherein, notwithstanding, I hold no paradox: for strictly his
power is the same with his will, and they both, with all the rest, do
make but one God.

SECT. 28

Therefore, that miracles have been I do believe; that they may yet be
wrought by the living I do not deny, but have no confidence in those
which are fathered on the dead; and this hath ever made me suspect
the efficacy of relics, to examine the bones, question the habits and
appurtenances of saints, and even of Christ himself. I cannot conceive why the cross that Helena found, and whereon Christ himself

---

transmutation: the Catholic doctrine of the transubstantiation of the bread and
    wine of the mass into the body and blood of Christ.
Cana: John 2:1–10.   *Devil*: Matt. 4:3.
Esdras: 2 Esd. 4:5.   *pose*: puzzle.
Helena: The alleged discovery by the mother of the Emperor Constantine of the
    cross of Christ at Jerusalem gave rise to enough relics to constitute many crosses.

died, should have power to restore others unto life; I excuse not Constantine from a fall off his horse, or a mischief from his enemies, upon the wearing those nails on his bridle which our Saviour bore upon the cross in his hands. I compute among your *piae fraudes* (nor many degrees before consecrated swords and roses) that which Baldwin, King of Jerusalem, returned the Genoese for their cost and pains in his war—to wit, the ashes of John the Baptist.[n] Those that hold the sanctity of their souls doth leave behind a tincture and sacred faculty on their bodies speak naturally of miracles, and do not salve the doubt.

Now one reason I tender so little devotion unto relics is, I think, the slender and doubtful respect I have always held unto antiquities. For that, indeed, which I admire is far before antiquity: that is, eternity, and that is God himself; who, though he be styled the ancient of days, cannot receive the adjunct of antiquity, who was before the world, and shall be after it, yet is not older than it: for in his years there is no climacter—his duration is eternity, and far more venerable than antiquity.

SECT. 29

But above all things I wonder how the curiosity of wiser heads could pass that great and indisputable miracle, the cessation of oracles;[n] and in what swoon their reasons lay, to content themselves and sit down with such far-fetched and ridiculous reasons as Plutarch allegeth for it. The Jews, that can believe the supernatural solstice of the sun in the days of Joshua, have yet the impudence to deny the eclipse (which even pagans confessed) at his death. But, for this, it is evident beyond all contradiction: the Devil himself confessed it. Certainly, it is not a warrantable curiosity to examine the verity of Scripture by the concordance of humane history, or seek to confirm the chronicle of Hester or Daniel by the authority of Megasthenes or Herodotus. I confess I have had an unhappy curiosity this way, till I laughed myself out of it with a piece of Justin where he delivers that

Constantine: who was given the nails by his mother.
piae fraudes: pious frauds.   *Baldwin*: first king of Jerusalem (1100–18).
ancient of days: Dan. 7:9.   *climacter*: critical stage or period.
Plutarch: in *The Cessation of Oracles*.   *Joshua*: Josh. 10:12–13.
his death: Jesus Christ's. Luke 23:44–5.
the Devil himself: in his oracle to Augustus.—B. See *Pseudodoxia Epidemica*, 7.12.
humane: classical.   *Hester*: Esther.
Megasthenes: a Greek historian of *c*. 300 B.C. to whom were attributed (wrongly) fragments of a chronology of Persia.
Herodotus: the first historian of Greece.   *Justin*: Justinus, 36.2.12.

the children of Israel for being scabbed were banished out of Egypt. And truly, since I have understood the occurrences of the world, and know in what counterfeit shapes and deceitful vizards times present represent on the stage things past, I do believe them little more than things to come. Some have been of my opinion, and endeavoured to write the history of their own lives; wherein Moses hath outgone them all, and left not only the story of his life, but—as some will have it—of his death also.

SECT. 30

It is a riddle to me how this story of oracles hath not wormed out of the world that doubtful conceit of spirits and witches—how so many learned heads should so far forget their metaphysics, and destroy the ladder and scale of creatures, as to question the existence of spirits. For my part, I have ever believed (and do now know) that there are witches.[n] They that doubt of these do not only deny them but spirits, and are obliquely and upon consequence a sort, not of infidels, but atheists. Those that to confute their incredulity desire to see apparitions, shall questionless never behold any, nor have the power to be so much as witches: the Devil hath them already in a heresy as capital as witchcraft, and to appear to them were but to convert them.

Of all the delusions wherewith he deceives mortality, there is not any that puzzleth me more than the legerdemain of changelings. I do not credit those transformations of reasonable creatures into beasts, or that the Devil hath a power to transpeciate a man into a horse, who tempted Christ—as a trial of his divinity—to convert but stones into bread. I could believe that spirits use with man the act of carnality, and that in both sexes; I conceive they may assume, steal, or contrive a body wherein there may be action enough to content decrepit lust, or passion to satisfy more active veneries; yet, in both, without a possibility of generation: and therefore that opinion that Antichrist should be born of the Tribe of Dan by conjunction with the Devil is ridiculous, and a conceit fitter for a rabbin than a Christian. I hold that the Devil doth really possess some men, the spirit

---

Moses: Deut. 34:5–8, written prophetically according to Philo Judaeus, *Life of Moses*, 2.291.
doubtful conceit of: sceptical opinion regarding.
scale of creatures: ordered hierarchy of created beings.
transpeciate: transform into another species.
stones into bread: Matt. 4:3.   *veneries*: sexual appetites.
Tribe of Dan: The theory was based on the mention in Gen. 49:17 and omission from Rev. 7:4–8.

of melancholy others, the spirit of delusion others; that as the Devil is concealed and denied by some, so God and good angels are pretended by others—whereof the late detection of the Maid of Germany hath left a pregnant example.

SECT. 31

Again, I believe that all that use sorceries, incantations, and spells, are not witches, or as we term them, magicians: I conceive there is a traditional magic, not learned immediately from the Devil but at second hand from his scholars, who, having once the secret betrayed, are able, and do empirically practise without his advice—they both proceeding upon the principles of nature, where actives aptly conjoined to disposed passives will, under any master, produce their effects. Thus, I think, at first a great part of philosophy was witchcraft, which, being afterward derived to one another, proved but philosophy, and was indeed no more but the honest effects of nature. What invented by us is philosophy, learned from him is magic.

We do surely owe the honour of many secrets to the discovery of good and bad angels. I could never pass that sentence of Paracelsus without an asterisk or annotation: *Ascendens constellatum multa revelat quaerentibus magnalia naturae*, i.e. *opera Dei*. I do think that many mysteries ascribed to our own inventions have been the courteous revelations of Spirits (for those noble essences in heaven bear a friendly regard unto their fellow natures on earth), and therefore believe that those many prodigies and ominous prognostics which forerun the ruins of states, princes, and private persons, are the charitable premonitions of good angels, which more careless enquiries term but the effects of chance and nature.

SECT. 32

Now, besides these particular and divided spirits there may be (for aught I know) an universal and common spirit to the whole world. It was the opinion of Plato, and it is yet of the hermetical philosophers; if there be a common nature that unites and ties the scattered and

---

Maid of Germany: Eva Flegen of Meurs, renowned for alleged abstinence from food for many years.
actives: heat and cold. *passives*: dryness and moisture.
derived: handed down.
Ascendens constellatum: Thereby is meant our good angel appointed us from our nativity.—B. The rising star reveals to those who seek many wonders of nature—a summary of Paracelsus, *Philosophia Sagax*, 1.3 (*Opera*, 1603–5. x.126).
opera Dei: the works of God. *Plato*: *Timaeus*, 30b, 34b.
hermetical philosophers: e.g. Paracelsus, op. cit., 1.1 (x.100).

divided individuals into one species, why may there not be one that
unites them all? However, I am sure there is a common spirit that
plays within us, yet makes no part of us, and that is the spirit of God,
the fire and scintillation of that noble and mighty essence which is the
life and radical heat of spirits and those essences that know not the
virtue of the sun, a fire quite contrary to the fire of hell. This is that
gentle heat that brooded on the waters, and in six days hatched the
world; this is that irradiation that dispels the mists of hell, the
clouds of horror, fear, sorrow, despair; and preserves the region of
the mind in serenity. Whosoever feels not the warm gale and gentle
ventilation of this spirit, though I feel his pulse, I dare not say he
lives; for truly, without this, to me there is no heat under the Tropic,
nor any light, though I dwelt in the body of the sun.

> As, when the labouring sun hath wrought his track
> Up to the top of lofty Cancer's back,
> The icy ocean cracks, the frozen pole
> Thaws with the heat of that celestial coal,
> So when thy absent beams begin to impart
> Again a solstice on my frozen heart,
> My winter's o'er, my drooping spirits sing,
> And every part revives into a spring.
> But if thy quickening beams awhile decline,
> And with their light bless not this orb of mine,
> A chilly frost surpriseth every member,
> And in the midst of June I feel December.
> O how this earthly temper doth debase
> The noble soul in this her humble place!
> Whose wingy nature ever doth aspire
> To reach that place whence first it took its fire.
> These flames I feel which in my heart do dwell
> Are not thy beams, but take their fire from hell:
> O quench them all, and let thy light divine
> Be as the sun to this poor orb of mine.
> And to thy sacred spirit convert those fires
> Whose earthly fumes choke my devout aspires.

SECT. 33

Therefore, for spirits, I am so far from denying their existence that I
could easily believe that not only whole countries but particular
persons have their tutelary and guardian angels. It is not a new

---

those essences: Souls did not need physical heat for their generation.
hatched the world: Gen. 1.   *aspires*: pantings, longings.

opinion of the Church of Rome but an old one of Pythagoras and Plato; there is no heresy in it, and, if not manifestly defined in Scripture, yet is it an opinion of a good and wholesome use in the course and actions of a man's life, and would serve as an hypothesis to salve many doubts whereof common philosophy affordeth no solution. Now if you demand my opinion and metaphysics of their natures, I confess them very shallow—most of them in a negative way, like that of God; or in a comparative, between ourselves and fellow creatures. For there is in this universe a stair or manifest scale of creatures, rising not disorderly, or in confusion, but with a comely method and proportion: between creatures of mere existence and things of life there is a large disproportion of nature; between plants and animals or creatures of sense, a wider difference; between them and man, a far greater; and if the proportion hold on, between man and angels there should be yet a greater.

We do not comprehend their natures, who retain the first definition of Porphyry, and distinguish them from ourselves by immortality: for before his fall man also was immortal; yet must we needs affirm that he had a different essence from the angels. Having, therefore, no certain knowledge of their natures, 'tis no bad method of the schools —whatsoever perfection we find obscurely in ourselves, in a more complete and absolute way to ascribe unto them. I believe they have an extemporary knowledge, and upon the first motion of their reason do what we cannot without study or deliberation; that they know things by their forms, and define by specifical differences what we describe by accidents and properties, and therefore probabilities to us may be demonstrations unto them; that they have knowledge not only of the specifical, but numerical forms of individuals, and understand by what reserved difference each single hypostasis (besides the relation to its species) becomes its numerical self. That as the soul hath a power to move the body it informs, so there's a faculty to move any, though inform none; ours upon restraint of time, place, and distance—but that invisible hand that conveyed Habakkuk to the lions' den, or Philip to Azotus, infringeth this rule, and hath a secret

Pythagoras: Diogenes Laertius, 8.32.   *Plato*: *Phaedo*, 107d.
their natures: i.e. angels'.   *I confess them*: i.e. my opinion and metaphysics.
scale of creatures: see note above, p. 32.
Porphyry: Porphyrius (233–c. 305), *Isagoge*, 3.6.
forms: inner natures.
specifical differences: innate distinctions peculiar to species.
accidents: non-essential, external attributes.   *numerical*: particular.
reserved: peculiar.   *hypostasis*: being, essence, entity, existence.
Habakkuk: Bel & Dr. 36, 39.   *Philip*: Acts 8:39–40.

conveyance wherewith mortality is not acquainted. If they have that intuitive knowledge whereby, as in reflection, they behold the thoughts of one another, I cannot peremptorily deny but they know a great part of ours. They that, to refute the invocation of saints, have denied that they have any knowledge of our affairs below, have proceeded too far, and must pardon my opinion till I can thoroughly answer that piece of Scripture, 'At the conversion of a sinner the angels of heaven rejoice.' I cannot with those in that great Father securely interpret the work of the first day—*Fiat lux*—to the creation of angels; though, I confess, there is not any creature that hath so near a glimpse of their nature as light in the sun and elements: we style it a bare accident, but where it subsists alone 'tis a spiritual substance, and may be an angel—in brief, conceive light invisible, and that is a spirit.

SECT. 34

These are certainly the magisterial and master pieces of the Creator; the flower or—as we may say—the best part of nothing; actually existing what we are but in hopes and probability: we are only that amphibious piece between a corporal and spiritual essence; that middle form that links those two together, and makes good the method of God and nature, that jumps not from extremes, but unites the incompatible distances by some middle and participating natures. That we are the breath and similitude of God, it is indisputable and upon record of Holy Scripture, but to call ourselves a microcosm or little world, I thought it only a pleasant trope of rhetoric till my nearer judgement and second thoughts told me there was a real truth therein: for first, we are a rude mass, and in the rank of creatures which only are, and have a dull kind of being not yet privileged with life or preferred to sense or reason; next, we live the life of plants, the life of animals, the life of men, and at last the life of spirits—running on in one mysterious nature those five kinds of existences which comprehend the creatures, not only of the world, but of the universe.

At the conversion: Luke 15:10.
great Father: Augustine, *City of God*, 11:32, concedes that he would not contend strongly against the opponents of his theory (11.9) that by light was meant angels.
Fiat lux: Let there be light. Gen. 1:3.   *accident*: non-essential quality.
magisterial: displaying the skill of a master.
part of nothing: i.e. part of that creation which was made out of nothing.
existing: embodying.   *we are only*: we alone are.
similitude of God: Gen. 2:7; Job 33:4; Jas. 3:9.
nearer judgement: closer apprehension.   *preferred*: raised.

Thus is man that great and true amphibium whose nature is disposed to live, not only like other creatures in divers elements, but in divided and distinguished worlds; for though there be but one world to sense, there are two to reason: the one visible, the other invisible—whereof Moses seems to have left no description, and of the other so obscurely that some parts thereof are yet in controversy. And truly, for the first chapters of Genesis I must confess a great deal of obscurity; though divines have (to the power of human reason) endeavoured to make all go in a literal meaning, yet those allegorical interpretations are also probable, and perhaps the mystical method of Moses, bred up in the hieroglyphical schools of the Egyptians.

SECT. 35

Now, for that immaterial world, methinks we need not wander so far as the first movable, for even in this material fabric the spirits walk as freely exempt from the affection of time, place, and motion, as beyond the extremest circumference. Do but extract from the corpulency of bodies, or resolve things beyond their first matter, and you discover the habitation of angels; which if I call the ubiquitary and omnipresent essence of God I hope I shall not offend divinity, for, before the creation of the world, God was really all things. For the angels he created no new world or determinate mansion, and therefore they are everywhere where is his essence, and do live at a distance even in himself. That God made all things for man is in some sense true, yet not so far as to subordinate the creation of those purer creatures unto ours, though as ministering spirits they do, and are willing to, fulfil the will of God in these lower and sublunary affairs of man. God made all things for himself, and it is impossible he should make them for any other end than his own glory. It is all he can receive, and all that is without himself, for honour, being an external adjunct, and in the honourer rather than in the person honoured, it was necessary to make a creature from whom he might

amphibium: animal living both on land and in water.
whereof: of which invisible world.
to the power of . . .: so far as . . . is capable.   *Egyptians*: Acts 7:22.
first movable: the outermost sphere in the medieval version of the Ptolemaic
    system of the universe, enclosing the spheres of earth, moon, sun, and planets,
    i.e. all that could be termed mundane.
extract from: deduce (Platonic inner forms) from, go deeper than.
corpulency: physical constitution.
first matter: material cause. See above, p. 15.
ubiquitary: ubiquitous, omnipresent.   *ministering spirits*: Heb. 1:14.
sublunary: beneath the moon, earthly.   *all things for himself*: Prov. 16:4.

receive this homage; and that is in the other world angels, in this, man—which when we neglect, we forget the very end of our creation, and may justly provoke God, not only to repent that he hath made the world, but that he hath sworn he would not destroy it.

That there is but one world is a conclusion of faith. Aristotle with all his philosophy hath not been able to prove it, and as weakly that the world was eternal—that dispute much troubled the pens of the ancient philosophers, but Moses decided that question, and all is salved with the new term of a creation, that is, a production of something out of nothing. And what is that? Whatsoever is opposite to something, or, more exactly, that which is truly contrary unto God; for he only is: all others have an existence with dependency, and are something but by a distinction. And herein is divinity conformant unto philosophy, and generation not only founded on contrarieties, but also creation—God being all things is contrary unto nothing, out of which were made all things; and so nothing became something, and omneity informed nullity into an essence.

SECT. 36

The whole Creation is a mystery, and particularly that of man: at the blast of his mouth were the rest of the creatures made, and at his bare word they started out of nothing; but in the frame of man (as the text describes it) he played the sensible operator, and seemed not so much to create, as make him. When he had separated the materials of other creatures, there consequently resulted a form and soul; but having raised the walls of man, he was driven to a second and harder creation of a substance like himself—an incorruptible and immortal soul.

For these two affections we have the philosophy and opinion of the heathens, the flat affirmative of Plato, and not a negative from Aristotle. There is another scruple cast in by divinity concerning its production, much disputed in the German auditories, and with that

---

to repent: Gen. 6:6.   *he hath sworn*: Gen. 9:11.
Aristotle: *De Caelo*, 1.8–9.   *eternal*: op. cit., 1.10–11.
distinction: qualification.   *generation not only*: not generation alone.
omneity: that which comprises all, i.e. God.
informed: fashioned.   *blast of his mouth*: Gen. 1:3–24.
the text: Gen. 2:7.
two affections: qualities of incorruptibility and immortality.
Plato: *Phaedrus*, 245c; *Phaedo*, 105sqq.
Aristotle: *De Anima*, 2.4, 3.5; *De Generatione Animalium*, 2.3.
auditories: assemblies.

indifferency and equality of arguments as leave the controversy un-
determined.[n] I am not of Paracelsus' mind, that boldly delivers a receipt to make a man without conjunction, yet cannot but wonder at
the multitude of heads that do deny traduction, having no other
argument to confirm their belief than that rhetorical sentence and
antimetathesis of Augustine: *Creando infunditur, infundendo creatur.*
Either opinion will consist well enough with religion; yet I should
rather incline to this, did not one objection haunt me; not wrung
from speculations and subtleties, but from common sense and
observation—not picked from the leaves of any author, but bred
amongst the weeds and tares of mine own brain. And this is a conclusion from the equivocal and monstrous productions in the
copulation of man with beast:[n] for if the soul of man be not transmitted and transfused in the seed of the parents, why are not those
productions merely beasts, but have also an impression and tincture
of reason in as high a measure as it can evidence itself in those improper organs?

Nor, truly, can I peremptorily deny that the soul, in this her sublunary estate, is wholly and in all acceptions inorganical, but that for
the performance of her ordinary actions is required, not only a
symmetry and proper disposition of organs, but a crasis and temper
correspondent to its operations; yet is not this mass of flesh and
visible structure the instrument and proper corpse of the soul, but
rather of sense, and that the hand of reason. In our study of anatomy
there is a mass of mysterious philosophy, and such as reduced the
very heathens to divinity;[n] yet amongst all those rare discoveries
and curious pieces I find in the fabric of man, I do not so much content myself as in that I find not, that is, no organ or instrument for
the rational soul; for in the brain, which we term the seat of reason,
there is not anything of moment more than I can discover in the
crany of a beast—and this is a sensible and no inconsiderable argument of the inorganity of the soul, at least in that sense we usually so

---

Paracelsus: *De Natura Rerum*, 1.
traduction: transmission of souls from parents to children.
antimetathesis: construction in which the terms change places.
Augustine: in fact Petrus Lombardus, *Sententiae*, 2.27.2. In creation it is infused,
    in infusion it is created.
equivocal: double-natured.   *sublunary*: earthly.
inorganical: not residing in or operating through any bodily organ.
crasis: blend, combination of humours or qualities.
that the hand of reason: the soul the agent of reason (as the body is of the senses).
crany: brain-case.
inorganity: condition of being without organs, incorporeal nature.

receive it. Thus we are men, and, we know not how, there is something in us that can be without us, and will be after us; though it is
strange that it hath no history, what it was before us, nor cannot tell
how it entered in us.

SECT. 37

Now, for these walls of flesh, wherein the soul doth seem to be im-
mured before the Resurrection—it is nothing but an elemental
composition, and a fabric that must fall to ashes. 'All flesh is grass'
is not only metaphorically but literally true; for all those creatures
we behold are but the herbs of the field, digested into flesh in them, or
more remotely carnified in ourselves. Nay, further, we are what we all
abhor, *anthropophagi* and cannibals, devourers not only of men but
of ourselves, and that not in an allegory but a positive truth: for all
this mass of flesh which we behold came in at our mouths; this
frame we look upon hath been upon our trenchers—in brief, we have
devoured ourselves.

I cannot believe the wisdom of Pythagoras did ever positively and
in a literal sense affirm his metempsychosis or impossible transmigration of the souls of men into beasts. Of all metamorphoses or
transmigrations I believe only one—that is, of Lot's wife (for that of
Nebuchadnezzar proceeded not so far); in all others I conceive there
is no further verity than is contained in their implicit sense and
morality. I believe that the whole frame of a beast doth perish, and is
left in the same state after death as before it was materialled unto
life; that the souls of men know neither contrary nor corruption;[n]
that they subsist beyond the body, and outlive death by the privilege
of their proper natures and without a miracle; that the souls of the
faithful, as they leave earth, take possession of heaven; that those
apparitions and ghosts of departed persons are not the wandering
souls of men but the unquiet walks of devils prompting and suggest-
ing us unto mischief, blood, and villainy, instilling and stealing into
our hearts that the blessed spirits are not at rest in their graves but
wander solicitous of the affairs of the world. That those phantasms
appear often, and do frequent cemeteries, charnel-houses, and
churches, it is because those are the dormitories of the dead, where
the Devil, like an insolent champion, beholds with pride the spoils
and trophies of his victory in Adam.

All flesh: Isa. 40:6.   *carnified*: made into flesh.
anthropophagi: eaters of human flesh.
Lot's wife: Gen. 19:26. See also *Pseudodoxia Epidemica*, 7.11.
Nebuchadnezzar: Dan. 4:33.   *materialled*: embodied.
stealing: introducing furtively.

SECT. 38

This is that dismal conquest we all deplore, that makes us so often cry *O Adam, quid fecisti?* I thank God I have not those strait ligaments or narrow obligations to the world as to dote on life, or be convulsed and tremble at the name of death. Not that I am insensible of the dread and horror thereof, or by raking into the bowels of the deceased, continual sight of anatomies, skeletons, or cadaverous relics, like vespilloes or grave-makers I am become stupid, or have forgot the apprehension of mortality; but that marshalling all the horrors, and contemplating the extremities thereof, I find not anything therein able to daunt the courage of a man, much less a well resolved Christian; and therefore am not angry at the error of our first parents, or unwilling to bear a part of this common fate, and, like the best of them, to die—that is, to cease to breathe, to take a farewell of the elements, to be a kind of nothing for a moment, to be within one instant of a spirit.

When I take a full view and circle of myself, without this reasonable moderator and equal piece of justice—death—I do conceive myself the miserablest person extant: were there not another life that I hope for, all the vanities of this world should not entreat a moment's breath from me; could the Devil work my belief to imagine I could never die, I would not outlive that very thought. I have so abject a conceit of this common way of existence, this retaining to the sun and elements, I cannot think this is to be a man, or to live according to the dignity of humanity. In expectation of a better, I can with patience embrace this life; yet in my best meditations do often desire death. I honour any man that contemns it, nor can I highly love any that is afraid of it; this makes me naturally love a soldier, and honour those tattered and contemptible regiments that will die at the command of a sergeant. For a pagan there may be some motives to be in love with life; but for a Christian to be amazed at death, I see not how he can escape this dilemma, that he is too sensible of this life, or hopeless of the life to come.

SECT. 39

Some divines count Adam thirty years old at his creation, because they suppose him created in the perfect age and stature of man; and

---

O Adam: O Adam, what have you done? 2 Esd. 7:48.
vespilloes: nocturnal corpse-bearers.
within one instant of: very nearly, about to become.
moderator: judge.   *conceit*: opinion.

surely we are all out of the computation of our age, and every man is some months elder than he bethinks him: for we live, move, have a being, and are subject to the actions of the elements and the malice of diseases in that other world—the truest microcosm—the womb of our mother. For, besides that general and common existence we are conceived to hold in our chaos and whilst we sleep within the bosom of our causes,[n] we enjoy a being and life in three distinct worlds, wherein we receive most manifest graduations. In that obscure world and womb of our mother our time is short, computed by the moon, yet longer than the days of many creatures that behold the sun, ourselves being not yet without life, sense, and reason, though for the manifestation of its actions it awaits the opportunity of objects, and seems to live there but in its root and soul of vegetation. Entering afterwards upon the scene of the world, we arise up and become another creature, performing the reasonable actions of man, and obscurely manifesting that part of divinity in us, but not in complement and perfection till we have once more cast our secundine— that is, this slough of flesh—and are delivered into the last world: that is, that ineffable place of Paul, that proper *ubi* of spirits.

The smattering I have of the philosophers' stone (which is something more than the perfect exaltation of gold) hath taught me a great deal of divinity, and instructed my belief how that immortal spirit and incorruptible substance of my soul may lie obscure, and sleep awhile within this house of flesh. Those strange and mystical transmigrations that I have observed in silkworms turned my philosophy into divinity: there is in these works of nature, which seem to puzzle reason, something divine, and hath more in it than the eye of a common spectator doth discover.

SECT. 40

I am naturally bashful, nor hath conversation, age, or travel been able to effront or enharden me; yet I have one part of modesty which I have seldom discovered in another—that is (to speak truly) I am not so much afraid of death as ashamed thereof: 'tis the very disgrace and ignominy of our natures, that in a moment can so disfigure us that our nearest friends, wife, and children, stand afraid and start at us. The birds and beasts of the field, that before in a natural fear obeyed us, forgetting all allegiance, begin to prey upon us. This very

not yet: already not.   *secundine*: afterbirth.
Paul: 2 Cor. 12:4.   *ubi*: place.
exaltation: refining.
enharden: embolden.   *effront*: make shameless.

conceit hath in a tempest disposed and left me willing to be swallowed up in the abyss of waters, wherein I had perished unseen, unpitied, without wondering eyes, tears of pity, lectures of mortality—and none had said *Quantum mutatus ab illo!* Not that I am ashamed of the anatomy of my parts, or can accuse nature for playing the bungler in any part of me, or my own vicious life for contracting any shameful disease upon me whereby I might not call myself as wholesome a morsel for the worms as any.

SECT. 41

Some, upon the courage of a fruitful issue wherein, as in the truest chronicle, they seem to outlive themselves, can with greater patience away with death. This conceit and counterfeit subsisting in our progenies seems to me a mere fallacy, unworthy the desires of a man that can but conceive a thought of the next world; who, in a nobler ambition, should desire to live in his substance in heaven rather than his name and shadow in the earth. And therefore at my death I mean to take a total adieu of the world, not caring for a monument, history, or epitaph—not so much as the bare memory of my name to be found anywhere but in the universal register of God. I am not yet so cynical as to approve the testament of Diogenes, nor do I altogether allow that rodomontado of Lucan:

> ... caelo tegitur, qui non habet urnam.
> He that unburied lies wants not his hearse,
> For unto him a tomb's the universe ...

but commend in my calmer judgement those ingenuous intentions that desire to sleep by the urns of their fathers, and strive to go the nearest way unto corruption.

I do not envy the temper of crows and daws, nor the numerous and weary days of our fathers before the Flood. If there be any truth in astrology, I may outlive a jubilee; as yet I have not seen one revolution of Saturn, nor hath my pulse beat thirty years, and yet, excepting

---

conceit: idea.
Quantum mutatus: How changed from that [Hector]! Virgil, *Aeneid*, 2.274.
away with: ignore.   *register of God*: book of life. Rev. 20:15.
Diogenes: who willed his friend not to bury him but to hang him up with a staff in
   his hand to fright away the crows. Cicero, *Tusculan Disputations*, 1.43(104).—*B.*
Lucan: *Pharsalia*, 7.819.
envy the temper: as did the dying Theophrastus. Cicero, op. cit., 3.28(69).
crows and daws: renowned for longevity. Pliny, *Natural History*, 7.48(153).
a jubilee: fifty years.
Saturn: formerly thought to take thirty years to complete its orbit round the sun.

44

one, have seen the ashes, and left under ground, all the kings of
Europe; have been contemporary to three Emperors, four Grand
Signiors, and as many Popes.[n] Methinks I have outlived myself, and
begin to be weary of the sun; I have shaked hands with delight in my
warm blood and canicular days; I perceive I do anticipate the vices of
age—the world to me is but a dream or mockshow, and we all therein
but pantaloons and antics to my severer contemplations.

SECT. 42

It is not, I confess, an unlawful prayer to desire to surpass the days of
our Saviour, or wish to outlive that age wherein he thought fittest to
die; yet if (as divinity affirms) there shall be no gray hairs in heaven,
but all shall rise in the perfect state of men, we do but outlive those
perfections in this world, to be recalled unto them by a greater
miracle in the next; and run on here but to be retrograde hereafter.
Were there any hopes to outlive vice, or a point to be superannuated
from sin, it were worthy our knees to implore the days of Methuselah.
But age doth not rectify, but incurvate our natures, turning bad dispositions into worser habits, and (like diseases) brings on incurable
vices; for every day as we grow weaker in age, we grow stronger in
sin, and the number of our days doth but make our sins innumerable.
The same vice committed at sixteen is not the same—though it agree
in all other circumstances—at forty, but swells and doubles from the
circumstance of our ages; wherein, besides the constant and inexcusable habit of transgressing, the maturity of our judgement cuts
off pretence unto excuse or pardon. Every sin, the oftener it is committed, the more it acquireth in the quality of evil: as it succeeds in
time, so it precedes in degrees of badness; for as they proceed they
ever multiply, and, like figures in arithmetic, the last stands for more
than all that went before it. And though I think no man can live well
once but he that could live twice, yet, for my own part, I would not
live over my hours past, or begin again the thread of my days—not
upon Cicero's ground, because I have lived them well, but for fear I
should live them worse. I find my growing judgement daily instruct

begin to be weary: *Macbeth*, V.v.49.
canicular days: dog-days, 3 July–11 August; thence figuratively the hottest, most
   unwholesome period.
that age: usually supposed, working from Luke 3:23, to be thirty-three.
Methuselah: 969 years. Gen. 5:27.
incurvate: bend.   precedes: ranks higher.
last stands for more: In writing the total of a sum, the figure representing the units
   is put down first, followed by those for tens, hundreds, etc.
Cicero's ground: *De Senectute*, 23(84).

me how to be better, but my untamed affections and confirmed vitiosity makes me daily do worse. I find in my confirmed age the same sins I discovered in my youth: I committed many then because I was a child, and because I commit them still I am yet an infant. Therefore I perceive a man may be twice a child before the days of dotage, and stand in need of Aeson's bath before threescore.

SECT. 43

And truly there goes a great deal of providence to produce a man's life unto threescore; there is more required than an able temper for those years. Though the radical humour contain in it sufficient oil for seventy, yet I perceive in some it gives no light past thirty. Men assign not all the causes of long life that write whole books thereof—they that found themselves on the radical balsam or vital sulphur of the parts determine not why Abel lived not so long as Adam.

There is, therefore, a secret glome or bottom of our days; 'twas his wisdom to determine them, but his perpetual and waking providence that fulfils and accomplisheth them; wherein the spirits, ourselves, and all the creatures of God, in a secret and disputed way do execute his will. Let them not therefore complain of immaturity that die about thirty: they fall but like the whole world, whose solid and well composed substance must not expect the duration and period of its constitution—when all things are completed in it, its age is accomplished, and the last and general fever may as naturally destroy it before six thousand, as me before forty. There is, therefore, some other hand that twines the thread of life than that of nature; we are not only ignorant in antipathies and occult qualities; our ends are as obscure as our beginnings: the line of our days is drawn by night, and the various effects therein by a pencil that is invisible; wherein, though we confess our ignorance, I am sure we do not err if we say it is the hand of God.

vitiosity: moral viciousness.
Aeson's bath: Medea made Aeson look young again (possibly by dyeing his hair). Ovid, *Metamorphoses*, 7.159–294.
balsam: supposed essence of organic bodies.
sulphur: one of the three principles (the others being termed 'salt' and 'mercury') supposed by post-Aristotelean chemists to be the basic constituents of matter. 'Sulphur' imparted potential heat or flammability to a substance.
glome or bottom: ball or skein (of thread).
six thousand: One rabbi Elias had predicted this to be the life span of the world. See below, p. 48, and *Pseudodoxia Epidemica*, 6.1.
antipathies: harmful hidden influences.

SECT. 44

I am much taken with two verses of Lucan, since I have been able
not only, as we do at school, to construe, but understand:

> Victurosque dei celant ut vivere durent,
> Felix esse mori.
> We're all deluded, vainly searching ways
> To make us happy by the length of days;
> For cunningly, to make's protract this breath,
> The gods conceal the happiness of death.

There be many excellent strains in that poet, wherewith his stoical
genius hath liberally supplied him; and truly there are singular pieces
in the philosophy of Zeno and doctrine of the Stoics, which, I perceive, delivered in a pulpit, pass for current divinity: yet herein are
they in extremes that can allow a man to be his own assassin, and so
highly extol the end and suicide of Cato; this is indeed not to fear
death, but yet to be afraid of life. It is a brave act of valour to contemn death, but where life is more terrible than death, it is then the
truest valour to dare to live. And herein religion hath taught us a
noble example, for all the valiant acts of Curtius, Scaevola or Codrus,
do not parallel or match that one of Job—and sure there is no torture
to the rack of a disease, nor any poniards in death itself like those in
the way or prologue unto it. *Emori nolo, sed me esse mortuum nihil
curo*—I would not die, but care not to be dead. Were I of Caesar's
religion, I should be of his desires, and wish rather to go off at one
blow, than to be sawed in pieces by the grating torture of a disease.

Men that look no further than their outsides think health an
appurtenance unto life, and quarrel with their constitutions for being
sick; but I that have examined the parts of man, and know upon what
tender filaments that fabric hangs, do wonder that we are not always
so; and considering the thousand doors that lead to death, do thank

Lucan: *Pharsalia*, 4.519–20.
Zeno: Zeno of Citium in Cyprus (*fl. c.* 300 B.C.), founder of the Stoic school.
Cato: Marcus Porcius Cato (95–46 B.C.), one of Lucan's heroes, was an ardent
   Stoic and opponent of Julius Caesar who killed himself with notable deliberate-
   ness on seeing his cause was lost.
Curtius: who jumped into a crevasse that Rome might last for ever. Livy, 7.6.
Scaevola: 'Left-handed', who thrust his right hand into a fire to show contempt
   for pain. Livy, 2.12.
Codrus: who tricked his enemies into killing him, so that they should lose.
   Cicero, *Tusc. Disp.*, 1.48(116).
Job: who refused to 'renounce God and die': Job 2:9–10, 13:14–15.
Emori nolo: Cicero, op. cit., 1.8(15).
Caesar's religion: Suetonius, *Julius*, 87.
thousand doors: Seneca, *Phoenissae*, 153.

my God that we can die but once. 'Tis not only the mischief of diseases and the villainy of poisons that make an end of us; we vainly accuse the fury of guns and the new inventions of death: 'tis in the power of every hand to destroy us, and we are beholding unto every one we meet he doth not kill us.

There is, therefore, but one comfort left—that though it be in the power of the weakest arm to take away life, it is not in the strongest to deprive us of death. God would not exempt himself from that: the misery of immortality in the flesh he undertook not, that was in it immortal. Certainly, there is no happiness within this circle of flesh, nor is it in the optics of these eyes to behold felicity: the first day of our jubilee is death. The Devil hath therefore failed of his desires; we are happier with death than we should have been without it: there is no misery but in himself, where there is no end of misery; and so indeed, in his own sense, the Stoic is in the right: he forgets that he can die who complains of misery—we are in the power of no calamity while death is in our own.

SECT. 45

Now besides this literal and positive kind of death, there are others whereof divines make mention—and those, I think, not merely metaphorical—as mortification, dying unto sin and the world. Therefore, I say, every man hath a double horoscope: one of his humanity, his birth; another of his Christianity, his baptism; and from this do I compute or calculate my nativity, not reckoning those *horae combustae* and odd days, or esteeming myself anything before I was my Saviour's, and enrolled in the register of Christ. Whosoever enjoys not this life, I count him but an apparition, though he wear about him the sensible affections of flesh. In these moral acceptions, the way to be immortal is to die daily, nor can I think I have the true theory of death when I contemplate a skull, or behold a skeleton with those vulgar imaginations it casts upon us; I have therefore enlarged that common *Memento mori* into a more Christian memorandum: *Memento quatuor novissima*—those four inevitable points of us all, death, judgement, heaven, and hell. Neither did the contemplations of the heathens rest in their graves without a further thought of

---

deprive us: Seneca, *Phoenissae*, 152–3.   *optics*: vision.
jubilee: expected life of fifty years.   *the Stoic*: Seneca, *On Providence*, 6.7.
horae combustae: wasted (lit. burnt) hours; astrologers' term for the time during
    which the moon is made invisible by the brightness of the sun.
affections: qualities, attributes.   *moral acceptions*: symbolic senses.
Memento mori: Remember you are to die.   *memorandum*: reminder.
Memento quatuor novissima: Remember the four last things.

Rhadamanth or some judicial proceeding after death, though in another way, and upon suggestion of their natural reasons. I cannot but marvel from what sibyl or oracle they stole the prophecy of the world's destruction by fire, or whence Lucan learned to say

> Communis mundo superest rogus, ossibus astra Misturus.—
> There yet remains to th' world one common fire
> Wherein our bones with stars shall make one pyre.

I believe the world grows near its end, yet is neither old nor decayed,[n] nor will ever perish upon the ruins of its own principles. As the work of creation was above nature, so is its adversary, annihilation, without which the world hath not its end, but its mutation. Now what fire should be able to consume it thus far without the breath of God, which is the truest consuming flame, my philosophy cannot inform me. Some believe there went not a minute to the world's creation, nor shall there go to its destruction; those six days, so punctually described, make not to them one moment, but rather seem to manifest the method and idea of that great work in the intellect of God, than the manner how he proceeded in its operation. I cannot dream that there should be at the last day any such judicial proceeding or calling to the bar as, indeed, the Scripture seems to imply, and the literal commentators do conceive: for unspeakable mysteries in the Scriptures are often delivered in a vulgar and illustrative way, and being written unto man, are delivered, not as they truly are, but as they may be understood—wherein, notwithstanding, the different interpretations according to different capacities may stand firm with our devotion, nor be any way prejudicial to each single edification.

SECT. 46

Now, to determine the day and year of this inevitable time is not only convincible and statute madness but also manifest impiety: how shall we interpret Elias' six thousand years, or imagine the secret communicated to a rabbi which God hath denied unto his angels? It had

Rhadamanth: in Greek myth the judge of the dead.
Lucan: *Pharsalia*, 7.814–15.
Scripture: e.g. Acts 17:31. cf. Matt. 10:15, 11:22, 24, 12:36; 2 Pet. 2:9, 3:7; 1 John 4:17; Jude 6.
convincible: that can be convicted.
statute: according to the legal definition.
Elias: a rabbinical commentator quoted in the Talmud, 6 (ed. I. Epstein, 1935, ii.657).
angels: Matt. 24:36.

been an excellent query to have posed the devil of Delphos, and must needs have forced him to some strange amphibology. It hath not only mocked the predictions of sundry astrologers in ages past, but the prophecies of many melancholy heads in these present, who neither understanding reasonably things past or present, pretend a knowledge of things to come—heads ordained only to manifest the incredible effects of melancholy, and to fulfil old prophecies rather than be the authors of new.

'In those days there shall come wars and rumours of wars' to me seems no prophecy, but a constant truth, in all times verified since it was pronounced. 'There shall be signs in the moon and stars'—how comes he then like a thief in the night, when he gives an item of his coming? That common sign drawn from the revelation of Antichrist is as obscure as any: in our common compute he hath been come these many years; but for my own part (to speak freely) I am half of opinion that Antichrist is the philosophers' stone in divinity, for the discovery and invention whereof, though there be prescribed rules and probable inductions, yet hath hardly any man attained the perfect discovery thereof. That general opinion that the world grows near its end hath possessed all ages past as nearly as ours; I am afraid that the souls that now depart cannot escape that lingering expostulation of the saints under the altar: *Quousque Domine?* 'How long, O Lord?' and groan in the expectation of that great jubilee.

SECT. 47

This is the day that must make good that great attribute of God, his justice; that must reconcile those unanswerable doubts that torment the wisest understandings, and reduce those seeming inequalities and respective distributions in this world to an equality and recompensive justice in the next. This is that one day that shall include and comprehend all that went before it, wherein, as in the last scene, all the actors must enter to complete and make up the catastrophe of this great piece. This is the day whose memory hath only power to make us honest in the dark, and to be virtuous without a witness. *Ipsa sui*

---

devil of Delphos: oracle at Delphi.
old prophecies: In those days there shall come liars and false prophets.—B.
    Matt. 24:11, Mark 13:22.
rumours of wars: Matt. 24:6, Mark 13:7, Luke 21:9.
moon and stars: Luke 21:25.   *thief in the night*: 1 Thess. 5:2.
revelation of Antichrist: 1 John 2:18; 2 Thess. 2:3 ff.
How long, O Lord: Rev. 6:9–10.   *respective*: discriminatory.
recompensive: compensatory.   *catastrophe*: denouement.
Ipsa sui pretium: Seneca, *De Vita Beata*, 9, and Claudian, *De Mallii Theodori*
    Consulatu, 1.

pretium virtus sibi—that virtue is her own reward—is but a cold
principle, and not able to maintain our variable resolutions in a constant and settled way of goodness.

I have practised that honest artifice of Seneca, and in my retired
and solitary imaginations, to detain me from the foulness of vice,
have fancied to myself the presence of my dear and worthiest friends,
before whom I should lose my head rather than be vicious; yet herein
I found that there was naught but moral honesty, and this was not to
be virtuous for his sake who must reward us at the last. I have tried
if I could reach that great resolution of his, to be honest without a
thought of heaven or hell; and indeed I found, upon a natural
inclination and inbred loyalty unto virtue, that I could serve her
without a livery; yet not in that resolved and venerable way but that
the frailty of my nature, upon an easy temptation, might be induced
to forget her. The life, therefore, and spirit of all our actions, is the
resurrection, and stable apprehension that our ashes shall enjoy the
fruit of our pious endeavours. Without this, all religion is a fallacy,
and those impieties of Lucian, Euripides, and Julian, are no blasphe-
mies, but subtle verities, and atheists have been the only philosophers.

SECT. 48

'How shall the dead arise?' is no question of my faith—to believe
only possibilities is not faith but mere philosophy. Many things are
true in divinity which are neither inducible by reason nor confirmable
by sense, and many things in philosophy confirmable by sense yet not
inducible by reason. Thus it is impossible by any solid or demonstra-
tive reasons to persuade a man to believe the conversion of the
needle to the north, though this be possible, and true, and easily
credible upon a single experiment unto the sense. I believe that our
estranged and divided ashes shall unite again; that our separated
dust, after so many pilgrimages and transformations into the parts of
minerals, plants, animals, elements, shall at the voice of God return
into their primitive shapes, and join again to make up their primary

resolutions: wills.   *Seneca*: *Epistulae Morales*, 11.8, 25.5–6.
resolution of his: ibid, 113.31.   *livery*: servant's payment.
Lucian: who made fun of the Greek deities, and allegedly of Christ in *The Lover
   of Lies*, 16.
Euripides: in whose *Madness of Hercules*, for example, Zeus is reproached as un-
   dutiful, deceitful, incompetent, stupid, and unjust.
Julian: the Roman emperor (361–3) who disestablished Christianity in favour of
   another cult.
inducible: capable of being inferred.
conversion of the needle: turning of the compass needle.

and predestinate forms. As at the Creation there was a separation of that confused mass into its species, so at the destruction thereof there shall be a separation into its distinct individuals. As at the Creation of the world all the distinct species that we behold lay involved in one mass till the fruitful voice of God separated this united multitude into its several species, so at the last day, when these corrupted relics shall be scattered in the wilderness of forms, and seem to have forgot their proper habits, God by a powerful voice shall command them back into their proper shapes, and call them out by their single individuals. Then shall appear the fertility of Adam and the magic of that sperm that hath dilated into so many millions.

I have often beheld as a miracle that artificial resurrection and revivification of mercury, how, being mortified into thousand shapes, it assumes again its own, and returns into its numerical self. Let us speak naturally, and like philosophers: the forms of alterable bodies in these sensible corruptions perish not; nor (as we imagine) wholly quit their mansions, but retire and contract themselves into their secret and unaccessible parts, where they may best protect themselves from the action of their antagonist. A plant or vegetable consumed to ashes, to a contemplative and school philosopher seems utterly destroyed, and the form to have taken his leave for ever; but to a sensible artist the forms are not perished, but withdrawn into their incombustible part, where they lie secure from the action of that devouring element. This is made good by experience, which can from the ashes of a plant revive the plant, and from its cinders recall it into its stalk and leaves again. What the art of man can do in these inferior pieces, what blasphemy is it to affirm the finger of God cannot do in these more perfect and sensible structures! This is that mystical philosophy from whence no true scholar becomes an atheist, but, from the visible effects of nature, grows up a real divine, and beholds, not in a dream as Ezekiel, but in an ocular and visible object, the types of his resurrection.

SECT. 49

Now, the necessary mansions of our restored selves are those two contrary and incompatible places we call heaven and hell; to define

---

mortified: dissolved in acid.   *numerical self*: characteristic state.
school: scholastic, i.e. limited to abstract logical deductions.
sensible artist: practical scientist.   *experience*: experiment.
revive the plant: referring probably to the mistaken belief that the frond-like patterns seen to form when a concoction of the ashes with water freezes are related to the shape of the original plant.
Ezekiel: Ezek. 37:1–14.

them, or strictly to determine what and where these are, surpasseth
my divinity. That elegant apostle which seemed to have a glimpse of
heaven hath left but a negative description thereof: 'Which neither
eye hath seen, nor ear hath heard, nor can enter into the heart of
man'—he was translated out of himself to behold it, but being returned into himself could not express it. Saint John's description—by
emeralds, chrysolites, and precious stones—is too weak to express
the material heaven we behold. Briefly, therefore, where the soul hath
the full measure and complement of happiness; where the boundless
appetite of that spirit remains completely satisfied, that it can neither
desire addition nor alteration—that, I think, is truly heaven. And this
can only be in the enjoyment of that essence whose infinite goodness
is able to terminate the desires of itself and the unsatiable wishes of
ours; wherever God will thus manifest himself, there is heaven,
though within the circle of this sensible world.

Thus the soul of man may be in heaven anywhere, even within the
limits of his own proper body; and when it ceaseth to live in the
body it may remain in its own soul—that is, its creator. And thus we
may say that Saint Paul, whether in the body or out of the body, was
yet in heaven. To place it in the empyreal or beyond the tenth sphere
is to forget the world's destruction; for when this sensible world
shall be destroyed, all shall then be here as it is now there—an
empyreal heaven, a quasi-vacuity; when to ask where heaven is, is to
demand where the presence of God is, or where we have the glory of
that happy vision. Moses, that was bred up in all the learning of the
Egyptians, committed a gross absurdity in philosophy when with
these eyes of flesh he desired to see God, and petitioned his maker
(that is truth itself) to a contradiction.

Those that imagine heaven and hell neighbours, and conceive a
vicinity between those two extremes upon consequence of the
parable where Dives discoursed with Lazarus in Abraham's bosom,
do too grossly conceive of those glorified creatures, whose eyes shall
easily outsee the sun, and behold without a perspective the extremest
distances; for if there shall be in our glorified eyes the faculty of sight
and reception of objects, I could think the visible species there to be
in as unlimitable a way as now the intellectual. I grant that two

elegant: who chose words carefully.   *Which neither eye*: 1 Cor. 2:9.
express it: 2 Cor. 12:2–4.   *Saint John's description*: Rev. 21:19–21.
Saint Paul: 2 Cor. 12:2–4.   *Egyptians*: Acts 7:22.
to see God: Exod. 33:18–23.   *Abraham's bosom*: Luke 16:23.
perspective: telescope.   *species*: images, appearances.

bodies placed beyond the tenth sphere or in a vacuity, according to Aristotle's philosophy could not behold each other, because there wants a body or medium to hand and transport the visible rays of the object unto the sense; but when there shall be a general defect of either medium to convey, or light to prepare and dispose that medium, and yet a perfect vision, we must suspend the rules of our philosophy, and make all good by a more absolute piece of optics.

SECT. 50

I cannot tell how to say that fire is the essence of hell; I know not what to make of purgatory, or conceive a flame that can either prey upon or purify the substance of a soul: those flames of sulphur mentioned in the Scriptures I take not to be understood of this present hell but of that to come, where fire shall make up the complement of our tortures, and have a body or subject wherein to manifest its tyranny. Some who have had the honour to be textuary in divinity are of opinion it shall be the same specifical fire with ours. This is hard to conceive; yet can I make good how even that may prey upon our bodies, and yet not consume us: for in this material world there are bodies that persist invincible in the powerfullest flames, and though by the action of fire they fall into ignition and liquation, yet will they never suffer a destruction.[n] I would gladly know how Moses with an actual fire calcined or burnt the Golden Calf into powder; for that mystical metal of gold, whose solary and celestial nature I admire, exposed unto the violence of fire grows only hot and liquefies, but consumeth not: so when the consumable and volatile pieces of our bodies shall be refined into a more impregnable and fixed temper like gold, though they suffer from the action of flames, they shall never perish, but lie immortal in the arms of fire.

And surely if this frame must suffer only by the action of this element, there will many bodies escape, and not only heaven, but earth will not be at an end, but rather a beginning; for at present it is not earth, but a composition of fire, water, earth, and air: but at that time, spoiled of these ingredients, it shall appear in a substance more like itself—its ashes. Philosophers that opinioned the world's destruction by fire did never dream of annihilation, which is beyond the power of sublunary causes; for the last and proper action of that

---

Aristotle's philosophy: *De Anima*, 2.7.
flames of sulphur: Rev. 14:10, 19:20, 21:8.
present hell: See below, Section 51.   *textuary*: regarded as authorities.
fall . . . liquation: burn and melt.   *Moses*: Exod. 32:20; Deut. 9:21.
sublunary: earthly.

element is but vitrification or a reduction of a body into glass; and therefore some of our chymics facetiously affirm that at the last fire all shall be crystallized and reverberated into glass, which is the utmost action of that element.

Nor need we fear this term 'annihilation', or wonder that God will destroy the works of his creation; for man subsisting, who is and will then truly appear a microcosm, the world cannot be said to be destroyed. For the eyes of God—and perhaps also of our glorified selves—shall as really behold and contemplate the world in its epitome or contracted essence, as now they do at large and in its dilated substance. In the seed of a plant, to the eyes of God and to the understanding of man, there exists—though in an invisible way—the perfect leaves, flowers, and fruit thereof; for things that are *in posse* to the sense are actually existent to the understanding. Thus God beholds all things, who contemplates as fully his works in their epitome as in their full volume, and beheld as amply the whole world in that little compendium of the sixth day as in the scattered and dilated pieces of those five before.

SECT. 51

Men commonly set forth the torments of hell by fire and the extremity of corporal afflictions, and describe hell in the same method that Mahomet doth heaven. This indeed makes a noise, and drums in popular ears; but if this be the terrible piece thereof, it is not worthy to stand in diameter with heaven, whose happiness consists in that part that is best able to comprehend it—that immortal essence, that translated divinity and colony of God, the soul.

Surely, though we place hell under earth, the Devil's walk and purlieu is about it: men speak too popularly who place it in those flaming mountains which to grosser apprehensions represent hell. The heart of man is the place the Devil dwells in: I feel sometimes a hell within myself; Lucifer keeps his court in my breast—Legion is revived in me. There are as many hells as Anaxagoras conceited worlds: there was more than one hell in Magdalen when there were

chymics: chemists, or rather alchemists.
reverberated: changed by heat.   *are in posse*: exist only potentially.
little compendium: man the microcosm.
Mahomet: It was a common reproach of Christians that the Islamic paradise promised unabashed fleshly pleasures.
flaming mountains: volcanoes.   *Legion*: the multiple devil of Mark 5:9.
Anaxagoras: Greek philosopher of the fifth century B.C.
Magdalen: Luke 8:2.

seven devils, for every devil is an hell unto himself—he holds enough of torture in his own *ubi*, and needs not the misery of circumference to afflict him; and thus a distracted conscience here is a shadow or introduction unto hell hereafter. Who can but pity the merciful intention of those hands that do destroy themselves? The Devil, were it in his power, would do the like; which being impossible, his miseries are endless, and he suffers most in that attribute wherein he is impassible, his immortality.

SECT. 52

I thank God—and with joy I mention it—I was never afraid of hell, nor never grew pale at the description of that place. I have so fixed my contemplations on heaven that I have almost forgot the idea of hell, and am afraid rather to lose the joys of the one than endure the misery of the other: to be deprived of them is a perfect hell, and needs, methinks, no addition to complete our afflictions. That terrible term hath never detained me from sin, nor do I owe any good action to the name thereof. I fear God, yet am not afraid of him; his mercies make me ashamed of my sins, before his judgements afraid thereof: these are the forced and secondary method of his wisdom, which he useth but as the last remedy, and upon provocation—a course rather to deter the wicked than incite the virtuous to his worship. I can hardly think there was ever any scared into heaven; they go the fairest way to heaven that would serve God without a hell: other mercenaries, that crouch unto him in fear of hell, though they term themselves the servants, are indeed but the slaves of the Almighty.

SECT. 53

And to be true, and speak my soul, when I survey the occurrences of my life, and call into account the finger of God, I can perceive nothing but an abyss and mass of mercies, either in general to mankind, or in particular to myself; and whether out of the prejudice of my affection, or an inverting and partial conceit of his mercies, I know not, but those which others term crosses, afflictions, judgements, misfortunes, to me, who enquire farther into them than their visible effects, they both appear, and in event have ever proved, the secret and dissembled favours of his affection.

It is a singular piece of wisdom to apprehend truly and without passion the works of God, and so well to distinguish his justice from

---

ubi: locality.   *of circumference*: surrounding, external.
impassible: not subject to harm.   *conceit*: conception.

his mercy as not to miscall those noble attributes; yet it is likewise an honest piece of logic so to dispute and argue the proceedings of God as to distinguish even his judgements into mercies. For God is merciful unto all, because better to the worst than the best deserve; and to say he punisheth none in this world, though it be a paradox, is no absurdity. To one that hath committed murder, if the judge should only ordain a fine, it were a madness to call this a punishment, and to repine at the sentence rather than admire the clemency of the judge. Thus, our offences being mortal, and deserving not only death but damnation, if the goodness of God be content to traverse and pass them over with a loss, misfortune or disease—what frenzy were it to term this a punishment rather than an extremity of mercy, and to groan under the rod of his judgements rather than admire the sceptre of his mercies! Therefore, to adore, honour, and admire him, is a debt of gratitude due from the obligation of our nature, states, and conditions; and with these thoughts, he, that knows them best, will not deny that I adore him. That I obtain heaven and the bliss thereof is accidental, and not the intended work of my devotion, it being a felicity I can neither think to deserve, nor scarce in modesty to expect. For these two ends of us all, either as rewards or punishments, are mercifully ordained and disproportionally disposed unto our actions, the one being so far beyond our deserts, the other so infinitely below our demerits.

SECT. 54

There is no salvation to those that believe not in Christ, that is, say some, since his nativity, and as divinity affirmeth, before also; which makes me much apprehend the end of those honest worthies and philosophers which died before his incarnation. It is hard to place those souls in hell whose worthy lives do teach us virtue on earth; methinks amongst those many subdivisions of hell, there might have been one limbo left for these. What a strange vision will it be to see their poetical fictions converted into verities, and their imagined and fancied Furies into real devils! How strange to them will sound the history of Adam, when they shall suffer for him they never heard of; when they that derive their genealogy from the gods shall know they are the unhappy issue of sinful man!

It is an insolent part of reason to controvert the works of God, or question the justice of his proceedings. Could humility teach others,

---

one limbo left: The first circle Dante comes to in his *Inferno*, 4, is reserved for the otherwise eminently worthy who for lack of baptism only are excluded from paradise, to suffer in this limbo not torture but grief.

as it hath instructed me, to contemplate the infinite and incomprehensible distance betwixt the Creator and the creature, or did we seriously perpend that one simile of Saint Paul: 'Shall the vessel say to the potter "Why hast thou made me thus?"' it would prevent these arrogant disputes of reason, nor would we argue the definitive sentence of God, either to heaven or hell. Men that live according to the right rule and law of reason, live but in their own kind—as beasts do in theirs, who justly obey the prescript of their natures—and therefore cannot reasonably demand a reward of their actions, as only obeying the natural dictates of their reason. It will therefore—and must—at last appear that all salvation is through Christ; which verity, I fear, these great examples of virtue must confirm, and make it good how the perfectest actions of earth have no title or claim unto heaven.

SECT. 55

Nor, truly, do I think the lives of these or of any other were ever correspondent or in all points conformable unto their doctrines: it is evident that Aristotle transgressed the rule of his own *Ethics*;[n] the Stoics, that condemn all passion, and command a man to laugh in Phalaris his bull, could not endure without a groan a fit of the stone or colic. The Sceptics, that affirmed they knew nothing, even in that opinion confuted themselves, and thought they knew more than all the world beside. Diogenes I hold to be the most vainglorious man of his time, and more ambitious in refusing all honours than Alexander in rejecting none. Vice and the Devil put a fallacy upon our reasons, and, provoking us too hastily to run from it, entangle and profound us deeper in it. The Duke of Venice, that weds himself unto the sea by a ring of gold, I will not argue of prodigality, because it is a solemnity of good use and consequence in the State.[n] But the philosopher that threw his money into the sea to avoid avarice was a notorious prodigal.

There is no road or ready way to virtue; it is not an easy point of art to disentangle ourselves from this riddle or web of sin. To perfect virtue, as to religion, there is required a panoplia or complete armour, that whilst we lie at close ward against one vice we lie not open to the veny of another. And indeed, wiser discretions, that have

---

Saint Paul: Rom. 9:20–1.
Phalaris: Sicilian tyrant of the sixth century B.C. who roasted his victims in a brazen bull.
Diogenes: Lucian, *Dialogues of the Dead*, 13.
philosopher: Crates, in Diogenes Laertius, 6.87.
complete armour: Eph. 6:13.   *veny*: attack.

the thread of reason to conduct them, offend without a pardon; whereas under heads may stumble without dishonour. There go so many circumstances to piece up one good action, that it is a lesson to be good, and we are forced to be virtuous by the book.

Again, the practice of men holds not an equal pace—yea, and often runs counter to their theory. We naturally know what is good, but naturally pursue what is evil; the rhetoric wherewith I persuade another cannot persuade myself; there is a depraved appetite in us, that will with patience hear the learned instructions of reason, but yet perform no farther than agrees to its own irregular humour. In brief, we all are monsters; that is, a composition of man and beast, wherein we must endeavour to be as the poets fancy that wise man Chiron, that is, to have the region of man above that of beast, and sense to sit but at the feet of reason. Lastly, I do desire with God that all, but yet affirm with men that few shall know salvation, that the bridge is narrow, the passage strait unto life; yet those who do confine the Church of God either to particular nations, churches, or families, have made it far narrower than our Saviour ever meant it.

SECT. 56

The vulgarity of those judgements that wrap the Church of God in Strabo's cloak, and restrain it unto Europe, seem to me as bad geographers as Alexander, who thought he had conquered all the world when he had not subdued the half of any part thereof. For we cannot deny the Church of God both in Asia and Africa if we do not forget the peregrinations of the Apostles, the death of their martyrs, the sessions of many and (even in our reformed judgement) lawful councils held in those parts in the minority and nonage of ours; nor must a few differences—more remarkable in the eyes of man than, perhaps, in the judgement of God—excommunicate from heaven one another, much less those Christians who are in a manner all martyrs, maintaining their faith in the noble way of persecution, and serving God in the fire, whereas we honour him but in the sunshine.

'Tis true we all hold there is a number of elect, and many to be saved; yet take our opinions together, and from the confusion thereof

---

under heads: lesser intellects.
what is evil: Rom. 7:19; Ovid, *Metamorphoses*, 7.20–1.
Chiron: wisest of the centaurs.   *desire with God*: 1 Tim. 2:3–4.
passage strait: Matt. 7:14.
Strabo's cloak: The Greek geographer Strabo, *Geographia*, 2.5.14, likened the then known inhabited world, of Europe, western Asia, and north-eastern Africa, to a short cloak spread out.
number of elect: Mark 13:20; Rev. 7:4, 9.

there will be no such thing as salvation, nor shall any one be saved: for first the Church of Rome condemneth us, we likewise them; the sub-reformists and sectaries sentence the doctrine of our Church as damnable; the Atomist or Familist reprobates all these—and all these them again. Thus, whilst the mercies of God do promise us heaven, our conceits and opinions exclude us from that place. There must be therefore more than one Saint Peter; particular churches and sects usurp the gates of heaven, and turn the key against each other: and thus we go to heaven against each other's wills, conceits and opinions, and with as much uncharity as ignorance do err, I fear, in points not only of our own, but one another's salvation.

SECT. 57

I believe many are saved who to man seem reprobated, and many are reprobated who in the opinion and sentence of man stand elected. There will appear at the last day strange and unexpected examples both of his justice and his mercy; and therefore, to define either is folly in man, and insolency even in the devils: those acute and subtle spirits, in all their sagacity, can hardly divine who shall be saved; which if they could prognostic, their labour were at an end, nor need they compass the earth seeking whom they may devour. Those who upon a rigid application of the Law sentence Solomon unto damnation, condemn not only him, but themselves and the whole world; for, by the letter and written Word of God, we are without exception in the state of death; but there is a prerogative of God, and an arbitrary pleasure above the letter of his own Law, by which alone we can pretend unto salvation, and through which Solomon might be as easily saved as those who condemn him.

SECT. 58

The number of those who pretend unto salvation, and those infinite swarms who think to pass through the eye of this needle, have much amazed me. That name and compellation of 'little flock' doth not

---

sub-reformists: those who would further reform an already reformed church.
sectaries: those who separate from a main church.
Atomist: perhaps a misreading of Adamist—the Adamites practised a return to primal innocence through nudity and sexual promiscuity.
Familist: member of the Family of Love which propagated a kind of mystical pantheism and the belief that Christians were by grace set free from obedience to moral laws.
prognostic: foretell.
compass the earth: Job 1:7, 2:2 (in Geneva and Bishops' Bibles).
devour: 1 Pet. 5:8.
Solomon: who was not baptized.   *little flock*: Luke 12:32.

comfort but deject my devotion, especially when I reflect upon mine
own unworthiness, wherein, according to my humble apprehensions,
I am below them all. I believe there shall never be an anarchy in
heaven, but as there are hierarchies amongst the angels,[n] so shall
there be degrees of priority amongst the saints. Yet is it, I protest, beyond my ambition to aspire unto the first ranks; my desires only are
—and I shall be happy therein—to be but the last man, and bring up
the rear in heaven.

SECT. 59

Again, I am confident and fully persuaded—yet dare not take my
oath—of my salvation: I am, as it were, sure, and do believe without
all doubt, that there is such a city as Constantinople; yet for me to
take my oath thereon were a kind of perjury, because I hold no
infallible warrant from my own sense to confirm me in the certainty
thereof. And truly, though many pretend an absolute certainty of
their salvation, yet, when an humble soul shall contemplate her own
unworthiness, she shall meet with many doubts, and suddenly find
how little we stand in need of the precept of Saint Paul—'Work out
your salvation with fear and trembling'.

That which is the cause of my election I hold to be the cause of my
salvation, which was the mercy and beneplacit of God before I was or
the foundation of the world. 'Before Abraham was, I am' is the say-
ing of Christ; yet is it true in some sense if I say it of myself, for I was
not only before myself, but Adam—that is, in the idea of God, and
the decree of that synod held from all eternity. And in this sense, I say,
the world was before the Creation, and at an end before it had a
beginning; and thus was I dead before I was alive—though my grave
be England, my dying place was paradise, and Eve miscarried of me
before she conceived of Cain.

SECT. 60

Insolent zeals that do decry good works, and rely only upon faith,
take not away merit; for, depending upon the efficacy of their faith,
they enforce the condition of God, and in a more sophistical way do
seem to challenge heaven. It was decreed by God that only those that
lapped in the water like dogs should have the honour to destroy the
Midianites; yet could none of those justly challenge, or imagine he
deserved that honour thereupon. I do not deny but that true faith

Saint Paul: Phil. 2:12.   *beneplacit*: good pleasure.
Before Abraham: John 8:58.   *zeals*: zealots.
Midianites: Judg. 7:4–7.

and such as God requires, is not only a mark or token, but also a means of our salvation; but where to find this is as obscure to me as my last end. And if our Saviour could object unto his own disciples and favourites a faith that, to the quantity of a grain of mustard seed, is able to remove mountains, surely that which we boast of is not anything, or at the most but a remove from nothing.

This is the tenor of my belief, wherein, though there be many things singular and to the humour of my irregular self, yet, if they square not with maturer judgements, I disclaim them, and do no further father them than the learned and best judgements shall authorize them.

our Saviour: Matt. 17:20.   *object*: put forward, propose for consideration.

The Second Part

Now, for that other virtue of charity, without which faith is a mere notion and of no existence—I have ever endeavoured to nourish the merciful disposition and humane inclination I borrowed from my parents, and regulate it to the written and prescribed laws of charity. And if I hold the true anatomy of myself, I am delineated and naturally framed to such a piece of virtue; for I am of a constitution so general that it consorts and sympathizeth with all things. I have no antipathy—or rather idiosyncrasy—in diet, humour, air, anything. I wonder not at the French for their dishes of frogs, snails, and toadstools, nor at the Jews for locusts and grasshoppers, but, being amongst them, make them my common viands; and I find they agree with my stomach as well as theirs; I could digest a salad gathered in a churchyard as well as in a garden. I cannot start at the presence of a serpent, scorpion, lizard, or salamander; at the sight of a toad or viper I find in me no desire to take up a stone to destroy them. I feel not in myself those common antipathies that I can discover in others. Those national repugnances do not touch me, nor do I behold with prejudice the French, Italian, Spaniard, or Dutch; but where I find their actions in balance with my countrymen's, I honour, love, and embrace them in the same degree. I was born in the eighth climate,[n] but seem for to be framed and constellated unto all; I am no plant that will not prosper out of a garden; all places, all airs make unto me one country—I am in England everywhere and under any meridian. I have been shipwracked, yet am not enemy with the sea or winds; I can study, play, or sleep in a tempest. In brief, I am averse from nothing: my conscience would give me the lie if I should say I absolutely detest or hate any essence but the Devil—or so at least abhor anything but that we might come to composition.

If there be any among those common objects of hatred I do contemn and laugh at, it is that great enemy of reason, virtue, and religion, the multitude—that numerous piece of monstrosity, which, taken asunder, seem men, and the reasonable creatures of God; but confused together, make but one great beast, and a monstrosity

---

constellated: constituted by the influence of the stars at birth.

more prodigious than Hydra. It is no breach of charity to call these
fools: it is the style all holy writers have afforded them, set down by
Solomon in canonical Scripture, and a point of our faith to believe so.
Neither, in the name of multitude, do I only include the base and
minor sort of people; there is a rabble even amongst the gentry, a
sort of plebeian heads whose fancy moves with the same wheel as
these; men in the same level with mechanics, though their fortunes
do somewhat gild their infirmities and their purses compound for
their follies. But as, in casting account, three or four men together
come short in account of one man placed by himself below them, so
neither are a troop of these ignorant doradoes of that true esteem and
value as many a forlorn person whose condition doth place him
below their feet. Let us speak like politicians: there is a nobility without heraldry—a natural dignity whereby one man is ranked with
another, another filed before him, according to the quality of his
desert, and pre-eminence of his good parts. Though the corruption
of these times, and the bias of present practice, wheel another way,
thus it was in the first and primitive commonwealths, and is yet in
the integrity and cradle of well-ordered polities, till corruption getteth
ground, ruder desires labouring after that which wiser considerations
contemn—everyone having a liberty to amass and heap up riches,
and they a licence or faculty to do or purchase anything.

SECT. 2

This general and indifferent temper of mine doth more nearly
dispose me to this noble virtue. It is a happiness to be born and
framed unto virtue, and to grow up from the seeds of nature rather
than the inoculation and forced grafts of education; yet if we are
directed only by our particular natures, and regulate our inclinations
by no higher rule than that of our reasons, we are but moralists—
divinity will still call us heathens. Therefore this great work of charity
must have other motives, ends, and impulsions: I give no alms to
satisfy the hunger of my brother, but to fulfil and accomplish the
will and command of my God; I draw not my purse for his sake that
demands it, but his that enjoined it; I relieve no man upon the
rhetoric of his miseries, nor to content mine own commiserating
disposition, for this is still but moral charity and an act that oweth

Solomon: Prov. 1:22, 8:5.   *mechanics*: the uneducated.
casting account: In a sum three or four lesser digits may go to make up one
   larger one.
doradoes: rich men (lit. gilded ones).   *politicians*: social theorists.
inoculation: grafting by budding.   *moralists*: merely moral men.

more to passion than reason. He that relieves another upon the bare suggestion and bowels of pity doth not this so much for his sake as for his own; for by compassion we make another's misery our own, and so by relieving them, we relieve ourselves also.

It is as erroneous a conceit to redress other men's misfortunes upon the common consideration of merciful natures, that it may be one day our own case; for this is a sinister and politic kind of charity, whereby we seem to bespeak the pities of men in the like occasions. And truly, I have observed that those professed eleemosynaries, though in a crowd or multitude, do yet direct and place their petitions on a few and selected persons; there is surely a physiognomy which those experienced and master mendicants observe, whereby they instantly discover a merciful aspect, and will single out a face wherein they spy the signatures and marks of mercy; for there are mystically in our faces certain characters which carry in them the motto of our souls, wherein he that cannot read ABC may read our natures.

I hold, moreover, that there is a phytognomy, or physiognomy not only of men, but of plants and vegetables, and in every one of them some outward figures which hang as signs or bushes of their inward forms. The finger of God hath left an inscription upon all his works—not graphical or composed of letters, but of their several forms, constitutions, parts, and operations, which aptly joined together do make one word that doth express their natures. By these letters God calls the stars by their names, and by this alphabet Adam assigned to every creature a name peculiar to its nature.

Now there are, besides these characters in our faces, certain mystical figures in our hands which I dare not call mere dashes, strokes *à la volée* or at random, because delineated by a pencil that never works in vain; and hereof I take more particular notice because I carry that in mine own hand which I could never read of nor discover in another. Aristotle, I confess, in his acute and singular book of physiognomy hath made no mention of chiromancy; yet I believe the Egyptians, who were nearer addicted to those abstruse and mystical sciences, had a knowledge therein, to which those vagabond and counterfeit Egyptians did after pretend, and perhaps retained a few corrupted principles which sometimes might verify their prognostics.

---

sinister: deceitful.   *eleemosynaries*: alms seekers.
bushes: signs.   *stars*: Ps. 147:4.
Adam: Gen. 2:19–20.   *à la volée*: at random.
book of physiognomy: not now attributed to Aristotle.
counterfeit Egyptians: gypsies.

It is the common wonder of all men how, among so many millions of faces, there should be none alike; now, contrary, I wonder as much how there should be any. He that shall consider how many thousand several words have been carelessly and without study composed out of twenty-four letters—withal how many hundred lines there are to be drawn in the fabric of one man—shall easily find that this variety is necessary; and it will be very hard that they shall so concur as to make one portrait like another. Let a painter carelessly limn out a million of faces, and you shall find them all different; yea, let him have his copy[1] before him, yet after all his art there will remain a sensible distinction: for the pattern or example of every thing is the perfectest in that kind; whereof we still come short, though we transcend or go beyond it, because herein it is wide and agrees not in all points unto its copy[2]. Nor doth the similitude of creatures disparage the variety of nature, nor any way confound the works of God. For even in things alike there is diversity, and those that do seem to accord do manifestly disagree. And thus is man like God; for in the same things that we resemble him, we are utterly different from him. There was never any thing so like another as in all points to concur; there will ever some reserved difference slip in to prevent the identity; without which two several things would not be alike, but the same—which is impossible.

SECT. 3

But to return from philosophy to charity: I hold not so narrow a conceit of this virtue as to conceive that to give alms is only to be charitable, or think a piece of liberality can comprehend the total of charity. Divinity hath wisely divided the acts thereof into many branches, and hath taught us, in this narrow way, many paths unto goodness: as many ways as we may do good, so many ways we may be charitable—there are infirmities not only of body, but of soul and fortunes, which do require the merciful hand of our abilities.

I cannot contemn a man for ignorance, but behold him with as much pity as I do Lazarus. It is no greater charity to clothe his body than apparel the nakedness of his soul. It is an honourable object to see the reasons of other men wear our liveries, and their borrowed understandings do homage to the bounty of ours. It is the cheapest way of beneficence, and, like the natural charity of the sun, illuminates another without obscuring itself. To be reserved and caitiff in

---

twenty-four letters: reckoning i/j, u/v as single letters.
copy[1]: model.   *copy*[2]: original or pattern.

this part of goodness is the sordidest piece of covetousness, and more contemptible than the pecuniary avarice. To this (as calling myself a scholar) I am obliged by the duty of my condition. I make not, therefore, my head a grave, but a treasure of knowledge; I intend no monopoly but a community in learning; I study not for my own sake only, but for theirs that study not for themselves. I envy no man that knows more than myself, but pity them that know less. I instruct no man as an exercise of my knowledge, or with an intent rather to nourish and keep it alive in mine own head than beget and propagate it in his; and in the midst of all my endeavours there is but one thought that dejects me, that my acquired parts must perish with myself, nor can be legacied among my honoured friends.

I cannot fall out or contemn a man for an error, or conceive why a difference in opinion should divide an affection; for controversies, disputes, and argumentations, both in philosophy and in divinity, if they meet with discreet and peaceable natures, do not infringe the laws of charity. In all disputes so much as there is of passion, so much there is of nothing to the purpose; for then reason, like a bad hound, spends upon a false scent, and forsakes the question first started. And this is one reason why controversies are never determined, for though they be amply proposed, they are scarce at all handled, they do so swell with unnecessary digressions; and the parenthesis on the party is often as large as the main discourse upon the subject.

The foundations of religion are already established, and the principles of salvation subscribed unto by all; there remain not many controversies worth a passion, and yet never any disputed without, not only in divinity, but in inferior arts. What a βατραχομυομαχία and hot skirmish is betwixt S and T in Lucian! How do the grammarians hack and slash for the genitive case in Jupiter. How do they break their own pates to salve that of Priscian! *Si foret in terris, rideret Democritus.* Yea, even amongst wiser militants, how many wounds have been given, and credits slain, for the poor victory of an opinion or beggarly conquest of a distinction! Scholars are men of

spends: gives tongue, barks.   *party*: part (of subject treated).
βατραχομυομαχία: battle of frogs and mice—title of a mock-heroic poem once attributed to Homer.
Lucian: in his mock trial, *The Consonants at Law.*
Jupiter: whether *Jovis* or *Jupiteris.*—B.   Priscian, *Grammatical Institutions*, 6, ruled that the shorter form was improper and archaic.
Priscian: to break his head was to violate the rules of grammar.
Democritus: Horace, *Epistles*, 2.1.194. If he were on earth, Democritus would laugh. D. was proverbial as a mocker of men's follies.

peace, they bear no arms; but their tongues are sharper than Actius
his razor; their pens carry farther, and give a louder report than
thunder—I had rather stand in the shock of a *basilisco* than in the
fury of a merciless pen.

It is not mere zeal to learning, or devotion to the Muses, that wiser
princes patron the arts and carry an indulgent aspect unto scholars,
but a desire to have their names eternized by the memory of their
writings, and a fear of the revengeful pen of succeeding ages; for
these are the men that, when they have played their parts and had
their exits, must step out and give the moral of their scenes, and
deliver unto posterity an inventory of their virtues and vices. And
surely there goes a great deal of conscience to the compiling of an
history, and there is no reproach to the scandal of a story. It is such
an authentic kind of falsehood that with authority belies our good
names to all nations and posterity.

SECT. 4

There is another offence unto charity which no author hath ever
written of, and few take notice of, and that's the reproach, not of
whole professions, mysteries and conditions, but of whole nations;
wherein by opprobrious epithets we miscall each other, and, by an
uncharitable logic, from a disposition in a few conclude a habit in all:

> Le mutin anglais, et le bravache écossais;
> Le bougre italien, et le fol français;
> Le poltron romain, le larron de Gascogne—
> L'Espagnol superbe, et l'Allemand ivrogne.

Saint Paul that calls the Cretans liars doth it but indirectly and upon
quotation of their own poet. It is as bloody a thought in one way as
Nero's was in another, for by a word we wound a thousand, and at
one blow assassin the honour of a nation. It is as complete a piece of

---

Actius his razor: with which he cut through a whetstone. Livy, 1.36.
basilisco: large cannon.   *eternized*: immortalized.
reproach to: reproach comparable to.   *authentic*: first-hand.
Le mutin: misremembered from J. Du Bellay,   *Les Regrets*, Sonnet 68.

> The English mutineer, and the Scots bully;
> The Italian bugger, and the French fool;
> The Roman coward, the thief of Gascony—
> The arrogant Spaniard, and the drunken Hun.

own poet: Epimenides. Titus 1:12.
Nero's: rather Caligula's, whose wish was that the Roman people might have one
  neck, to be severed at a stroke. Suetonius, *Caligula*, 30.
assassin: assassinate.

madness to miscall and rave against the times, or think to recall men
to reason by a fit of passion: Democritus, that thought to laugh the
times into goodness, seems to me as deeply hypochondriac as
Heraclitus that bewailed them. It moves not my spleen to behold the
multitude in their proper humours—that is, in their fits of folly and
madness—as well understanding that wisdom is not profaned unto
the world, and 'tis the privilege of a few to be virtuous.

They that endeavour to abolish vice destroy also virtue, for con-
traries, though they destroy one another, are yet the life of one
another: thus virtue, abolish vice, is an idea. Again, the community
of sin doth not disparage goodness; for when vice gains upon the
major part, virtue in whom it remains becomes more excellent, and
being lost in some, multiplies its goodness in others which remain
untouched, and persists entire in the general inundation. I can
therefore behold vice without a satire, content only with an admon-
ition or instructive reprehension; for noble natures, and such as are
capable of goodness, are railed into vice, that might as easily be
admonished into virtue; and we should be all so far the orators of
goodness as to protect her from the power of vice, and maintain the
cause of injured truth.

No man can justly censure or condemn another, because, indeed,
no man truly knows another. This I perceive in myself, for I am in the
dark to all the world, and my nearest friends behold me but in a
cloud. Those that know me but superficially think less of me than I
do of myself; those of my near acquaintance think more; God, who
truly knows me, knows that I am nothing, for he only beholds me—
and all the world—who looks not on us through a derived ray or a
trajection of a sensible species, but beholds the substance without the
help of accidents, and the forms of things as we their operations.
Further, no man can judge another, because no man knows himself;
for we censure others but as they disagree from that humour which
we fancy laudable in ourselves, and commend others but for that
wherein they seem to quadrate and consent with us. So that, in conclusion, all is but that we all condemn, self-love.

'Tis the general complaint of these times—and perhaps of those
past—that charity grows cold, which I perceive most verified in
those which most do manifest the fires and flames of zeal, for it is

profaned: made commonly available.   *community*: commonness.
railed: driven by abuse.   *derived*: reflected from a surface.
trajection: transmission.   *species*: image.
accidents: non-essential properties, outward characteristics.
forms: inner natures.

a virtue that best agrees with coldest natures and such as are com-
plexioned for humility. But how shall we expect charity towards
others when we are uncharitable to ourselves? 'Charity begins at
home' is the voice of the world; yet is every man his own greatest
enemy, and, as it were, his own executioner. *Non occides* is the
commandment of God, yet scarce observed by any man; for I
perceive every man is his own Atropos, and lends a hand to cut the
thread of his own days. Cain was not therefore the first murderer,
but Adam, who brought in death; whereof he beheld the practice and
example in his own son Abel, and saw that verified in the experience
of another which faith could not persuade him in the theory of himself.

SECT. 5

There is I, think, no man that apprehends his own miseries less than
myself, and no man that so nearly apprehends another's. I could
lose an arm without a tear, and with few groans, methinks, be
quartered into pieces; yet can I weep most seriously at a play, and
receive with a true passion the counterfeit griefs of those known and
professed impostors.

It is a barbarous part of inhumanity to add unto any afflicted
party's misery, or endeavour to multiply in any man a passion whose
single nature is already above his patience. This was the greatest
affliction of Job, and those oblique expostulations of his friends a
deeper injury than the downright blows of the Devil. It is not the
tears of our own eyes only, but of our friends also, that do exhaust
the current of our sorrows, which, falling into many streams, runs
more peaceably, and is contented with a narrower channel. It is an
act within the power of charity to translate a passion out of one
breast into another, and to divide a sorrow almost out of itself; for
an affliction, like a dimension, may be so divided as, if not indivisible,
at least to become insensible.

Now with my friend I desire not to share or participate, but to
engross his sorrows, that by making them mine own I may more
easily discuss them; for in mine own reason and within myself I can
command that which I cannot entreat without myself and within
the circle of another. I have often thought those noble pairs and
examples of friendship not so truly histories of what had been as

---

Non occides: the Sixth Commandment, Thou shalt not kill. Exod. 20:13.
Atropos: the Greek Fate represented as cutting the thread of life.
Cain: Gen. 4:8.   *a dimension*: anything measurable.
discuss: dispel.   *entreat*: persuade by pleading.

fictions of what should be, but I now perceive nothing in them but possibilities, nor anything in the heroic examples of Damon and Pythias, Achilles and Patroclus, which, methinks, upon some grounds I could not perform within the narrow compass of myself.

That a man should lay down his life for his friend seems strange to vulgar affections and such as confine themselves within that worldly principle, 'Charity begins at home'. For mine own part, I could never remember the relations that I hold unto myself, nor the respect that I owe unto mine own nature, in the cause of God, my country and my friends. Next to these three, I do embrace myself. I confess I do not observe that order that the schools ordain our affections—to love our parents, wives, children, and then our friends—for excepting the injunctions of religion, I do not find in myself such a necessary and indissoluble sympathy to all those of my blood. I hope I do not break the Fifth Commandment if I conceive I may love my friend before the nearest of my blood, even those to whom I owe the principles of life. I never yet cast a true affection on a woman,[n] but I have loved my friend as I do virtue, my soul, my God.

From hence methinks I do conceive how God loves man, what happiness there is in the love of God. Omitting all other, there are three most mystical unions: two natures in one person; three persons in one nature; one soul in two bodies. For though indeed they be really divided, yet are they so united as they seem but one, and make rather a duality than two distinct souls.

SECT. 6

There are wonders in true affection; it is a body of enigmas, mysteries, and riddles, wherein two so become one as they both become two. I love my friend before myself, and yet methinks I do not love him enough; some few months hence my multiplied affection will make me believe I have not loved him at all. When I am from him, I am dead till I be with him; when I am with him, I am not satisfied, but would still be nearer him: united souls are not satisfied with embraces, but desire to be truly each other, which being impossible, their desires

Damon and Pythias: who, celebrated in an Elizabethan play by R. Edwards, were prepared to die for each other.
Patroclus: whose death, in Homer's *Iliad*, caused the sulking Achilles to resume his role in the siege of Troy.
Fifth Commandment: Honour thy father and thy mother. Exod. 20:12.
two natures: the divine and the human in the incarnate Christ.
three persons: in the Christian Trinity.

are infinite, and must proceed without a possibility of satisfaction. Another misery there is in affection, that whom we truly love like our own selves, we forget their looks, nor can our memory retain the idea of their faces; and it is no wonder, for they are ourselves, and our affections make their looks our own. This noble affection falls not on vulgar and common constitutions, but on such as are marked for virtue; he that can love his friend with this noble ardour will in a competent degree affect all.

Now if we can bring our affections to look beyond the body and cast an eye upon the soul, we have found out the true object not only of friendship but charity; and the greatest happiness that we can bequeath the soul is that wherein we all do place our last felicity, salvation; which though it be not in our power to bestow, it is in our charity and pious invocations to desire, if not procure and further. I cannot contentedly frame a prayer for myself in particular without a catalogue of my friends, nor request a happiness wherein my sociable disposition doth not desire the fellowship of my neighbour. I never hear the toll of a passing-bell—though in my mirth—without my prayers and best wishes for the departing spirit; I cannot go to cure the body of my patient but I forget my profession, and call unto God for his soul; I cannot see one say his prayers but, instead of imitating him, I fall into a supplication for him, who perhaps is no more to me than a common nature; and if God hath vouchsafed an ear to my supplications, there are surely many happy that never saw me, and enjoy the blessing of mine unknown devotions. To pray for enemies (that is, for their salvation) is no harsh precept, but the practice of our daily and ordinary devotions. I cannot believe the story of the Italian; our bad wishes and malevolous desires proceed no further than this life: it is the Devil and uncharitable votes of hell that desire our misery in the world to come.

SECT. 7

To do no injury, nor take none, was a principle which to my former years and impatient affections seemed to contain enough of morality; but my more settled years and Christian constitution have fallen upon severer resolutions. I can hold there is no such thing as injury; that if there be, there is no such injury as revenge, and no such revenge as the contempt of an injury; that to hate another is to

---

affect: love.
the Italian: who, having promised to spare a man's life if he foreswore his religion, then killed him in a state of mortal sin.
affections: disposition.   *no such thing as injury*: i.e. to oneself.

malign himself; that the truest way to love another is to despise ourselves.

I were unjust unto mine own conscience if I should say I am at variance with anything like myself. I find there are many pieces in this one fabric of man; this frame is raised upon a mass of antipathies. I am one, methinks, but as the world, wherein, notwithstanding, there are a swarm of distinct essences, and in them another world of contrarieties. We carry private and domestic enemies within, public and more hostile adversaries without. The Devil, that did but buffet Saint Paul, plays, methinks, at sharp with me; let me be nothing if within the compass of myself I do not find the Battle of Lepanto—passion against reason, reason against faith, faith against the Devil, and my conscience against all. There is another man within me, that's angry with me, rebukes, commands, and dastards me.

I have no conscience of marble to resist the hammer of more heavy offences, nor yet so soft and waxen as to take the impression of each single peccadillo or scape of infirmity. I am of a strange belief, that it is as easy to be forgiven some sins as to commit others. For my original sin, I hold it to be washed away in my baptism; for my actual transgressions, I compute and reckon with God but from my last repentance, sacrament, or general absolution, and therefore am not terrified with the sins or madness of my youth.

I thank the goodness of God I have no sins that want a name; I am not singular in offences—my transgressions are epidemical and from the common breath of our corruption. For there are certain tempers of body which, matched with an humorous depravity of mind, do hatch and produce vitiosities whose newness and monstrosity of nature admits no name; this was the temper of that lecher that carnalled with a statua, and the constitution of Nero in his sphinctrian recreations. For the heavens are not only fruitful in new and unheard-of stars, the earth in plants and animals, but men's minds also in villainy and vices. Now the dullness of my reason, and the vulgarity of my disposition, never prompted my invention, nor solicited my affection unto any of these; yet even those common and quotidian

Saint Paul: 2 Cor. 12:7.   *at sharp*: with unbated sword, in deadly earnest.
Battle of Lepanto: at which, in 1570, the Christian Venetians decisively defeated
    the Muslim Turks.
dastards: makes a coward of.   *scape*: careless offence.
humorous: constitutional.   *lecher*: Pliny, *Natural History*, 36.4(21).
carnalled: had sexual intercourse.   *statua*: statue.
Nero: specifically the Emperor Tiberius (Claudius Nero Caesar), in Suetonius,
    Tiberius, 43, and Tacitus, *Annals*, 6.1, though Nero partook of similar pleasures.
sphinctrian: anal.   *vulgarity*: ordinariness.

infirmities that so necessarily attend me, and do seem to be my very
nature, have so dejected me, so broken the estimation that I should
have otherwise of myself, that I repute myself the most abjectest
piece of mortality. Divines prescribe a fit of sorrow to repentance:
there goes indignation, anger, contempt and hatred into mine—
passions of a contrary nature which neither seem to suit with this
action nor my proper constitution. It is no breach of charity to ourselves to be at variance with our vices, nor to abhor that part of us
which is an enemy to the ground of charity, our God; wherein we do
but imitate our great selves the world, whose divided antipathies and
contrary faces do yet carry a charitable regard unto the whole, by
their particular discords preserving the common harmony, and keeping in fetters those powers whose rebellions, once masters, might be
the ruin of all.

SECT. 8

I thank God, amongst those millions of vices I do inherit and hold
from Adam I have escaped one (and that a mortal enemy to charity),
the first and father sin, not only of man, but of the Devil—pride, a
vice whose name is comprehended in a monosyllable, but in its
nature not circumscribed with a world. I have escaped it in a condition that can hardly avoid it—those petty acquisitions and reputed
perfections that advance and elevate the conceits of other men add
no feathers unto mine. I have seen a grammarian tower and plume
himself over a single line in Horace, and show more pride in the
construction of one ode than the author in the composure of the
whole book.

For my own part, besides the jargon and patois of several provinces, I understand no less than six languages; yet I protest I have no
higher conceit of myself than had our fathers before the confusion
of Babel, when there was but one language in the world, and none to
boast himself either linguist or critic. I have not only seen several
countries, beheld the nature of their climes, the chorography of their
provinces, topography of their cities, but understood their several
laws, customs and policies; yet cannot all this persuade the dullness
of my spirit unto such an opinion of myself as I behold in nimbler
and conceited heads that never looked a degree beyond their nests. I
know the names, and somewhat more, of all the constellations in my
horizon; yet I have seen a prating mariner, that could only name the

---

our great selves: our macrocosmic embodiment.
construction: explanation.

pointers and the North star, out-talk me, and conceit himself a whole sphere above me. I know most of the plants of my country and of those about me; yet methinks I do not know so many as when I did but know an hundred, and had scarcely ever simpled further than Cheapside. For indeed, heads of capacity, and such as are not full with a handful or easy measure of knowledge, think they know nothing till they know all; which being impossible, they fall upon the opinion of Socrates, and only know they know not anything. I cannot think that Homer pined away upon the riddle of the fisherman, or that Aristotle, who understood the uncertainty of knowledge, and confessed so often the reason of man too weak for the works of nature, did ever drown himself upon the flux and reflux of Euripus. We do but learn today what our better advanced judgements will unteach us tomorrow, and Aristotle doth but instruct us as Plato did him—that is, to confute himself.

I have run through all sects, yet find no rest in any; though our first studies and junior endeavours may style us Peripatetics, Stoics, or Academics, yet I perceive the wisest heads prove at last almost all Sceptics, and stand like Janus in the field of knowledge. I have, therefore, one common and authentic philosophy I learned in the schools, whereby I discourse and satisfy the reason of other men; another, more reserved and drawn from experience, whereby I content mine own. Solomon, that complained of ignorance in the height of knowledge, hath not only humbled my conceits but discouraged my endeavours.

There is yet another conceit that hath sometimes made me shut my books, which tells me it is a vanity to waste our days in the blind pursuit of knowledge; it is but attending a little longer, and we shall enjoy that by instinct and infusion which we endeavour at here by labour and inquisition: it is better to sit down in a modest ignorance, and rest contented with the natural blessing of our own

---

pointers: two stars in the Great Bear through which a line may be drawn pointing approximately to the Pole star.
simpled: sought medicinal herbs.
Cheapside: the London street where stall holders sold plants for healing and cooking.   *Socrates*: Plato, *Apology*, 21d.
Homer: to whom the fishermen said that what they had caught, they had thrown away, and what they had not caught, they had with them. Having failed to catch any fish, they had resorted to delousing themselves. See *Pseudodoxia Epidemica*, 7.13.
flux and reflux of Euripus: the tides of the strait between Boeotoia and Euboea. See *Pseudodoxia Epidemica*, 7.13.
Janus: whose statues represented him looking two ways at once.
Solomon: Eccles. 8:16–17.

reasons, than buy the uncertain knowledge of this life—with sweat
and vexation—which death gives every fool gratis, and is an accessory
of our glorification.

SECT. 9

I was never yet once, and commend their resolutions who never
marry twice; not that I disallow of second marriage—as neither, in
all cases, of polygamy, which considering some times, and the
unequal number of both sexes, may be also necessary. The whole
world was made for man, but the twelfth part of man for woman:
man is the whole world and the breath of God, woman the rib and
crooked piece of man. I could be content that we might procreate
like trees, without conjunction, or that there were any way to perpetuate the world without this trivial and vulgar way of coition. It
is the foolishest act a wise man commits in all his life, nor is there
anything that will more deject his cooled imagination when he shall
consider what an odd and unworthy piece of folly he hath committed.
I speak not in prejudice, nor am averse from that sweet sex, but naturally amorous of all that is beautiful: I can look a whole day with
delight upon a handsome picture, though it be but of an horse.

It is my temper—and I like it the better—to affect all harmony;
and sure there is music, even in the beauty and the silent note which
Cupid strikes, far sweeter than the sound of an instrument. For there
is a music wherever there is a harmony, order, or proportion; and
thus far we may maintain the music of the spheres: for those well
ordered motions and regular paces, though they give no sound unto
the ear, yet to the understanding they strike a note most full of harmony. Whosoever is harmonically composed delights in harmony,[n]
which makes me much distrust the symmetry of those heads which de-
claim against all church music. For myself, not only from my obedience but my particular genius, I do embrace it; for even that vulgar
and tavern music which makes one man merry, another mad, strikes in
me a deep fit of devotion and a profound contemplation of the first
Composer—there is something in it of divinity more than the ear discovers. It is an hieroglyphical and shadowed lesson of the whole world
and creatures of God—such a melody to the ear as the whole world,
well understood, would afford the understanding. In brief, it is a sensible fit of that harmony which intellectually sounds in the ears of God.

---

death gives: 1 Cor. 13:8–12.
spheres: the spheres of the pre-Copernican system were supposed as they revolved
   to emit heavenly harmonies.
fit: musical section.

I will not say with Plato the soul is an harmony, but harmonical, and hath its nearest sympathy unto music. Thus some, whose temper of body agrees, and humours the constitution of their souls, are born poets—though indeed all are naturally inclined unto rhythm. This made Tacitus in the very first line of his story fall upon a verse; and Cicero, the worst of poets, but declaiming for a poet, falls in the very first sentence upon a perfect hexameter.

I feel not in me those sordid and unchristian desires of my profession: I do not secretly implore and wish for plagues, rejoice at famines, revolve ephemerides and almanacs in expectation of malignant aspects, fatal conjunctions, and eclipses; I rejoice not at unwholesome springs, nor unseasonable winters; my prayer goes with the husbandman's—I desire everything in its proper season, that neither men nor the times be out of temper. Let me be sick myself, if sometimes the malady of my patient be not a disease unto me; I desire rather to cure his infirmities than my own necessities; where I do him no good methinks it is scarce honest gain, though I confess 'tis but the worthy salary of our well intended endeavours. I am not only ashamed but heartily sorry that, besides death, there are diseases incurable; yet not for my own sake, or that they be beyond my art, but for the general cause and sake of humanity, whose common cause I apprehend as mine own.

And to speak more generally, those three noble professions which all civil commonwealths do honour are raised upon the fall of Adam, and are not any exempt from their infirmities: there are not only diseases incurable in physic, but cases indissoluble in law, vices incorrigible in divinity. If General Councils may err, I do not see why particular courts should be infallible; their perfectest rules are raised upon the erroneous reason of man, and the laws of one do but condemn the rules of another—as Aristotle oft-times the opinions of his predecessors because, though agreeable to reason, yet were not consonant to his own rules and the logic of his proper principles. Again, to speak nothing of the sin against the Holy Ghost (whose

---

Plato: *Phaedo*, 86b–d.
Tacitus: *Annals*, 1.1: Urbem Romam in principio reges habuere.—*B.*
Cicero: *Pro Archia Poeta*: In qua me non inficior mediocriter esse.—*B.*
revolve: ponder over.   *aspects*: relative positions of planets.
conjunctions: astrologically significant proximities of heavenly bodies.
indissoluble: unresolvable.
General Councils: alluding to the *Book of Common Prayer*, 'Articles of Religion', 21.
Holy Ghost: Matt. 12:31–2; Mark 3:29; Luke 12:10.

cure not only, but whose nature is unknown), I can cure the gout or
stone in some, sooner than divinity, pride or avarice in others. I can
cure vices by physic when they remain incurable by divinity, and
shall obey my pills when they contemn their precepts. I boast nothing,
but plainly say, we all labour against our own cure: for death is the
cure of all diseases. There is no catholicon or universal remedy I
know but this, which though nauseous to queasy stomachs, yet to
prepared appetites is nectar, and a pleasant potion of immortality.

SECT. 10

For my conversation, it is—like the sun's—with all men, and with a
friendly aspect to good and bad. Methinks there is no man bad, and
the worst, best; that is, while they are kept within the circle of those
qualities wherein they are good. There is no man's mind of such
discordant and jarring a temper to which a tuneable disposition may
not strike a harmony. *Magnae virtutes nec minora vitia*—it is the
posy of the best natures, and may be inverted on the worst; there are
in the most depraved and venomous dispositions certain pieces that
remain untouched, which by an antiperistasis become more excellent,
or by the excellency of their antipathies are able to preserve themselves from the contagion of their enemy vices, and persist entire
beyond the general corruption.

For it is also thus in nature. The greatest balsams do lie enveloped
in the bodies of most powerful corrosives; I say, moreover—and I
ground upon experience—that poisons contain within themselves
their own antidote and that which preserves them from the venom of
themselves; without which they were not deleterious to others only,
but to themselves also. But it is the corruption that I fear within me,
not the contagion of commerce without me; 'tis that unruly regiment
within me that will destroy me. 'Tis I that do infect myself; the man
without a navel yet lives in me: I feel that original canker corrode
and devour me; and therefore *Defenda me Dios de me*—Lord deliver
me from myself—is a part of my litany and the first voice of my retired
imaginations.

There is no man alone, because every man is a microcosm and
carries the whole world about him. *Nunquam minus solus quam cum*

---

their precepts: the divines'.
good and bad: Matt. 5:45.
Magnae virtutes: Great virtues, nor lesser vices. Plutarch, *Demetrius*, 1.7.
antiperistasis: reaction or contrast.
man without a navel: Adam. See *Pseudodoxia Epidemica*, 5.5.
lives in me: Thomas à Kempis, *Imitation of Christ*, 3.34.3.
Nunquam minus: Never less alone than when alone. Cicero, *De Officiis*, 3.1.1.

solus, though it be the apophthegm of a wise man, is yet true in the mouth of a fool; for indeed, though in a wilderness, a man is never alone, not only because he is with himself and his own thoughts, but because he is with the Devil, who ever consorts with our solitude, and is that unruly rebel that musters up those disordered motions which accompany our sequestered imaginations. And to speak more narrowly, there is no such thing as solitude, nor anything that can be said to be alone and by itself but God, who is his own circle, and can subsist by himself: all others—besides their dissimilary and hetero-geneous parts, which in a manner multiply their natures—cannot subsist without the concourse of God and the society of that hand which doth uphold their natures. In brief, there can be nothing truly alone and by itself which is not truly one, and such is only God: all others do transcend an unity, and so by consequence are many.

SECT. 11

Now, for my life, it is a miracle of thirty years, which to relate were not a history but a piece of poetry, and would sound to common ears like a fable. For the world, I count it, not an inn, but an hospital, and a place not to live but to die in. The world that I regard is myself; it is the microcosm of mine own frame that I cast mine eye on; for the other, I use it but like my globe, and turn it round sometimes for my recreation. Men that look upon my outside, perusing only my condition and fortunes, do err in my altitude, for I am above Atlas his shoulders: the earth is a point not only in respect of the heavens above us, but of that heavenly and celestial part within us. That mass of flesh that circumscribes me limits not my mind; that surface that tells the heavens it hath an end cannot persuade me I have any: I take my circle to be above three hundred and sixty; though the number of the arc do measure my body, it comprehendeth not my mind—whilst I study to find how I am a microcosm or little world, I find myself something more than the great.

There is surely a piece of divinity in us—something that was before the elements, and owes no homage unto the sun. Nature tells me I am the image of God, as well as Scripture; he that understands not thus much hath not his introduction or first lesson, and is yet to begin the

his own circle: See above, p. 10.   *dissimilary*: various.
concourse: concurrence.   *Atlas*: who in Greek myth supported the heavens.
that surface . . . an end: the finite sphere that bounds the earth in relation to the
     rest of the universe.
three hundred and sixty: the number of degrees in a circle ('arc').
owes no homage: because not nurtured by physical heat.
Scripture: Genesis 1:26, 27; 9:6; 1 Cor. 11:7.

alphabet of man. Let me not injure the felicity of others if I say I am as happy as any—*Ruat caelum: fiat voluntas tua* salveth all, so that whatsoever happens, it is but what our daily prayers desire. In brief, I am content, and what should providence add more? Surely this is it we call happiness, and this do I enjoy; with this I am happy in a dream, and as content to enjoy a happiness in a fancy as others in a more apparent truth and reality.

There is surely a nearer apprehension of anything that delights us in our dreams than in our waked senses. Without this I were unhappy, for my awaked judgement discontents me, ever whispering unto me that I am from my friend; but my friendly dreams in the night requite me, and make me think I am within his arms. I thank God for my happy dreams as I do for my good rest, for there is a satisfaction in them unto reasonable desires and such as can be content with a fit of happiness; and surely it is not a melancholy conceit to think we are all asleep in this world, and that the conceits of this life are as mere dreams to those of the next, as the phantasms of the night to the conceits of the day. There is an equal delusion in both, and the one doth but seem to be the emblem or picture of the other; we are somewhat more than ourselves in our sleeps, and the slumber of the body seems to be but the waking of the soul. It is the ligation of sense, but the liberty of reason; and our awaking conceptions do not match the fancies of our sleeps.

At my nativity, my ascendant was the watery sign of Scorpio; I was born in the planetary hour of Saturn, and I think I have a piece of that leaden planet in me. I am in no way facetious, nor disposed for the mirth and galliardise of company; yet in one dream I can compose a whole comedy—behold the action, apprehend the jests, and laugh myself awake at the conceits thereof. Were my memory as faithful as my reason is then fruitful I would never study but in my dreams, and this time also would I choose for my devotions; but our grosser memories have then so little hold of our abstracted understandings that they forget the story, and can only relate to our awaked souls a confused and broken tale of what hath passed.

Ruat caelum: Let the sky fall: thy will be done.   *fit*: short period.
waking of the soul: Paracelsus, *De Philosophia*, 5 (*Opera*, 1603–5, ii.54).
ascendant: zodiacal constellation just rising.
Scorpio: allegedly causing the mind and disposition to be active yet reserved and thoughtful.
Saturn: supposedly making people melancholy, fond of solitude, bashful, firm in friendship, grave, often ascetic, and, in Scorpio, petulant, subtle, inconstant, and envious; ingenious, profound, and clever; and unfortunate at sea.
galliardise: gaiety.

Aristotle, who hath written a singular tract of sleep, hath not me-thinks thoroughly defined it, nor yet Galen, though he seem to have corrected it; for those noctambuloes or night-walkers, though in their sleep, do yet enjoy the action of their senses. We must therefore say that there is something in us that is not in the jurisdiction of Morpheus; and that those abstracted and ecstatic souls do walk about in their own corpse, as spirits with the bodies they assume, wherein they seem to hear, see, and feel, though indeed the organs are destitute of sense, and their natures of those faculties that should inform them. Thus, it is observed that men sometimes upon the hour of their departure do speak and reason above themselves. For then the soul begins to be freed from the ligaments of the body, begins to reason like herself, and to discourse in a strain above mortality.

SECT. 12

We term sleep a death, and yet it is waking that kills us, and destroys those spirits that are the house of life. 'Tis indeed a part of life that best expresseth death, for every man truly lives so long as he acts his nature, or someway makes good the faculties of himself. Themistocles, therefore, that slew his soldier in his sleep, was a merciful executioner; 'tis a kind of punishment the mildness of no laws hath invented—I wonder the fancy of Lucan and Seneca did not discover it. It is that death by which we may be literally said to die daily; a death which Adam died before his mortality; a death whereby we live a middle and moderating point between life and death—in fine, so like death I dare not trust it without my prayers and an half adieu unto the world, and take my farewell in a colloquy with God.

> The night is come like to the day:
> Depart not thou great God away.
> Let not my sins, black as the night,
> Eclipse the lustre of thy light.
> Keep still in my horizon, for to me
> The sun makes not the day, but thee.

Aristotle: *Of Sleep and Waking*, 1: a sort of lack of motion.
Galen: who in *De Motu Musculorum*, 2.4, points out that not all a sleeper's
    muscles are still.
noctambuloes: sleep-walkers.   *Morpheus*: Greek god of dreams.
Themistocles: rather Iphicrates in Frontinus, *Strategematon*, 3.12.2–3.
Lucan and Seneca: forced by Nero to kill themselves, but allowed to choose the
    method. Tacitus, *Annals*, 15.63–4, 70.
die daily: 1 Cor. 15:31.

Thou, whose nature cannot sleep,
On my temples sentry keep;
Guard me 'gainst those watchful foes
Whose eyes are open while mine close.
Let no dreams my head infest
But such as Jacob's temples blessed.
While I do rest, my soul advance;
Make my sleep a holy trance
That I may, my rest being wrought,
Awake into some holy thought,
And with as active vigour run
My course as doth the nimble sun.
Sleep is a death—O make me try
By sleeping what it is to die,
And as gently lay my head
On my grave as now my bed.
Howe'er I rest, great God, let me
Awake again at last with thee:
And thus assured, behold I lie
Securely, or to wake or die.
These are my drowsy days, in vain
I do now wake to sleep again.
O come that hour when I shall never
Sleep again, but wake for ever!

This is the dormitive I take to bedward; I need no other laudanum
than this to make me sleep; after which I close mine eyes in security,
content to take my leave of the sun, and sleep unto the Resurrection.

SECT. 13

The method I should use in distributive justice, I often observe in
commutative, and keep a geometrical proportion in both; whereby,
becoming equable to others, I become unjust to myself, and supererogate in that common principle, 'Do unto others as thou wouldst be
done unto thyself'. I was not born unto riches, neither is it, I think,
my star to be wealthy; or if it were, the freedom of my mind and
frankness of my disposition were able to contradict and cross my
fates: for to me avarice seems not so much a vice, as a deplorable
piece of madness; to conceive ourselves urinals, or be persuaded that

Jacob's temples: Gen. 28:12–15.   *dormitive*: means of inducing sleep.
The method . . . in both: I often repay people as I should reward them, giving
   several times more than is deserved. See Aristotle, *Nicomachean Ethics*, 5.3–4.
supererogate: do more than duty requires.
Do unto others: Matt. 7:12; Luke 6:31.   *star*: astrological destiny.

we are dead, is not so ridiculous, nor so many degrees beyond the power of hellebore as this.

The opinions of theory, and positions of men, are not so void of reason as their practised conclusions: some have held that snow is black,[n] that the earth moves, that the soul is air, fire, water[n]—but all this is philosophy, and there is no delirium if we do but speculate the folly and indisputable dotage of avarice. To that subterraneous idol and god of the earth I do confess I am an atheist; I cannot persuade myself to honour that the world adores; whatsoever virtue its prepared substance may have within my body,[n] it hath no influence nor operation without. I would not entertain a base design, or an action that should call me villain, for the Indies; and for this only do I love and honour my own soul, and have methinks two arms too few to embrace myself.

Aristotle is too severe, that will not allow us to be truly liberal without wealth and the bountiful hand of fortune; if this be true, I must confess I am charitable only in my liberal intentions and bountiful well-wishes. But if the example of the mite be not only an act of wonder, but an example of the noblest charity, surely poor men may also build hospitals, and the rich alone have not erected cathedrals. I have a private method which others observe not; I take the opportunity of myself to do good: I borrow occasion of charity from mine own necessities, and supply the wants of others when I am in most need myself; for it is an honest stratagem to take advantage of ourselves, and so to husband the acts of virtue that where they are defective in one circumstance they may repay their want and multiply their goodness in another.

I have not Peru in my desires, but a competence and ability to perform those good works to which he hath inclined my nature. He is rich who hath enough to be charitable, and it is hard to be so poor that a noble mind may not find a way to this piece of goodness. 'He that giveth to the poor lendeth to the Lord'—there is more rhetoric in that one sentence than in a library of sermons; and indeed if those sentences were understood by the reader with the same emphasis as they are delivered by the author, we needed not those volumes of instructions, but might be honest by an epitome.

---

hellebore: anciently administered to the insane. Horace, *Satires*, 2.3.82: By far the greatest dose of hellebore is to be given to the avaricious.
speculate: consider.   *god of the earth*: gold.
Aristotle: Although, in *Nicomachean Ethics*, 1.8, he suggests that possessions are necessary to happiness since without them it is difficult to be generous, he observes, in 4.1, that the liberality of a gift is relative to the means of the giver.
example of the mite: Mark 12:42–4, Luke 21:2–4.
He that giveth: Prov. 19:17.   *emphasis*: implied meaning.

Upon this motive only, I cannot behold a beggar without relieving his necessities with my purse or his soul with my prayers; these scenical and accidental differences between us cannot make me forget that common and untouched part of us both; there is under these centos and miserable outsides, these mutilate and semi-bodies, a soul of the same alloy with our own, whose genealogy is God as well as ours, and in as fair a way to salvation as ourselves. Statists that labour to contrive a commonwealth without poverty take away the object of charity, not understanding only the commonwealth of a Christian, but forgetting the prophecy of Christ.

SECT. 14

Now there is another part of charity which is the basis and pillar of this, and that is the love of God, for whom we love our neighbour; for this I think charity: to love God for himself, and our neighbour for God. All that is truly amiable is God, or, as it were, a divided piece of him that retains a reflex or shadow of himself. Nor is it strange that we should place affection on that which is invisible: all that we truly love is thus; what we adore under affection of our senses deserves not the honour of so pure a title. Thus we adore virtue though to the eyes of sense she be invisible. Thus that part of our noble friends that we love is not that part that we embrace, but that insensible part that our arms cannot embrace. God, being all goodness, can love nothing but himself; he loves us but for that part which is, as it were, himself and the traduction of his Holy Spirit.

Let us call to assize the love of our parents, the affection of our wives and children, and they are all dumb shows and dreams, without reality, truth, or constancy; for first there is a strong bond of affection between us and our parents, yet how easily dissolved! We betake ourselves to a woman, forgetting our mothers in a wife, and the womb that bare us in that that shall bear our image. This woman blessing us with children, our affection leaves the level it held before, and sinks from our bed unto our issue and picture of posterity, where affection holds no steady mansion. They, growing up in years, desire our ends, or, applying themselves to a woman, take a lawful way to love another better than ourselves. Thus I perceive a man may be buried alive, and behold his grave in his own issue.

---

scenical and accidental: superficial and non-essential.
centos: patchwork pieces.　　*statists*: political theorists.
not understanding only: not only not understanding.
prophecy of Christ: Luke 6:20.
traduction: offspring.　　*sinks*: passes down.

SECT. 15

I conclude, therefore, and say there is no happiness under (or, as Copernicus will have it, above) the sun, nor any crambe in that repeated verity and burthen of all the wisdom of Solomon: 'All is vanity and vexation of spirit'—there is no felicity in that the world adores. Aristotie, whilst he labours to refute the ideas of Plato, falls upon one himself; for his *summum bonum* is a chimaera, and there is no such thing as his felicity. That wherein God himself is happy; the holy angels are happy; in whose defect the devils are unhappy—that dare I call happiness: whatsoever conduceth unto this may with an easy metaphor deserve that name; whatsoever else the world terms happiness is to me a story out of Pliny, an apparition or neat delusion, wherein there is no more of happiness than the name.

Bless me in this life with but the peace of my conscience, command of my affections, the love of thyself and my dearest friends, and I shall be happy enough to pity Caesar. These are, O Lord, the humble desires of my most reasonable ambition, and all I dare call happiness on earth, wherein I set no rule or limit to thy hand or providence: dispose of me according to the wisdom of thy pleasure. Thy will be done, though in my own undoing.

FINIS

crambe: distasteful repetition.
Solomon: Eccles. 1:14; 2:11, 17; 4:4, 16; 6:9.
Aristotle: *Nicomachean Ethics*, 1.6 ff.   *summum bonum*: chief good.
Pliny: whose *Natural History* contains many credulous errors.
neat: clever.   *Thy will be done*: cf. Matt. 26:42.

A Letter

sent upon the information of animadversions to come forth upon the imperfect and surreptitious copy of *Religio Medici,* whilst this true one was going to the press.

Honourable Sir,

Give your servant, who hath ever honoured you, leave to take notice of a book at present in the press, entitled (as I am informed) *Animadversions* upon a treatise lately printed under the name of *Religio Medici*: hereof I am advertised you have descended to be the author. Worthy sir, permit your servant to affirm there is contained therein nothing that can deserve the reason of your contradictions, much less the candour of your *Animadversions*; and to certify the truth thereof, that book (whereof I do acknowledge myself the author) was penned many years past, and (what cannot escape your apprehension) with no intention for the press, or the least desire to oblige the faith of any man to its assertions.

But what hath more especially emboldened my pen unto you at present is that the same piece, contrived in my private study and as an exercise unto myself rather than exercitation for any other, having passed from my hand under a broken and imperfect copy, by frequent transcription it still ran forward in corruption, and—after the addition of some things, omission of others, and transposition of many—without my assent or privacy the liberty of these times committed it unto the press, from whence it issued so disguised, the author without distinction could not acknowledge it.

Having thus miscarried, within a few weeks I shall, God willing, deliver unto the press the true and intended original (whereof in the meantime your worthy self may command a view); otherwise whenever that copy shall be extant, it will most clearly appear how far the text hath been mistaken, and all observations, glosses, or exercitations thereon will in a great part impugn the printer or transcriber rather than the author. If after that you shall esteem it worth your vacant hours to discourse thereon, you shall but take that liberty which I assume myself, that is, freely to abound in your sense as I have done in my own. However you shall determine, you

---

descended: condescended.
privacy: knowledge.
distinction: making certain qualifications.
abound: expatiate.

shall sufficiently honour me in the vouchsafe of your refute, and I oblige the whole world in the occasion of your pen.

Norwich,
March 3,
1642.   Your servant,
                                                T. B.

Worthy Sir,

Speedily, upon the receipt of your letter of the third current, I sent to find out the printer that Mr. Crooke (who delivered me yours) told me was printing something under my name concerning your treatise of *Religio Medici*, and to forbid him any further proceeding therein; but my servant could not meet with him; whereupon I have left with Mr. Crooke a note to that purpose, entreating him to deliver it to the printer.

I verily believe there is some mistake in the information given you, and that what is printing must be from some other pen than mine, for such reflections as I made upon your learned and ingenious discourse are so far from meriting the press as they can tempt nobody to a serious reading of them. They were notes hastily set down as I suddenly ran over your excellent piece, which is of so weighty subject, and so strongly penned, as requireth much time and sharp attention but to comprehend it. Whereas what I writ was the employment but of one sitting, and there was not twenty-four hours between my receiving my Lord of Dorset's letter that occasioned what I said and the finishing my answer to him; and yet part of that time was taken up in procuring your book—which he desired me to read and give him an account of—for till then I was so unhappy as never to have heard of that worthy discourse.

If that letter ever come to your view, you will see the high value I set upon your great parts; and if it should be thought I have been something too bold in differing from your sense, I hope I shall easily obtain pardon when it shall be considered that his Lordship assigned it me as an exercitation, to oppose in it for his entertainment such passages as I might judge capable thereof; wherein what liberty I took is to be attributed to the security of a private letter, and to my not knowing (nor my Lord's) the person whom it concerned.

vouchsafe: favour.   *refute*: disproof.
current: of the present month.   *strongly*: intensely.
parts: abilities.

But sir, now that I am so happy as to have that knowledge, I dare
assure you that nothing shall ever issue from me but savouring of all
honour, esteem, and reverence, both to yourself and that worthy
production of yours. If I had the vanity to give myself reputation by
entering the lists in public with so eminent and learned a man as you
are, yet I know right well I am no ways able to do it—it would be a
very unequal congress. I pretend not to learning: those slender
notions I have are but disjointed pieces I have by chance gleaned up
here and there; to encounter such a sinewy opposite, or make
animadversions upon so smart a piece as yours is, requireth a solid
stock and exercise in school learning. My superficial besprinkling will
serve only for a private letter or familiar discourse with lay auditors.

With longing I expect the coming abroad of the true copy of that
book whose false and stolen one hath already given me so much
delight. And so, assuring you I shall deem it a great good fortune to
deserve your favour and friendship, I kiss your hand and rest

Winchester House,
the 20 of March,
1642.
                                               your most humble servant,
                                               Kenelm Digby.

unequal congress: Virgil, *Aeneid*, 1.475: unequally matched with Achilles.

To such as have, or shall peruse the *Observations* upon a former corrupt copy of this book.

There are some men that Politian speaks of *Cui quam recta manus, tam fuit et facilis,* and it seems the author to the observations upon this book would arrogate as much to himself; for they were, by his own confession, but the conceptions of one night—a hasty birth—and so it proves, for what is really controllable he generally omitteth, and what is false upon the error of the copy he doth not always take notice of; and wherein he would contradict, he mistaketh or traduceth the intention, and (besides a parenthesis sometimes upon the author) only meddleth with those points from whence he takes a hint to deliver his prepared conceptions. But the gross of his book is made out by discourses collateral and digressions of his own, not at all emergent from this discourse; which is easily perceptible unto the intelligent reader.

Thus much I thought good to let thee understand, without the author's knowledge, who, slighting the refute, hath enforcedly published (as a sufficient confutation) his own book. And in this I shall not make so bold with him as the Observator hath done with that noble knight whose name he hath wrongfully prefixed, as I am informed, to his slight animadversions: but I leave him to repentance, and thee to thy satisfaction.

Farewell.

Yours, A. B.

Politian: Agnolo Poliziano, 'Epitaph on Ioctus the Painter', 2 (*Opera*, 1553, p. 621): Whose hand was as accurate as it was fluent.
controllable: open to objection.
gross: bulk.   *slighting the refute*: disdaining disproof.
Observator: author of the *Observations*.

Hydriotaphia

To my worthy and honoured friend
Thomas Le Gros of Crostwick, Esquire[n]

When the funeral pyre was out, and the last valediction over, men took a lasting adieu of their interred friends, little expecting the curiosity of future ages should comment upon their ashes; and, having no old experience of the duration of their relics, held no opinion of such after-considerations.

But who knows the fate of his bones, or how often he is to be buried? Who hath the oracle of his ashes, or whither they are to be scattered? The relics of many lie, like the ruins of Pompey's, in all parts of the earth; and, when they arrive at your hands, these may seem to have wandered far, who, in a direct and meridian travel, have but few miles of known earth between yourself and the Pole.

That the bones of Theseus should be seen again in Athens was not beyond conjecture and hopeful expectation; but that these should arise so opportunely to serve yourself was an hit of fate, and honour beyond prediction.

We cannot but wish these urns might have the effect of theatrical vessels, and great Hippodrome urns in Rome—to resound the acclamations and honour due unto you. But these are sad and sepul-chral pitchers, which have no joyful voices; silently expressing old mortality, the ruins of forgotten times; and can only speak with life how long, in this corruptible frame, some parts may be uncorrupted —yet able to outlast bones long unborn, and noblest pile among us.

We present not these as any strange sight, or spectacle unknown to your eyes who have beheld the best of urns and noblest variety of ashes; who are yourself no slender master of antiquities, and can daily command the view of so many imperial faces: which raiseth your thoughts unto old things, and consideration of times before you,

---

oracle: oracular knowledge.
Pompey's: Pompey's sons are buried in Asia and Europe, but Libyan earth covers him. Martial, 5.74.1–2.—*B.*
direct: little directly but sea between your house and Greenland.—B.
bones of Theseus: brought back by Cimon. Plutarch, *Cimon*, 8.6.—*B.*
hit: stroke.
Hippodrome urns: the great urns in the Hippodrome at Rome, conceived to resound the voices of people at their shows.—B.
noblest pile: worthily possessed by that true gentleman Sir Horatio Townshend, my honoured friend.—B., referring to Raynham Hall, Norfolk.

when even living men were antiquities; when the living might exceed
the dead, and to depart this world could not be properly said, to go
unto the greater number. And so run up your thoughts upon the
ancient of days, the antiquary's truest object, unto whom the eldest
parcels are young, and earth itself an infant; and, without Egyptian
account, makes but small noise in thousands.

We were hinted by the occasion, not catched the opportunity to
write of old things, or intrude upon the antiquary. We are coldly
drawn unto discourses of antiquities, who have scarce time before us
to comprehend new things, or make out learned novelties. But seeing
they arose as they lay, almost in silence among us (at least in short
account suddenly passed over), we were very unwilling they should
die again, and be buried twice among us.

Beside, to preserve the living, and make the dead to live, to keep
men out of their urns, and discourse of human fragments in them, is
not impertinent unto our profession; whose study is life and death,
who daily behold examples of mortality, and of all men least need
artificial mementoes, or coffins by our bedside, to mind us of our
graves.

'Tis time to observe occurrences, and let nothing remarkable
escape us; the supinity of elder days hath left so much in silence, or
time hath so martyred the records, that the most industrious heads
do find no easy work to erect a new *Britannia*.

'Tis opportune to look back upon old times, and contemplate
our forefathers. Great examples grow thin, and to be fetched from
the past world. Simplicity flies away, and iniquity comes at long
strides upon us. We have enough to do to make up ourselves from
present and past times, and the whole stage of things scarce serveth
for our instruction. A complete piece of virtue must be made up from
the centos of all ages, as all the beauties of Greece could make but
one handsome Venus.

When the bones of King Arthur were digged up, the old race might

---

greater number: Petronius, 42.5.—B.
Egyptian account: which makes the world so many years old.—B., referring to
    estimates varying from 10,000 to 100,000 years.
supinity: laziness.
a new Britannia: wherein Mr. Dugdale hath excellently well endeavoured, and
    worthy to be countenanced by ingenious and noble persons.—B., referring to
    Camden's *Britannia* (1586, etc.), and W. Dugdale's *Monasticon Anglicanum*
    (1655), and *Antiquities of Warwickshire* (1656).
Venus: Cicero, *De Inventione*, 2.1, tells how Zeuxis used the five most beautiful
    girls in Croton as models for his painting of Helen.
King Arthur: in the time of Henry II. Camden, *Britannia*, 'Somerset'.—B.

think they beheld therein some originals of themselves: unto these of our urns none here can pretend relation, and can only behold the relics of those persons who, in their life giving the law unto their predecessors, after long obscurity now lie at their mercies. But remembering the early civility they brought upon these countries, and forgetting long past mischiefs, we mercifully preserve their bones, and piss not upon their ashes.

In the offer of these antiquities we drive not at ancient families, so long outlasted by them: we are far from erecting your worth upon the pillars of your forefathers, whose merits you illustrate. We honour your old virtues—conformable unto times before you—which are the noblest armory. And having long experience of your friendly conversation, void of empty formality, full of freedom, constant and generous honesty, I look upon you as a gem of the old rock, and must profess myself, even to urn and ashes,

Norwich.
May 1.   your ever faithful friend and servant,
                                      Thomas Browne.

piss not: Horace, *Ars Poetica*, 471.
old rock: The finest diamond comes from ancient rock.—*B.*

En sum: Propertius, 4.11.14: See, I am a burden which is lifted by five fingers.

Hydriotaphia

Urn-Burial,

OR

A Brief Discourse of the Sepulchral Urns lately found in Norfolk

CHAPTER I

In the deep discovery of the subterranean world, a shallow part would satisfy some enquirers who, if two or three yards were open about the surface, would not care to rake the bowels of Potosi and regions towards the centre. Nature hath furnished one part of the earth, and man another. The treasures of time lie high, in urns, coins, and monuments, scarce below the roots of some vegetables. Time hath endless rarities, and shows of all varieties; which reveals old things in heaven, makes new discoveries in earth, and even earth itself a discovery. That great antiquity America lay buried for thousands of years, and a large part of the earth is still in the urn unto us.

Though, if Adam were made out of an extract of the earth, all parts might challenge a restitution, yet few have returned their bones far lower than they might receive them; not affecting the graves of giants—under hilly and heavy coverings—but, content with less than their own depth, have wished their bones might lie soft, and the earth be light upon them. Even such as hope to rise again would not be content with central interment, or so desperately to place their relics as to lie beyond discovery, and in no way to be seen again: which happy contrivance hath made communication with our forefathers, and left unto our view some parts which they never beheld themselves.

Though earth hath engrossed the name, yet water hath proved the smartest grave; which in forty days swallowed almost mankind and the living creation—fishes not wholly escaping, except the salt ocean were handsomely contempered by admixture of the fresh element.

Many have taken voluminous pains to determine the state of the soul upon disunion, but men have been most fantastical in the singular contrivances of their corporal dissolution; whilst the soberest nations have rested in two ways—of simple inhumation and burning.

Potosi: the rich mountain of Peru.—B., referring to its silver-mines.
Adam: traditionally formed of dust from the four quarters of the earth.
receive them: i.e. from the surface of the earth which provided their nourishment.
graves of giants: the popular explanation of burial-mounds.
forty days: Gen. 7:17–23.   *contempered*: modified.

That carnal interment or burying was of the elder date, the old examples of Abraham and the patriarchs are sufficient to illustrate, and were without competition if it could be made out that Adam was buried near Damascus (or Mount Calvary, according to some tradition). God himself, that buried but one, was pleased to make choice of this way, collectible from Scripture expression and the hot contest between Satan and the archangel about discovering the body of Moses. But the practice of burning was also of great antiquity, and of no slender extent. For (not to derive the same from Hercules) noble descriptions there are hereof in the Grecian funerals of Homer, in the formal obsequies of Patroclus and Achilles; and, somewhat elder, in the Theban war, and solemn combustion of Menoeceus and Archemorus, contemporary unto Jair the eighth judge of Israel. Confirmable also among the Trojans, from the funeral pyre of Hector, burnt before the gates of Troy; and the burning of Penthesilea, the Amazonian queen; and long continuance of that practice in the inward countries of Asia—while as low as the reign of Julian we find that the King of Chionia burnt the body of his son, and interred the ashes in a silver urn.

The same practice[n] extended also far west, and, besides Herulians, Getes, and Thracians, was in use with most of the Celtae, Sarmatians, Germans, Gauls, Danes, Swedes, Norwegians, not to omit some use thereof among Carthaginians and Americans; of greater antiquity among the Romans than most opinion, or Pliny seems to allow: for (beside the old Table Laws of burning or burying within the City, of making the funeral fire with planed wood, or quenching the fire with wine), Manlius the Consul burnt the body of his son; Numa, by special clause of his will, was not burnt but buried; and Remus was solemnly burned, according to the description of Ovid.

Abraham: Gen. 25:9.   *collectible*: inferable.
Moses: Deut. 34:6; Jude 9.   *Hercules*: said to have cremated one Argeus.
Patroclus and Achilles: Homer, *Iliad*, 23.161–257; *Odyssey*, 24.65–84.
Menoeceus and Archemorus: Statius, *Thebaid*, 12.60–104, 6.54–248.
Jair: Judg. 10:3–5.   *Hector*: *Iliad*, 24.782–804.
Penthesilea: Quintus Smyrnaeus, *Posthomerica*, 1.789–803.—*B*.
low: recently.   *Julian*: Roman emperor, 361–3.
Chionia: Grumbates, King of Chionia, a country near Persia.—*B*.
Herulians, Getes, and Thracians: nations of eastern Europe.
Pliny: *Natural History*, 7.54(187).
Table Laws: the Twelve Tables, a Roman code of the fifth century B.C.
Manlius: Titus Manlius Torquatus, who had his son beheaded for disobeying a
    military order. Livy, 8.7.   *Numa*: Plutarch, *Numa*, 22.2.
Ovid: *Fasti*, 4.856: Finally the pyre being built, the flame was applied.—*B*.

Cornelius Sylla was not the first whose body was burned in Rome, but of the Cornelian family; which, being indifferently, not frequently, used before, from that time spread, and became the prevalent practice —not totally pursued in the highest run of cremation, for, when even crows were funerally burnt, Poppaea, the wife of Nero, found a peculiar grave interment. Now, as all customs were founded upon some bottom of reason, so there wanted not grounds for this, according to several apprehensions of the most rational dissolution. Some, being of the opinion of Thales that water was the original of all things, thought it most equal to submit unto the principle of putrefaction, and conclude in a moist relentment. Others conceived it most natural to end in fire, as due unto the master principle in the composition according to the doctrine of Heraclitus: and therefore heaped up large piles, more actively to waft them toward that element; whereby they also declined a visible degeneration into worms, and left a lasting parcel of their composition.

Some apprehended a purifying virtue in fire, refining the grosser commixture, and firing out the ethereal particles so deeply immersed in it. And such as by tradition or rational conjecture held any hint of the final pyre of all things, or that this element at last must be too hard for all the rest, might conceive most naturally of the fiery dissolution. Others, pretending no natural grounds, politicly declined the malice of enemies upon their buried bodies. Which consideration led Sylla unto this practice, who, having thus served the body of Marius, could not but fear a retaliation upon his own, entertained after in the civil wars and revengeful contentions of Rome.

But as many nations embraced, and many left it indifferent, so others too much affected, or strictly declined this practice. The Indian Brahmins seemed too great friends unto fire, who burnt themselves alive, and thought it the noblest way to end their days in fire, according to the expression of the Indian burning himself at Athens, in his last words upon the pyre unto the amazed spectators: 'Thus I make myself immortal.'

But the Chaldeans, the great idolaters of fire, abhorred the burning of their carcasses, as a pollution of that deity. The Persian magi

Cornelian family: Pliny, 7.54(187); Cicero, *Laws*, 2.22(56).
run: currency, popularity.   *crows*: Pliny, 10.60(122).
Poppaea: Tacitus, *Annals*, 16.6.
Thales: Greek philosopher of the sixth century B.C.
relentment: dissolution.   *Heraclitus*: Greek philosopher of c. 500 B.C.
Marius: Pliny, Cicero, locc. citt.
immortal: and therefore the inscription of his tomb was made accordingly.—B.

declined it upon the like scruple, and being only solicitous about
their bones, exposed their flesh to the prey of birds and dogs. And
the Parsees now in India, which expose their bodies unto vultures,
and endure not so much as *feretra* or biers of wood, the proper fuel of
fire, are led on with such niceties. But whether the ancient Germans,
who burned their dead, held any such fear to pollute their deity of
Herthus, or the earth, we have no authentic conjecture.

The Egyptians were afraid of fire, not as deity, but a devouring
element, mercilessly consuming their bodies, and leaving too little
of them; and therefore by precious embalmments, depositure in dry
earths, or handsome enclosure in glasses, contrived the notablest
ways of integral conservation. And from such Egyptian scruples,
imbibed by Pythagoras, it may be conjectured that Numa and the
Pythagorical sect first waived the fiery solution.

The Scythians, who swore by wind and sword—that is, by life and
death—were so far from burning their bodies that they declined all
interment, and made their graves in the air; and the ichthyophagi,
or fish-eating nations about Egypt, affected the sea for their grave,
thereby declining visible corruption, and restoring the debt of their
bodies. Whereas the old heroes in Homer dreaded nothing more than
water or drowning, probably upon the old opinion of the fiery substance of the soul, only extinguishable by that element; and therefore the poet emphatically implieth the total destruction in this kind
of death, which happened to Ajax Oileus.

The old Balearians had a peculiar mode, for they used great urns
and much wood, but no fire in their burials, while they bruised the
flesh and bones of the dead, crowded them into urns, and laid heaps
of wood upon them. And the Chinois, without cremation or urnal
interment of their bodies, make use of trees and much burning,
while they plant a pine-tree by their grave, and burn great numbers
of printed draughts of slaves and horses over it, civilly content with
their companies in effigy which barbarous nations exact unto reality.

Christians abhorred this way of obsequies, and though they sticked
not to give their bodies to be burnt in their lives, detested that mode
after death; affecting rather a depositure than absumption, and
properly submitting unto the sentence of God, to return not unto
ashes but unto dust again, conformable unto the practice of the
patriarchs, the interment of our Saviour, of Peter, Paul, and the
ancient martyrs. And so far at last declining promiscuous interment

---

Ajax Oileus: *Odyssey*, 4. 499–511.   *Chinois*: Chinsor.
depositure: laying down.   *absumption*: being taken away.

with pagans, that some have suffered ecclesiastical censures for making no scruple thereof.

The Mussulman believers will never admit this fiery resolution, for they hold a present trial from their black and white angels in the grave, which they must have made so hollow that they may rise upon their knees.

The Jewish nation, though they entertained the old way of inhumation, yet sometimes admitted this practice—for the men of Jabesh burnt the body of Saul—and by no prohibited practice, to avoid contagion or pollution, in time of pestilence burnt the bodies of their friends; and when they burnt not their dead bodies, yet sometimes used great burnings near and about them, deducible from the expressions concerning Jehoram, Zedekiah, and the sumptuous pyre of Asa; and were so little averse from pagan burning that the Jews lamenting the death of Caesar, their friend and revenger on Pompey, frequented the place where his body was burnt for many nights together. And as they raised noble monuments and mausoleums for their own nation, so they were not scrupulous in erecting some for others, according to the practice of Daniel, who left that lasting sepulchral pile in Ecbatana for the Median and Persian kings.

But even in times of subjection and hottest use, they conformed not unto the Roman practice of burning; whereby the prophecy was secured concerning the body of Christ, that it should not see corruption, or a bone should not be broken: which we believe was also providentially prevented, from the soldier's spear, and nails that passed by the little bones both in his hands and feet; nor of ordinary contrivance that it should not corrupt on the cross, according to the laws of Roman crucifixion—or an hair of his head perish, though observable in Jewish customs to cut the hairs of malefactors.

Nor, in their long cohabitation with Egyptians, crept into a

---

ecclesiastical censures: e.g. a second-century Spanish bishop, Martialis.—*B.*
present: immediate.   *Saul*: 1 Sam. 31:12.
pestilence: Amos 6:10.—*B.*   *Jehoram*: 2 Chron. 21:19.
Zedekiah: Jer. 34:5.   *Asa*: 2 Chron. 16:14.
Caesar: Suetonius, *Julius¸* 84.5.
noble monuments: as that magnificent sepulchral monument erected by Simon. 1 Macc. 13:27–9.—*B.*
sepulchral pile: Josephus, *Jewish Antiquities*, 10.10.7(264–5): 'a building marvellously wrought', whereof a Jewish priest had always the custody unto Josephus his days.—*B.*
see corruption: Ps. 16:10, Acts 2:31.
bone should not be broken: John 19:36.
hair of his head perish: Christ's prophecy concerning his apostles. Luke. 21:18.

custom of their exact embalming, wherein, deeply slashing the muscles, and taking out the brains and entrails, they had broken the subject of so entire a resurrection, nor fully answered the types of Enoch, Elijah, or Jonah. Which yet to prevent or restore was of equal facility unto that rising power, able to break the fasciations and bands of death, to get clear out of the cerecloth and an hundred pounds of ointment, and out of the sepulchre before the stone was rolled from it.

But though they embraced not this practice of burning, yet entertained they many ceremonies agreeable unto Greek and Roman obsequies. And he that observeth their funeral feasts, their lamentations at the grave, their music, and weeping mourners; how they closed the eyes of their friends, how they washed, anointed, and kissed the dead; may easily conclude these were not mere pagan civilities. But whether that mournful burthen and treble calling out after Absalom had any reference unto the last conclamation and triple valediction used by other nations, we hold but a wavering conjecture.

Civilians make sepulture but of the law of nations: others do naturally found it and discover it also in animals. They that are so thick-skinned as still to credit the story of the phoenix may say something for animal burning: more serious conjectures find some examples of sepulture in elephants, cranes, the sepulchral cells of pismires, and practice of bees—which civil society carrieth out their dead, and hath exequies, if not interments.

CHAP. II

The solemnities, ceremonies, rites of their cremation or interment, so solemnly delivered by authors, we shall not disparage our reader to repeat. Only the last and lasting part in their urns, collected bones and ashes, we cannot wholly omit; or decline that subject which occasion lately presented in some discovered among us.

In a field of old Walsingham, not many months past, were digged up between forty and fifty urns, deposited in a dry and sandy soil, not a yard deep, nor far from one another: not all strictly of one

---

subject: substance, material.
Enoch, Elijah: who ascended to heaven entire. Gen. 5:24; Ecclus. 44:16, 49:14; Heb. 11:5; 2 Kgs. 2:11.
Jonah: whose deliverance whole from the whale's belly was used as a type of the Resurrection. Matt. 12:40.
fasciations: bindings.
Absalom: O Absalom, Absalom, Absalom! 2 Sam. 18:33.—*B.*
conclamation: calling out together. *civilians*: authorities on civil law.

figure, but most answering these described; some containing two pounds of bones—distinguishable in skulls, ribs, jaws, thigh-bones, and teeth—with fresh impressions of their combustion, besides the extraneous substances, like pieces of small boxes, or combs handsomely wrought, handles of small brass instruments, brazen nippers, and in one some kind of opal.

Near the same plot of ground, for about six yards compass, were digged up coals and incinerated substances; which begat conjecture that this was the *ustrina* or place of burning their bodies, or some sacrificing place unto the manes, which was properly below the surface of the ground, as the *arae* and altars unto the gods and heroes above it.

That these were the urns of Romans, from the common custom and place where they were found, is no obscure conjecture: not far from a Roman garrison, and but five miles from Brancaster, set down by ancient record under the name of Branodunum; and where the adjoining town, containing seven parishes, in no very different sound (but Saxon termination) still retains the name of Burnham— which being an early station, it is not improbable the neighbour parts were filled with habitations, either of Romans themselves, or Britons Romanized, which observed the Roman customs.

Nor is it improbable that the Romans early possessed this country, for though we meet not with such strict particulars of these parts before the new institution of Constantine and military charge of the Count of the Saxon shore, and that, about the Saxon invasions, the Dalmatian horsemen were in the garrison of Brancaster; yet, in the time of Claudius, Vespasian, and Severus, we find no less than three legions dispersed through the province of Britain; and as high as the reign of Claudius a great overthrow was given unto the Iceni by the Roman lieutenant Ostorius. Not long after, the country was so molested that, in hope of a better state, Prasutagus bequeathed his kingdom unto Nero and his daughters; and Boadicea his queen fought the last decisive battle with Paulinus. After which time, and conquest of Agricola the lieutenant of Vespasian, probable it is they wholly possessed this country, ordering it into garrisons or

opal: in one sent me by my worthy friend Dr. Thomas Witherley of Walsingham.—B.

arae: altars proper to demi-gods and heroes.   *country*: region.

Constantine: Roman emperor, 306–37.

Claudius, Vespasian, and Severus: Roman emperors 41–54, 69–79, and 193–211, respectively.

as high: as early.   *Ostorius*: Tacitus, *Annals,* 12.31.

Paulinus: Tacitus, *Annals*, 14.31–7.   *conquest of Agricola*: in A.D. 83 or 84.

habitations, best suitable with their securities. And so some Roman habitations not improbable in these parts as high as the time of Vespasian, where the Saxons after seated, in whose thin-filled maps we yet find the name of Walsingham. Now if the Iceni were but Gammadims, Anconians, or men that lived in an angle, wedge, or elbow of Britain, according to the original etymology, this country will challenge the emphatical appellation, as most properly making the elbow or iken of Icenia.

That Britain was notably populous is undeniable from that expression of Caesar. That the Romans themselves were early in no small numbers, seventy thousand, with their associates, slain by Boadicea, affords a sure account. And though many Roman habitations are now unknown, yet some by old works, rampiers, coins, and urns, do testify their possessions. Some urns have been found at Caister, some also about Southcreek, and, not many years past, no less than ten in a field at Buxton, not near any recorded garrison. Nor is it strange to find Roman coins of copper and silver among us: of Vespasian, Trajan, Adrian, Commodus, Antoninus, Severus, etc.; but the greater number of Diocletian, Constantine, Constans, Valens, with many of Victorinus, Postumus, Tetricus, and the thirty tyrants in the reign of Gallienus. And some as high as Adrianus have been found about Thetford or Sitomagus, mentioned in the *Itinerary of Antoninus* as the way from Venta or Caister unto London. But the most frequent discovery is made at the two Caisters by Norwich and Yarmouth, at Burgh Castle, and Brancaster.

Besides the Norman, Saxon, and Danish pieces of Cuthred,

Gammadims, Anconians: The Gammadims of Ezek. 27:11 had been identified with the inhabitants of Anconia, glossed as 'Elbow-land', a place on a headland or bay.

Caesar: *Gallic War*, 5.12: The multitude of men is numberless, and the buildings very numerous, much like the Gauls'.—*B.*

seventy thousand: Tacitus, *Annals*, 14.33.   *rampiers*: ramparts.

Buxton: in the ground of my worthy friend Rob Jegon, Esq., wherein some things contained were preserved by the most worthy Sir William Paston, Bt.—*B.*

as high as Adrianus: as early as the reign of Hadrian (117–38).

Thetford: wrongly identified here with the Sitomagus of the *Antonine Itinerary*, which was probably NE. of Ipswich.

Venta: Caister St. Edmunds.

Yarmouth: most at Caister-on-Sea by Yarmouth, found in a place called East Bloodyburgh Furlong, belonging to Mr. Thomas Wood, a person of civility, industry, and knowledge in this way, who hath made observation of remarkable things about him, and from whom we have received divers silver and copper coins.—*B.*

Brancaster: belonging to that noble gentleman, and true example of worth, Sir Ralph Hare, Baronet, my honoured friend.—*B.*

Canutus, William, Matilda, and others, some British coins of gold have been dispersedly found, and no small number of silver pieces near Norwich, with a rude head upon the obverse, and an ill-formed horse on the reverse, with inscriptions: *Ic., Duro., T.* (whether implying Iceni, Durotriges, *tascia*, or Trinobantes, we leave to higher conjecture). Vulgar chronology will have Norwich Castle as old as Julius Caesar; but his distance from these parts, and its Gothic form of structure, abridgeth such antiquity. The British coins afford conjecture of early habitation in these parts, though the city of Norwich arose from the ruins of Venta, and though perhaps not without some habitation before, was enlarged, builded, and nominated by the Saxons. In what bulk or populosity it stood in the old East Angle monarchy, tradition and history are silent. Considerable it was in the Danish eruptions, when Sueno burnt Thetford and Norwich, and Ulfketel, the governor thereof, was able to make some resistance, and after endeavoured to burn the Danish navy.

How the Romans left so many coins in countries of their conquests seems of hard resolution, except we consider how they buried them under ground, when upon barbarous invasions they were fain to desert their habitations in most part of their empire; and the strictness of their laws forbidding to transfer them to any other uses (wherein the Spartans were singular who, to make their copper money useless, contempered it with vinegar). That the Britons left any some wonder, since their money was iron and iron rings before Caesar; and those of after stamp by permission, and but small in bulk and bigness. That so few of the Saxons' remain, because overcome by succeeding conquerors upon the place, their coins by degrees passed into other stamps, and the marks of after ages.

Than the time of these urns deposited, or precise antiquity of these relics, nothing of more uncertainty. For since the lieutenant of

---

Matilda: a piece of Maud the Empress, said to be found in Buckenham Castle, with this inscription: *Elle n'a elle.*—B. (Probably a counter rather than a coin.)
near Norwich: at Thorpe next Norwich.—*B.*   *tascia*: a tribute penny.
arose from the ruins: Norwich replaced Venta, but on a different site.
populosity: size of population.
Danish navy: This struggle, between Swein Forkbeard, King of Norway, and Ulfkell Snilling, took place in 1003.
Spartans: According to Plutarch, *Lycurgus*, 9, the money was not copper but iron.—*B.*
contempered: tempered.
Caesar: Gallic War, 5.12, where he mentions also bronze and gold coins.
after stamp: later mintage.

Claudius seems to have made the first progress into these parts; since Boadicea was overthrown by the forces of Nero, and Agricola put a full end to these conquests—it is not probable the country was fully garrisoned or planted before: and, therefore, however these urns might be of later date, not likely of higher antiquity.

And the succeeding emperors desisted not from their conquests in these and other parts, as testified by history and medal inscription yet extant—the province of Britain, in so divided a distance from Rome, beholding the faces of many imperial persons, and in large account no fewer than Caesar, Claudius, Britannicus, Vespasian, Titus, Adrian, Severus, Commodus, Geta, and Caracalla.

A great obscurity herein, because no medal or emperor's coin enclosed which might denote the date of their interments—observable in many urns, and found in those of Spitalfields by London, which contained the coins of Claudius, Vespasian, Commodus, Antoninus, attended with lachrymatories, lamps, bottles of liquor, and other appurtenances of affectionate superstition, which in these rural interments were wanting.

Some uncertainty there is from the period or term of burning, or the cessation of that practice. Macrobius affirmeth it was disused in his days. But most agree, though without authentic record, that it ceased with the Antonini—most safely to be understood after the reign of those emperors which assumed the name of Antoninus, extending unto Heliogabalus, not strictly after Marcus; for about fifty years later we find the magnificent burning and consecration of Severus. And if we so fix this period or cessation, these urns will challenge above thirteen hundred years.

But whether this practice was only then left by emperors and great persons, or generally about Rome and not in other provinces, we hold no authentic account. For after Tertullian, in the days of Minucius it was obviously objected upon Christians that they condemned the practice of burning; and we find a passage in Sidonius which asserteth that practice in France unto a lower account. And perhaps

---

Macrobius: Macrobius Theodosius (*fl. c.* A.D. 400), *Saturnalia,* 7.7.5.—*B.*
Heliogabalus: or Elagabalus, murdered in 222.
Marcus: Marcus Aurelius, who died in 180.
Severus: Septimius Severus, who died in 211. The date is confused with that of the death of Severus Alexander, 235.
Tertullian: Christian writer, second–third centuries.
Minucius: Minucius Felix (second–third centuries), *Octavius,* 11.4: They curse pyres and condemn the disposal of bodies by fire.—*B.*
Sidonius: Sidonius Apollinaris (430–c. 479), *Letters,* 3.3.8.—*B.*
asserteth: places.

not fully disused till Christianity fully established, which gave the final extinction to these sepulchral bonfires.

Whether they were the bones of men or women or children, no authentic decision from ancient custom in distinct places of burial (although not improbably conjectured that the double sepulture or burying-place of Abraham had in it such intention); but from exility of bones, thinness of skulls, smallness of teeth, ribs, and thigh-bones, not improbable that many thereof were persons of minor age, or women. Confirmable also from things contained in them: in most were found substances resembling combs, plates like boxes, fastened with iron pins, and handsomely overwrought like the necks or bridges of musical instruments, long brass plates overwrought like the handles of neat implements, brazen nippers to pull away hair, and in one a kind of opal yet maintaining a bluish colour.

Now, that they accustomed to burn or bury with them things wherein they excelled, delighted, or which were dear unto them, either as farewells unto all pleasure, or vain apprehension that they might use them in the other world, is testified by all antiquity. Observable from the gem or beryl ring upon the finger of Cynthia, the mistress of Propertius, when, after her funeral pyre, her ghost appeared unto him. And notably illustrated from the contents of that Roman urn preserved by Cardinal Farnese, wherein, besides great number of gems with heads of gods and goddesses, were found an ape of agate, a grasshopper, an elephant of amber, a crystal ball, three glasses, two spoons, and six nuts of crystal. And beyond the contents of urns, in the monument of Childeric I, and fourth king from Pharamond, casually discovered three years past at Tournai, restoring unto the world much gold richly adorning his sword, two hundred rubies, many hundred imperial coins, three hundred golden bees, the bones and horseshoe of his horse interred with him, according to the barbarous magnificence of those days in their sepulchral obsequies. Although, if we steer by the conjecture of many, and Septuagint expression, some trace thereof may be found even with the ancient Hebrews, not only from the sepulchral treasure of David, but the circumcision knives which Joshua also buried.

---

lower: more recent.
Abraham: Gen. 23:9, Vulgate version, may be translated: He may give me a
    double burying-place.
Propertius: *Elegies*, 4.7.9.   *Childeric I*: King of the Salian Franks, 458–81.
Pharamond: founder of the Merovingian dynasty.
David: Josephus, *Antiquities*, 7.15.3(392–3).
circumcision knives: in the Septuagint version of Josh. 24:30.

Some men, considering the contents of these urns, lasting pieces and toys included in them, and the custom of burning with many other nations, might somewhat doubt whether all urns found among us were properly Roman relics, or some not belonging unto our British, Saxon, or Danish forefathers.

In the form of burial among the ancient Britons, the large discourses of Caesar, Tacitus, and Strabo, are silent; for the discovery whereof, with other particulars, we much deplore the loss of that letter which Cicero expected or received from his brother Quintus, as a resolution of British customs; or the account which might have been made by Scribonius Largus, the physician accompanying the Emperor Claudius—who might have also discovered that frugal bit of the old Britons which, in the bigness of a bean, could satisfy their thirst and hunger.

But that the Druids and ruling priests used to burn and bury is expressed by Pomponius; that Belinus, the brother of Brennus, and king of Britons, was burnt, is acknowledged by Polydorus; that they held that practice in Gallia, Caesar expressly delivereth. Whether the Britons (probably descended from them, of like religion, language and manners) did not sometimes make use of burning; or whether at least such as were after civilized unto the Roman life and manners conformed not unto this practice, we have no historical assertion or denial; but since, from the account of Tacitus, the Romans early wrought so much civility upon the British stock that they brought them to build temples, to wear the gown, and study the Roman laws and language, that they conformed also unto their religious rites and customs in burials seems no improbable conjecture.

That burning the dead was used in Sarmatia is affirmed by Gaguinus;[n] that the Sueons and Gothlanders used to burn their princes and great persons is delivered by Saxo and Olaus; that this was the old German practice is also asserted by Tacitus. And though we are bare in historical particulars of such obsequies in this island,

Cicero: *Letters to Quintus*, 2.16(15).4.
Scribonius Largus: first-century A.D. author of a work on medicinal compounds.
frugal bit: Dio Cassius, 77.12.4.—*B*.
Pomponius: Pomponius Mela (*c*. 43 A.D.), *De Situ Orbis*, 3.2(19).
Polydorus: Polydore Vergil, *English History*, 1 (Camden Soc., 36, 1846, pp. 46–7).
Caesar: *Gallic War*, 6.16, describing live human sacrifice.
account of Tacitus: *Agricola*, 21.   *Sarmatia*: a large region of NE. Europe.
Sueons and Gothlanders: Swedes and Goths.
Saxo: Saxo Grammaticus, *Historia Danica*, 5.
Olaus: Olaus Magnus, *History of the Goths*, 16.37.
asserted by Tacitus: *Germania*, 27.

or that the Saxons, Jutes, and Angles burnt their dead, yet came they from parts where 'twas of ancient practice—the Germans using it, from whom they were descended. And even in Jutland, and Schleswig in Anglia Cimbrica, urns with bones were found not many years before us.

But the Danish and northern nations have raised an era or point of compute from their custom of burning their dead: some deriving it from Unguinus, some from Frotho the Great, who ordained by law that princes and chief commanders should be committed unto the fire, though the common sort had the common grave interment. So Starkatterus, that old hero, was burnt, and Ringo royally burnt the body of Harald the King, slain by him.

What time this custom generally expired in that nation we discern no assured period. Whether it ceased before Christianity, or upon their conversion by Ansgarius the Gaul, in the time of Ludovicus Pius, the son of Charles the Great, according to good computes; or whether it might not be used by some persons, while, for a hundred and eighty years, paganism and Christianity were promiscuously embraced among them, there is no assured conclusion. About which times the Danes were busy in England, and particularly infested this country, where many castles and strongholds were built by them or against them, and great number of names and families still derived from them. But since this custom was probably disused before their invasion or conquest, and the Romans confessedly practised the same since their possession of this island, the most assured account will fall upon the Romans, or Britons Romanized.

However, certain it is that urns conceived of no Roman original are often digged up both in Norway and Denmark, handsomely described and graphically represented by the learned physician Wormius; and in some parts of Denmark in no ordinary number, as stands delivered by authors exactly describing those countries. And they contained not only bones, but many other substances in them, as knives, pieces of iron, brass, and wood—and one of Norway a brass gilded jews' harp.

Anglia Cimbrica: a district in Schleswig.
an era: *Roisold, Brendetyde, Ildtyde*, signifying the Age of Burning.—*B.*
compute: reckoning.   *Unguinus*: eighth king after Frotho the Great.
Frotho the Great: legendary Danish king reigning at the birth of Christ.
Starkatterus: a legendary hero in Saxo Grammaticus.
Ringo: fifteenth king after Frotho.   *Harald*: fourteenth king after Frotho.
Ludovicus Pius: Louis I, Emperor of the West, 814–40.
original: origin.
Wormius: Olaus Worm, *Monumenta Danica* (1643).—*B.*

Nor were they confused or careless in disposing the noblest sort, while they placed large stones in circle about the urns or bodies which they interred—somewhat answerable unto the monument of Rollright Stones in England, or sepulchral monument probably erected by Rollo (who after conquered Normandy); where 'tis not improbable somewhat might be discovered. Meanwhile, to what nation or person belonged that large urn found at Ashbury, containing mighty bones and a buckler; what those large urns found at Little Massingham, or why the Anglesey urns are placed with their mouths downward, remains yet undiscovered.

CHAP. III

Plastered and whited sepulchres were anciently affected in cadaverous and corruptive burials, and the rigid Jews were wont to garnish the sepulchres of the righteous. Ulysses, in *Hecuba*, cared not how meanly he lived, so he might find a noble tomb after death. Great persons affected great monuments, and the fair and larger urns contained no vulgar ashes, which makes that disparity in those which time discovereth among us. The present urns were not of one capacity, the largest containing above a gallon, some not much above half that measure; nor all of one figure, wherein there is no strict conformity, in the same or different countries—observable from those represented by Casalius, Bosio, and others, though all found in Italy: while many have handles, ears, and long necks, but most imitate a circular figure, in a spherical and round composure; whether from any mystery, best duration or capacity, were but a conjecture. But the common form—with necks—was a proper figure, making our last bed like our first; nor much unlike the urns of our nativity, while we lay in the nether part of the earth, and inward vault of our microcosm. Many urns are red, these but of a black colour, somewhat smooth, and dully sounding, which begat some doubt whether they were burnt, or only baked in oven or sun, according to the ancient way in many bricks, tiles, pots, and testaceous works (and as the word *testa* is properly

Rollright Stones: in Oxfordshire.—B.
erected by Rollo: suggested by Camden, *Britannia*.
Ashbury: in Cheshire.—B., citing J. Twyne, *De Rebus Albionicis* (1590), who, p. 75, describes such a find in Kent.
Little Massingham: in Norfolk.—B.
Anglesey urns: Holinshed, *Chronicles*, 1.1.8 (1577, f.16ʳ).—B.
rigid Jews: Matt. 23:29.—B.   *Hecuba*: Euripides, *Hecuba*, 317–20.—B.
Casalius: J. B. Casalius, *De Urbis*, 2.21 (1650, p. 350).
Bosio: A. Bosio, *Roma Sotterranea*, 3.23 (1632, pp. 197–201).
nether part of the earth: Ps. 63:9.—B.
testaceous: earthenware.   *testa*: piece of baked clay.

to be taken, when occurring without addition, and chiefly intended by Pliny when he commendeth bricks and tiles of two years old, and to make them in the spring). Nor only these concealed pieces, but the open magnificence of antiquity ran much in the artifice of clay: hereof the house of Mausolus was built; thus old Jupiter stood in the Capitol; and the statua of Hercules, made in the reign of Tarquinius Priscus, was extant in Pliny's days. And such as declined burning, or funeral urns, affected coffins of clay, according to the mode of Pythagoras, and way preferred by Varro. But the spirit of great ones was above these circumscriptions, affecting copper, silver, gold, and porphyry urns, wherein Severus lay, after a serious view and sentence on that which should contain him. Some of these urns were thought to have been silvered over, from sparklings in several pots, with small tinsel parcels—uncertain whether from the earth or the first mixture in them.

Among these urns we could obtain no good account of their coverings: only one seemed arched over with some kind of brickwork. Of those found at Buxton, some were covered with flints, some in other parts with tiles; those at Yarmouth Caister were closed with Roman bricks; and some have proper earthen covers adapted and fitted to them. But in the Homerical urn of Patroclus, whatever was the solid tegument, we find the immediate covering to be a purple piece of silk; and such as had no covers might have the earth closely pressed into them, after which disposure were probably some of these, wherein we found the bones and ashes half mortared unto the sand and sides of the urn, and some long roots of quitch, or dog's-grass wreathed about the bones.

No lamps, included liquors, lachrymatories or tear-bottles, attended these rural urns, either as sacred unto the manes, or passionate expressions of their surviving friends, while, with rich flames and hired tears, they solemnized their obsequies, and in the most lamented monuments made one part of their inscriptions. Some find

---

Pliny: *Natural History*, 35.49(170).
Mausolus: according to Pliny, 36.6(47), the tomb was of brick faced with marble.
Pliny's days: *Nat. Hist.*, 35.45(157).   *coffins of clay*: Pliny, 35.46(160).
Varro: Marcus Terentius Varro (116–27 B.C.), 'the most learned of Romans'.
serious view and sentence: 'Thou shalt hold that man whom the world could not hold.'—Dio Cassius, 77.15.4.—*B*.
Buxton: see above, p. 102.   *Yarmouth Caister*: see above, p. 102.
Patroclus: *Iliad*, 23.254, terms the covering 'a soft linen cloth'. 24.796 names soft purple robes for Hector's urn.
tegument: covering.   *included*: in containers.
inscriptions: *Cum lacrimis posuere* (With tears they deposited).—*B*.

sepulchral vessels containing liquors which time hath incrassated
into jellies (for, beside these lachrymatories, notable lamps, with
vessels of oils and aromatical liquors, attended noble ossuaries), and
some yet retaining a vinosity and spirit in them—which if any have
tasted they have far exceeded the palates of antiquity: liquors not to
be computed by years of annual magistrates, but by great conjunctions and the fatal periods of kingdoms. The draughts of consulary date were but crude unto these, and Opimian wine but in the
must unto them.

In sundry graves and sepulchres we meet with rings, coins, and
chalices: ancient frugality was so severe that they allowed no gold to
attend the corpse, but only that which served to fasten their teeth.
Whether the opaline stone in this urn were burnt upon the finger of
the dead, or cast into the fire by some affectionate friend, it will
consist with either custom; but other incinerable substances were
found so fresh that they could feel no singe from fire. These upon
view were judged to be wood, but, sinking in water and tried by the
fire, we found them to be bone or ivory. In their hardness and yellow
colour they most resembled box, which in old expressions found the
epithet of eternal, and perhaps in such conservatories might have
passed uncorrupted.

That bay-leaves were found green in the tomb of St. Humbert, after
an hundred and fifty years, was looked upon as miraculous. Remarkable it was unto old spectators that the cypress of the temple of
Diana lasted so many hundred years: the wood of the Ark and olive
rod of Aaron were older at the Captivity. But the cypress of the ark
of Noah, was the greatest vegetable antiquity, if Josephus were not
deceived by some fragments of it in his days (to omit the moor-logs
and fir-trees found underground in many parts of England, the
undated ruins of winds, floods, or earthquakes—and which in
Flanders still show from what quarter they fell, as generally lying in a
north-east position).

But though we found not these pieces to be wood, according to
first apprehension, yet we missed not altogether of some woody

---

incrassated: thickened.   vinosity: vinous quality.
periods of kingdoms: about 500 years. Plato, Republic, 8(546).—B.
of consulary date: dated by the consuls in office at the time of their vintage.
Opimian wine: The vintage of 121 B.C., in the consulate of Opimius, was renowned
    for its quality. Petronius, 34.6.—B.
ancient frugality: in the Twelve Tables, 11.
opaline stone: see above, pp. 101, 105.   incinerable: reducible to ashes.
conservatories: preserving vessels.   temple of Diana: Pliny, 16.79(215).
Ark and olive rod: Heb. 9:4.   Josephus: Antiquities, 1.3.5(92), 20.2.2(25).

substance; for the bones were not so clearly picked but some coals were found amongst them—a way to make wood perpetual, and a fit associate for metal, whereon was laid the foundation of the great Ephesian temple, and which were made the lasting tests of old boundaries and landmarks. Whilst we look on these, we admire not observations of coals found fresh after four hundred years. In a long-deserted habitation even egg-shells have been found fresh, not tending to corruption.

In the monument of King Childeric the iron relics were found all rusty and crumbling into pieces; but our little iron pins, which fastened the ivory works, held well together, and lost not their magnetical quality, though wanting a tenacious moisture for the firmer union of parts: although it be hardly drawn into fusion, yet that metal soon submitteth unto rust and dissolution. In the brazen pieces we admired, not the duration, but the freedom from rust, and ill savour upon the hardest attrition; but now, exposed unto the piercing atoms of air, in the space of a few months they begin to spot and betray their green entrails.

We conceive not these urns to have descended thus naked as they appear, or to have entered their graves without the old habit of flowers. The urn of Philopoemen was so laden with flowers and ribbons that it afforded no sight of itself. The rigid Lycurgus allowed olive and myrtle. The Athenians might fairly except against the practice of Democritus—to be buried up in honey—as fearing to embezzle a great commodity of their country, and the best of that kind in Europe; but Plato seemed too frugally politic, who allowed no larger monument than would contain four heroic verses, and designed the most barren ground for sepulture (though we cannot commend the goodness of that sepulchral ground which was set at no higher rate than the mean salary of Judas). Though the earth had confounded the ashes of these ossuaries, yet the bones were so smartly burnt that some thin plates of brass were found half melted among them: whereby we apprehend they were not of the meanest carcasses, perfunctorily fired, as sometimes in military, and commonly in pestilence, burnings; or after the manner of abject corpses, huddled forth and carelessly burnt without the Esquiline Port at Rome—

Ephesian temple: Pliny, 36.21(95).   *tests*: proofs.
habitation: at Elmham.—B.   *Philopoemen*: Plutarch, *Philopoemen*, 21.3.
Lycurgus: legendary legislator of Sparta.
Democritus: Varro, *Satyrae Menippeae*, 81.   *Plato*: *Laws*, 958d–e.
Judas: Matt. 27: 5–8.   *confounded*: mixed with.
Esquiline Port: where the bodies of the poor, criminals, or those otherwise held in contempt, were burnt or thrown to the dogs.

which was an affront contrived upon Tiberius, while they but half burnt his body, and in the Amphitheatre, according to the custom in notable malefactors (whereas Nero seemed not so much to fear his death as that his head should be cut off, and his body not burnt entire).

Some, finding many fragments of skulls in these urns, suspected a mixture of bones: in none we searched was there cause of such conjecture, though sometimes they declined not that practice. The ashes of Domitian were mingled with those of Julia, of Achilles with those of Patroclus—all urns contained not single ashes. Without confused burnings they affectionately compounded their bones, passionately endeavouring to continue their living unions; and when distance of death denied such conjunctions, unsatisfied affections conceived some satisfaction to be neighbours in the grave, to lie urn by urn, and touch but in their names. And many were so curious to continue their living relations that they contrived large and family urns, wherein the ashes of their nearest friends and kindred might successively be received—at least some parcels thereof, while their collateral memorials lay in minor vessels about them.

Antiquity held too light thoughts from objects of mortality, while some drew provocatives of mirth from anatomies, and jugglers showed tricks with skeletons; when fiddlers made not so pleasant mirth as fencers, and men could sit with quiet stomachs while hanging was played before them. Old considerations made few mementoes by skulls and bones upon their monuments. In the Egyptian obelisks and hieroglyphical figures, it is not easy to meet with bones. The sepulchral lamps speak nothing less than sepulture, and in their literal draughts prove often obscene and antic pieces. Where we find *D. M.* it is obvious to meet with sacrificing pateras and vessels of libation, upon old sepulchral monuments. In the Jewish hypogeum and subterranean cell at Rome was little observable beside the variety of lamps and frequent draughts of the holy candlestick.

Tiberius: Suetonius, *Tiberius*, 75.3, says the insulting proposal was not carried out.

Nero: Suetonius, *Nero*, 49.4.   *Julia*: Suetonius, *Domitian*, 17.3.

Patroclus: Homer, *Odyssey*, 24.76–7.

anatomies: referring to the silver skeleton on Trimalchio's dinner-table in Petronius, 34, and his verses thereon.—*B.*

hanging was played: A barbarous pastime at feasts, when men stood upon a rolling globe with their necks in a rope fastened to a beam, and a knife in their hands ready to cut it when the stone was rolled away; wherein if they failed, they lost their lives to the laughter of the spectators. Athenaeus, 4.14(155).—*B.*

D.M.: *Diis manibus*: To the deified souls of the dead.—*B.*

pateras: offering dishes.   *hypogeum*: vault.

candlestick: sevenfold. Exod. 25:31–40.

In authentic draughts of Antony and Jerome we meet with thigh-bones and death's-heads, but the cemeterial cells of ancient Christians and martyrs were filled with draughts of Scripture stories: not declining the flourishes of cypress, palms, and olive, and the mystical figures of peacocks, doves, and cocks, but iterately affecting the portraits of Enoch, Lazarus, Jonas, and the vision of Ezekiel, as hopeful draughts and hinting imagery of the Resurrection—which is the life of the grave, and sweetens our habitations in the land of moles and pismires.

Gentile inscriptions precisely delivered the extent of men's lives: seldom the manner of their deaths, which history itself so often leaves obscure in the records of memorable persons. There is scarce any philosopher but dies twice or thrice in Laertius, nor almost any life without two or three deaths in Plutarch—which makes the tragical ends of noble persons more favourably resented by compassionate readers, who find some relief in the election of such differences.

The certainty of death is attended with uncertainties, in time, manner, places. The variety of monuments hath often obscured true graves, and cenotaphs confounded sepulchres; for, beside their real tombs, many have found honorary and empty sepulchres. The variety of Homer's monuments made him of various countries; Euripides had his tomb in Attica, but his sepulture in Macedonia; and Severus found his real sepulchre in Rome, but his empty grave in Gallia.

He that lay in a golden urn, eminently above the earth, was not like to find the quiet of these bones. Many of these urns were broke by a vulgar discoverer in hope of enclosed treasure. The ashes of Marcellus were lost above ground upon the like account. Where profit hath prompted, no age hath wanted such miners; for which the most barbarous expilators found the most civil rhetoric: 'Gold once out of the earth is no more due unto it; what was unreasonably

---

Antony: who lived as a hermit in a tomb.
Jerome: who, as a youth, visited the Roman catacombs on Sundays.
iterately: repeatedly.   *Enoch*: translated to heaven. Gen. 5:24, etc.
Lazarus: raised from the dead. John 11:43–4.
Jonas: see note above, p. 100.   *Ezekiel*: Ezek. 37:1–14.
Laertius: Diogenes Laertius, *Lives of the Philosophers*.
resented: felt.   *confounded*: been confused with.
Homer: Pausanias, 10.24.3.   *Euripides*: Pausanias, 1.2.2.—*B.*
Severus: *Augustan History*, 'Severus Alexander', 63.3.—*B.*
golden urn: ibid., 'Septimius Severus', 24.2.
Marcellus: Plutarch, *Marcellus*, 30.2–3.—*B.*   *expilators*: pillagers.
civil rhetoric: the commission of the Gothish king Theodoric for finding out
    sepulchral treasure. Cassiodorus, *Variae*, 4.34.—*B.*

committed to the ground is reasonably resumed from it. Let monuments and rich fabrics, not riches, adorn men's ashes—the commerce of the living is not to be transferred unto the dead. It is no injustice to take that which none complains to lose, and no man is wronged where no man is possessor.'

What virtue yet sleeps in this *terra damnata* and aged cinders were petty magic to experiment: these crumbling relics and long-fired particles superannuate such expectations. Bones, hairs, nails, and teeth of the dead, were the treasures of old sorcerers. In vain we revive such practices. Present superstition too visibly perpetuates the folly of our forefathers; wherein, unto old observation, this island was so complete that it might have instructed Persia.

Plato's historian of the other world lies twelve days incorrupted, while his soul was viewing the large stations of the dead: how to keep the corpse seven days from corruption by anointing and washing, without exenteration, were an hazardable piece of art in our choicest practice. How they made distinct separation of bones and ashes from fiery admixture hath found no historical solution, though they seemed to make a distinct collection, and overlooked not Pyrrhus his toe. Some provision they might make by fictile vessels, coverings, tiles, or flat stones, upon and about the body (and in the same field, not far from these urns, many stones were found underground), as also by careful separation of extraneous matter, composing and raking up the burnt bones with forks, observable in that notable lamp of Galvanus. Marlianus, who had the sight of the *vas ustrinum*, or vessel wherein they burnt the dead, found in the Esquiline Field at Rome, might have afforded clearer solution. But their insatisfaction herein begat that remarkable invention in the funeral pyres of some princes, by incombustible sheets made with a texture of asbestos (incremable flax, or salamander's wool), which preserved their bones and ashes incommixed.

How the bulk of a man should sink into so few pounds of bones and ashes may seem strange unto any who considers not its constitution, and how slender a mass will remain, upon an open and

---

terra damnata: alchemical term for the residue after calcination (lit. damned earth).
superannuate such expectations: outlive such hopes.
Persia: Pliny, 30.4(13).   *Plato's historian*: Er in the *Republic*, 10(614b).
Pyrrhus his toe: which could not be burnt. Pliny, 7.2(20).—*B.*
lamp of Galvanus: decorated with representations of ancient funeral rites.
Marlianus: J.B. Marlianus, *Romae Topographia* (1544, p. 8).
vas ustrinum: cremation vessel.   *Esquiline Field*: see note above, p. 111.
incremable: unburnable.

urging fire, of the carnal composition. Even bones themselves, reduced into ashes, do abate a notable proportion; and, consisting much of a volatile salt, when that is fired out, make a light kind of cinders, although their bulk be disproportionable to their weight, when the heavy principle of salt is fired out and the earth almost only remaineth—observable in sallow, which makes more ashes than oak, and discovers the common fraud of selling ashes by measure, and not by ponderation.

Some bones make best skeletons: some bodies quick and speediest ashes. Who would expect a quick flame from hydropical Heraclitus? The poisoned soldier, when his belly brake, put out two pyres (in Plutarch); but in the plague of Athens one private pyre served two or three intruders, and the Saracens burnt in large heaps by the King of Castile showed how little fuel sufficeth. Though the funeral pyre of Patroclus took up an hundred foot, a piece of an old boat burnt Pompey; and if the burthen of Isaac were sufficient for an holocaust, a man may carry his own pyre.

From animals are drawn good burning lights, and good medicines against burning; though the seminal humour seems of a contrary nature to fire, yet the body completed proves a combustible lump, wherein fire finds flame even from bones, and some fuel almost from all parts (though the metropolis of humidity seems least disposed unto it, which might render the skulls of these urns less burned than other bones). But all flies or sinks before fire almost in all bodies; when the common ligament is dissolved, the attenuable parts ascend, the rest subside in coal, calx or ashes.

To burn the bones of the King of Edom for lime seems no irrational ferity; but to drink of the ashes of dead relations, a passionate prodigality. He that hath the ashes of his friend hath an everlasting treasure: where fire taketh leave, corruption slowly enters. In bones well burnt, fire makes a wall against itself—experimented in cupels and

---

skeletons: old bones, according to Lyserus, *Culter Anatomicus*, 5, 'Praeloquium' (1653, p. 175); those of young persons not tall nor fat, according to Realdus Columbus, cited by Lyserus.—*B.*
Heraclitus: Diogenes Laertius, 9.3.   *Plutarch*: *Tiberius Gracchus*, 13.4–5.
Athens: Thucydides, 2.52.4.—*B.*   *Patroclus*: Homer, *Iliad*, 23.164.
Pompey: Plutarch, *Pompey*, 80.2.   *Isaac*: Gen. 22:6.
against burning: frog-spawn, whites of eggs.—*B.*
metropolis: the brain. Hippocrates, *De Carnibus*.—*B.*
attenuable: rarefiable.   *Edom*: Amos 2:1.
ferity: barbarity.
drink of the ashes: as Artemisia of her husband Mausolus, to become his living tomb. Valerius Maximus, 4.6 Externa 1.—*B.*

tests of metals, which consist of such ingredients. What the sun compoundeth, fire analyseth, not transmuteth. That devouring agent leaves almost always a morsel for the earth, whereof all things are but a colony; and which, if time permits, the mother element will have in their primitive mass again.

He that looks for urns and old sepulchral relics must not seek them in the ruins of temples, where no religion anciently placed them. These were found in a field, according to ancient custom in noble or private burial: the old practice of the Canaanites, the family of Abraham, and the burying-place of Joshua in the borders of his possessions; and also agreeable unto Roman practice, to bury by highways, whereby their monuments were under eye, memorials of themselves, and mementoes of mortality unto living passengers, whom the epitaphs of great ones were fain to beg to stay and look upon them—a language, though sometimes used, not so proper in church inscriptions. The sensible rhetoric of the dead, to exemplarity of good life, first admitted the bones of pious men and martyrs within church walls; which, in succeeding ages, crept into promiscuous practice: while Constantine was peculiarly favoured to be admitted unto the church porch, and the first thus buried in England was in the days of Cuthred.

Christians dispute how their bodies should lie in the grave: in urnal interment they clearly escaped this controversy. Though we decline the religious consideration, yet in cemeterial and narrower burying-places, to avoid confusion and cross position, a certain posture were to be admitted, which even pagan civility observed. The Persians lay north and south, the Megarians and Phoenicians placed their heads to the east; the Athenians, some think, towards the west, which Christians still retain—and Beda will have it to be the posture of our Saviour. (That he was crucified with his face towards the west we will not contend with tradition and probable account; but we applaud not the hand of the painter in exalting his cross so high above those on either side, since hereof we find no authentic account

---

tests: cupels (vessels of bone-ash for the refining of gold and silver) in iron containers.

Canaanites: Gen. 23:5-20.   Abraham: Gen. 49:29-32.
Joshua: Josh. 24:30.   inscriptions: Siste viator—Stop traveller.—B.
exemplarity of: exemplify.   Constantine: who died in 337.

Cuthred: Overlord of the West Saxons, 740-54. In 758, Cuthbert, Archbishop of Canterbury, was buried in the Cathedral.
Megarians: who lived on the Isthmus of Corinth.
Beda: the Venerable Bede, on Mark 16.

in history, and even the crosses found by Helena pretend no such distinction from longitude or dimension.)

To be gnawed out of our graves, to have our skulls made drinking-bowls, and our bones turned into pipes to delight and sport our enemies, are tragical abominations escaped in burning burials.[n]

Urnal interments and burnt relics lie not in fear of worms, or to be an heritage for serpents. In carnal sepulture, corruptions seem peculiar unto parts, and some speak of snakes out of the spinal marrow. But while we suppose common worms in graves, 'tis not easy to find any there: few in churchyards above a foot deep, fewer or none in churches, though in fresh decayed bodies. Teeth, bones, and hair, give the most lasting defiance to corruption. In an hydropical body ten years buried in a churchyard, we met with a fat concretion, where the nitre of the earth, and the salt and lixivious liquor of the body, had coagulated large lumps of fat into the consistence of the hardest castile soap; whereof part remaineth with us.[n] After a battle with the Persians, the Roman corpses decayed in few days while the Persian bodies remained dry and uncorrupted. Bodies in the same ground do not uniformly dissolve, nor bones equally moulder; whereof in the opprobrious disease we expect no long duration. The body of the Marquess of Dorset seemed sound and handsomely cereclothed, that after seventy-eight years was found uncorrupted. Common tombs preserve not beyond powder: a firmer consistence and compage of parts might be expected from arefaction, deep burial or charcoal. The greatest antiquities of mortal bodies may remain in petrified bones, whereof (though we take not in the pillar of Lot's wife, or metamorphosis of Ortelius), some may be older than pyramids, in the petrified relics of the general inundation. When Alexander opened the tomb of Cyrus, the remaining bones discovered his proportion, whereof urnal fragments afford but a bad conjecture, and have this disadvantage of grave interments, that they

Helena: mother of Constantine, claimed to have found Christ's actual cross.
longitude: length.
lixivious: alkaline.   *Persian bodies*: Ammianus Marcellinus, 19.9.9.
opprobrious disease: syphilis, which rots even living bodies.
Dorset: whose body, being buried 1530, was, 1608, upon the cutting open of the cerecloth, found perfect and nothing corrupted; the flesh not hardened, but, in colour, proportion, and softness, like an ordinary corpse newly to be interred. —B.
compage: holding together.   *arefaction*: drying.
Lot's wife: Gen. 19:26.
Ortelius: In his map of Russia, A. Ortelius, *Theatrum Orbis Terrarum* (1574), shows in the east a group of natives turned to stone.—B.
Alexander: Arrian, *Anabasis*, 6.29.

leave us ignorant of most personal discoveries. For, since bones afford not only rectitude and stability but figure unto the body, it is no impossible physiognomy to conjecture at fleshy appendencies, and after what shape the muscles and carnous parts might hang in their full consistences. A full spread *cariola* shows a well-shaped horse behind; handsome-formed skulls give some analogy of fleshy resemblance. A critical view of bones makes a good distinction of sexes. Even colour is not beyond conjecture since it is hard to be deceived in the distinction of negroes' skulls. Dante's characters are to be found in skulls as well as faces. Hercules is not only known by his foot: other parts make out their comproportions, and inferences upon whole or parts. And since the dimensions of the head measure the whole body, and the figure thereof gives conjecture of the principal faculties, physiognomy outlives ourselves, and ends not in our graves.

Severe contemplators, observing these lasting relics, may think them good monuments of persons past, little advantage to future beings; and, considering that power which subdueth all things unto itself, that can resume the scattered atoms, or identify out of anything, conceive it superfluous to expect a resurrection out of relics. But—the soul subsisting—other matter, clothed with due accidents, may salve the individuality. Yet the saints, we observe, arose from graves and monuments about the Holy City. Some think the ancient patriarchs so earnestly desired to lay their bones in Canaan as hoping to make a part of that resurrection, and, though thirty miles from Mount Calvary, at least to lie in that region which should produce the first-fruits of the dead. And if, according to learned conjecture,[n] the bodies of men shall rise where their greatest relics remain, many are not like to err in the topography of their resurrection, though their bones or bodies be after translated by angels into the field of

---

appendencies: appendages.   *carnous*: fleshy.

cariola: that part in the skeleton of an horse which is made by the haunch-bones. —B.

negroes' skulls: for their extraordinary thickness.—B.

Dante's characters: The poet Dante, in his view of purgatory (*Purgatorio*, 23.31–3), found gluttons so meagre and extenuated that he conceited them to have been in the Siege of Jerusalem; and that it was easy to have discovered *homo* or *omo* in their faces—M being made by the two lines of their cheeks arching over the eyebrows to the nose, and their sunk eyes making O O, which makes up *omo*. —B.

Hercules: Aulus Gellius, I.l.

comproportions: corresponding dimensions.

identify: create an individual being.

Holy City: Matt. 27:52–3.   *Canaan*: Gen. 49:29.

Ezekiel's vision, or, as some will order it, into the valley of judgement, or Jehoshaphat.

CHAP. IV

Christians have handsomely glossed the deformity of death by careful consideration of the body, and civil rites which take off brutal terminations; and, though they conceived all reparable by a resurrection, cast not off all care of interment. For since the ashes of sacrifices burnt upon the altar of God were carefully carried out by the priests, and deposed in a clean field; since they acknowledged their bodies to be the lodging of Christ, and temples of the Holy Ghost, they devolved not all upon the sufficiency of soul existence: and therefore with long services and full solemnities concluded their last exequies—wherein, to all distinctions, the Greek devotion seems most pathetically ceremonious.

Christian invention hath chiefly driven at rites which speak hopes of another life, and hints of a resurrection. And if the ancient Gentiles held not the immortality of their better part and some subsistence after death, in several rites, customs, actions, and expressions, they contradicted their own opinions—wherein Democritus went high, even to the thought of a resurrection, as scoffingly recorded by Pliny. What can be more express than the expression of Phocylides? Or who would expect from Lucretius a sentence of Ecclesiastes? Before Plato could speak, the soul had wings in Homer, which fell not, but flew out of the body into the mansions of the dead; who also observed that handsome distinction of *demas* and *soma*, for the body conjoined to the soul, and body separated from it. Lucian spoke much truth in jest when he said, that part of Hercules which proceeded from Alcmena perished, that from Jupiter remained immortal. Thus Socrates was content that his friends should bury his body, so they would not think they buried Socrates; and regarding only his

---

Ezekiel's vision: Ezek. 37:1–14.   *Jehoshaphat*: Joel 3:2, 12.
take off: do away with.   *sacrifices*: Lev. 4:12.
deposed: deposited.   *Holy Ghost*: 1 Cor. 6:19.
Pliny: 7.55(189): Similar is the vanity of revival promised by Democritus, who
 did not himself revive. What lunacy it is, alas, to think life renewed by death.
 —*B.*
Phocylides: *Gnomai*, 103–4: We hope that perhaps the remains of the departed
 may return from the earth into the light.—*B.*
Lucretius: 2.999–1000: For that returns to the earth which was before in the
 earth.—*B.*
Ecclesiastes: 12:7.   *Homer*: *Odyssey*, 11.222.
fell not: Plato, *Phaedrus*, 246.   *demas*: living body.
soma: corpse.   *Lucian*: *Hermotimus*, 7.
Socrates: *Phaedo*, 115e.

immortal part, was indifferent to be burnt or buried. From such considerations Diogenes might contemn sepulture; and, being satisfied that the soul could not perish, grow careless of corporal interment. The Stoics, who thought the souls of wise men had their habitation about the moon, might make slight account of subterraneous deposition; whereas the Pythagoreans and transcorporating philosophers, who were to be often buried, held great care of their interment. And the Platonics rejected not a due care of the grave, though they put their ashes to unreasonable expectations in their tedious term of return and long set revolution.

Men have lost their reason in nothing so much as their religion, wherein stones and clouts make martyrs; and since the religion of one seems madness unto another, to afford an account or rationale of old rites requires no rigid reader. That they kindled the pyre aversely, or turning their face from it, was an handsome symbol of unwilling ministration; that they washed their bones with wine and milk, that the mother wrapped them in linen, and dried them in her bosom, the first fostering part, and place of their nourishment; that they opened their eyes towards heaven before they kindled the fire, as the place of their hopes or original, were no improper ceremonies. Their last valediction, thrice uttered by the attendants, was also very solemn; and somewhat answered by Christians, who thought it too little if they threw not the earth thrice upon the interred body. That in strewing their tombs the Romans affected the rose, the Greeks amaranthus and myrtle; that the funeral pyre consisted of sweet fuel —cypress, fir, larix, yew, and trees perpetually verdant—lay silent expressions of their surviving hopes. Wherein Christians, which deck their coffins with bays, have found a more elegant emblem: for that tree, seeming dead, will restore itself from the root, and its dry and exsuccous leaves resume their verdure again (which, if we mistake not, we have also observed in furze). Whether the planting of yew in churchyards hold not its original from ancient funeral rites, or as an emblem of resurrection from its perpetual verdure, may also admit conjecture.

They made use of music to excite or quiet the affections of their friends, according to different harmonies. But the secret and

---

Diogenes: the cynic. Diogenes Laertius, 6.79.
transcorporating: who believed in the transmigration of souls.
revolution: the Platonic year. See above, p. 7.
last valediction: Farewell, farewell: we, in the order which nature allows, shall follow.—*B.*
larix: larch.   *exsuccous*: sapless.

symbolical hint was the harmonical nature of the soul; which, delivered from the body, went again to enjoy the primitive harmony of heaven, from whence it first descended—which, according to its progress traced by antiquity, came down by Cancer, and ascended by Capricornus.

They burnt not children before their teeth appeared, as apprehending their bodies too tender a morsel for fire, and that their gristly bones would scarce leave separable relics after the pyral combustion. That they kindled not fire in their houses for some days after was a strict memorial of the late afflicting fire; and, mourning without hope, they had an happy fraud against excessive lamentation, by a common opinion that deep sorrows disturbed their ghosts.

That they buried their dead on their backs, or in a supine position, seems agreeable unto profound sleep, and common posture of dying; contrary to the most natural way of birth, nor unlike our pendulous posture in the doubtful state of the womb. Diogenes was singular, who preferred a prone situation in the grave; and some Christians like neither, who decline the figure of rest, and make choice of an erect posture.

That they carried them out of the world with their feet forward, not inconsonant unto reason, as contrary unto the native posture of man, and his production first into it; and also agreeable unto their opinions: while they bid adieu unto the world, not to look again upon it; whereas Mahometans, who think to return to a delightful life again, are carried forth with their heads forward, and looking toward their houses.

They closed their eyes as parts which first die, or first discover the sad effects of death. But their iterated clamations to excite their dying or dead friends, or revoke them unto life again, was a vanity of affection; as not presumably ignorant of the critical tests of death, by apposition of feathers, glasses, and reflection of figures, which dead eyes represent not; which, however not strictly verifiable in fresh and warm cadavers, could hardly elude the test in corpses of four or five days.

That they sucked in the last breath of their expiring friends was surely a practice of no medical institution, but a loose opinion that

Capricornus: Macrobius, *In Somnium Scipionis*, 1.12, regarded these two constellations as the exit and entrance of heaven.
ghosts: Hurt not my spirit. Tibullus, 1.1.67.—*B*.
nor unlike: nor like, and unlike.
Diogenes: the cynic. Diogenes Laertius, 6.31–2.
Christians: Russians, etc.—*B.*　　　　*clamations*: callings.
excitate: arouse.　　　　*revoke*: recall.
five days: at least by some difference from living eyes.—*B.*

the soul passed out that way, and a fondness of affection—from some Pythagorical foundation—that the spirit of one body passed into another, which they wished might be their own.

That they poured oil upon the pyre was a tolerable practice while the intention rested in facilitating the accension; but to place good omens in the quick and speedy burning, to sacrifice unto the winds for a dispatch in this office, was a low form of superstition.

The archimime or jester attending the funeral train, and imitating the speeches, gesture, and manners of the deceased, was too light for such solemnities, contradicting their funeral orations and doleful rites of the grave.

That they buried a piece of money with them as a fee of the Elysian ferryman, was a practice full of folly. But the ancient custom of placing coins in considerable urns, and the present practice of burying medals in the noble foundations of Europe, are laudable ways of historical discoveries in actions, persons, chronologies; and posterity will applaud them.

We examine not the old laws of sepulture exempting certain persons from burial or burning. But hereby we apprehend that these were not the bones of persons planet-struck, or burnt with fire from heaven; no relics of traitors to their country, self-killers, or sacrilegious malefactors—persons in old apprehension unworthy of the earth, condemned unto the Tartaras of hell, and bottomless pit of Pluto, from whence there was no redemption.

Nor were only many customs questionable in order to their obsequies, but also sundry practices, fictions, and conceptions, discordant or obscure, of their state and future beings. Whether unto eight or ten bodies of men to add one of a woman, as being more inflammable, and unctuously constituted for the better pyral combustion, were any rational practice; or whether the complaint of Periander's wife be tolerable—that wanting her funeral burning, she suffered intolerable cold in hell (according to the constitution of the infernal house of Pluto, wherein cold makes a great part of their tortures)—it cannot pass without some question.

Why the female ghosts appear unto Ulysses before the heroes and masculine spirits; why the psyche or soul of Tiresias is of the

fondness of affection: foolish assumption.
accension: kindling.   *archimime or jester*: Suetonius, *Vespasian*, 19.2.
ferryman: Charon, who in Greek myth ferried the dead across the Styx to Hades.
planet-struck: killed supposedly by the influence of a malign planet.
Tartaras: lowest regions.   *in order to*: regarding.
Periander's wife: Melissa, in Herodotus, 5.92.
Ulysses: *Odyssey*, 11.225 ff.   *Tiresias*: *Odyssey*, 11.90.—*B.*

masculine gender (who, being blind on earth, sees more than all the rest in hell); why the funeral suppers consisted of eggs, beans, smallage, and lettuce, since the dead are made to eat asphodels about the Elysian meadows; why, since there is no sacrifice acceptable, nor any propitiation for the covenant of the grave, men set up the deity of Morta, and fruitlessly adored divinities without ears—it cannot escape some doubt.

The dead seem all alive in the humane Hades of Homer, yet cannot well speak, prophesy, or know the living, except they drink blood, wherein is the life of man. And therefore the souls of Penelope's paramours conducted by Mercury chirped like bats, and those which followed Hercules made a noise but like a flock of birds.

The departed spirits know things past and to come, yet are ignorant of things present: Agamemnon foretells what should happen unto Ulysses, yet ignorantly enquires what is become of his own son. The ghosts are afraid of swords in Homer, yet Sibylla tells Aeneas, in Virgil, the thin habit of spirits was beyond the force of weapons. The spirits put off their malice with their bodies, and Caesar and Pompey accord in Latin hell, yet Ajax in Homer endures not a conference with Ulysses. And Deiphobus appears all mangled in Virgil's ghosts, yet we meet with perfect shadows among the wounded ghosts of Homer.

Since Charon, in Lucian, applauds his condition among the dead, whether it be handsomely said of Achilles, that living contemner of death, that he had rather be a ploughman's servant than emperor of the dead. How Hercules his soul is in hell, and yet in heaven; and Julius his soul in a star, yet seen by Aeneas in hell—except the ghosts were but images and shadows of the soul received in higher mansions, according to the ancient division of body, soul, and image or simulacrum of them both. The particulars of future

---

asphodels: in Lucian, *Downward Journey*, 2.—*B.*
Morta: one of the Fates, called by the Greeks Atropos, and portrayed as a blind hag.
humane: classical.
life of man: Lev. 17:11, 14.
Hercules: *Odyssey*, 11.605.
Agamemnon: *Odyssey*, 11.443–61.
force of weapons: *Aeneid*, 6.290–4.
Ajax: *Odyssey*, 11.543–64.
drink blood: *Odyssey*, 11.95–9, etc.
Mercury: *Odyssey*, 24.6–9.
departed spirits: Dante, *Inferno*, 10.97–108.
afraid of swords: *Odyssey*, 11.48–50.
Caesar and Pompey: *Aeneid*, 6.826–7.
Deiphobus: *Aeneid*, 6.494–7.
Lucian: Charon, in the dialogue so named, scorns the supposed glories of human life.
Achilles: *Odyssey*, 11.485–91.
Hercules: *Odyssey*, 11.601–4.
Julius: the deified Caesar. Horace, *Odes*, 1.12.46–8.
seen by Aeneas: *Aeneid*, 6.826 ff.
ancient division: *Iliad*, 23.103–4.

beings must needs be dark unto ancient theories, which Christian philosophy yet determines but in a cloud of opinions. A dialogue between two infants in the womb concerning the state of this world might handsomely illustrate our ignorance of the next, whereof methinks we yet discourse in Plato's den, and are but embryon philosophers.

Pythagoras escapes in the fabulous hell of Dante, among that swarm of philosophers; wherein, whilst we meet with Plato and Socrates, Cato is to be found in no lower place than purgatory. Among all the set, Epicurus is most considerable, whom men make honest without an Elysium; who contemned life without encouragement of immortality; and, making nothing after death, yet made nothing of the king of terrors.

Were the happiness of the next world as closely apprehended as the felicities of this, it were a martyrdom to live; and unto such as consider none hereafter, it must be more than death to die—which makes us amazed at those audacities that durst be nothing, and return into their chaos again. Certainly, such spirits as could contemn death when they expected no better being after, would have scorned to live had they known any. And therefore we applaud not the judgment of Machiavel that Christianity makes men cowards; or that, with the confidence of but half dying, the despised virtues of patience and humility have abased the spirits of men, which pagan principles exalted: but rather regulated the wildness of audacities in the attempts, grounds, and eternal sequels of death; wherein men of the boldest spirits are often prodigiously temerarious. Nor can we extenuate the valour of ancient martyrs, who contemned death in the uncomfortable scene of their lives, and in their decrepit martyrdoms did probably lose not many months of their days, or parted with life when it was scarce worth the living. For (beside that long time past holds no consideration unto a slender time to come), they had no small disadvantage from the constitution of old age, which naturally makes men fearful—complexionally superannuated from the bold and courageous thoughts of youth and fervent years. But the contempt of death from corporal animosity promoteth not our felicity: they may set in the orchestra and noblest seats of heaven

---

Plato's den: *Republic,* 7(514 ff.).   *embryon*: embryonic.
Dante: In *Inferno*, 4, Pythagoras is not mentioned.—*B.*
Cato: *Purgatorio*, 1.31 ff.   *Machiavel*: N. Machiavelli, *Discorsi*, 2.2.
extenuate: belittle.
complexionally superannuated from: having in temperament outgrown.
corporal animosity: loathing of physical existence.

who have held up shaking hands in the fire, and humanly contended for glory.

Meanwhile, Epicurus lies deep in Dante's hell, wherein we meet with tombs enclosing souls which denied their immortalities. But whether the virtuous heathen who lived better than he spake, or, erring in the principles of himself, yet lived above philosophers of more specious maxims, lie so deep as he is placed (at least so low as not to rise against Christians who, believing or knowing that truth, have lastingly denied it in their practice and conversation), were a query too sad to insist on.

But all or most apprehensions rested in opinions of some future being, which, ignorantly or coldly believed, begat those perverted conceptions, ceremonies, sayings, which Christians pity or laugh at. Happy are they which live not in that disadvantage of time when men could say little for futurity but from reason, whereby the noblest minds fell often upon doubtful deaths and melancholy dissolutions. With these hopes Socrates warmed his doubtful spirits against that cold potion; and Cato, before he durst give the fatal stroke, spent part of the night in reading the immortality of Plato, thereby confirming his wavering hand unto the animosity of that attempt.

It is the heaviest stone that melancholy can throw at a man, to tell him he is at the end of his nature; or that there is no further state to come, unto which this seems progressional, and otherwise made in vain. Without this accomplishment the natural expectation and desire of such a state were but a fallacy in nature. Unsatisfied considerators would quarrel the justice of their constitutions, and rest content that Adam had fallen lower; whereby, by knowing no other original, and deeper ignorance of themselves, they might have enjoyed the happiness of inferior creatures, who in tranquillity possess their constitutions as having not the apprehension to deplore their own natures. And being framed below the circumference of these hopes, or cognition of better being, the wisdom of God hath necessitated their contentment; but the superior ingredient and obscured part of ourselves, whereto all present felicities afford no resting contentment, will be able at last to tell us we are more than our present selves, and evacuate such hopes in the fruition of their own accomplishments.

Dante's hell: *Inferno*, 10.13–15.
Cato: Plutarch, *Cato Minor*, 68.2, 70.1.
considerators: thinkers.

Socrates: Plato, *Phaedo*.
immortality of Plato: *Phaedo*.
superior ingredient: soul.

CHAP. V

Now since these dead bones have already outlasted the living ones of Methuselah, and, in a yard under ground and thin walls of clay, outworn all the strong and specious buildings above it, and quietly rested under the drums and tramplings of three conquests—what prince can promise such diuturnity unto his relics, or might not gladly say,

Sic ego componi versus in ossa velim.

Time, which antiquates antiquities, and hath an art to make dust of all things, hath yet spared these minor monuments. In vain we hope to be known by open and visible conservatories, when to be unknown was the means of their continuation, and obscurity their protection. If they died by violent hands, and were thrust into their urns, these bones become considerable; and some old philosophers would honour them, whose souls they conceived most pure which were thus snatched from their bodies, and to retain a stronger propension unto them; whereas they weariedly left a languishing corpse, and with faint desires of reunion. If they fell by long and aged decay, yet, wrapped up in the bundle of time, they fall into indistinction, and make but one blot with infants. If we begin to die when we live, and long life be but a prolongation of death, our life is a sad composition: we live with death, and die not in a moment. How many pulses made up the life of Methuselah were work for Archimedes: common counters sum up the life of Moses his man. Our days become considerable, like petty sums, by minute accumulations; where numerous fractions make up but small round numbers, and our days of a span long make not one little finger.

If the nearness of our last necessity brought a nearer conformity unto it, there were a happiness in hoary hairs, and no calamity in half senses. But the long habit of living indisposeth us for dying,

one little finger: according to the ancient arithmetic of the hand wherein the little finger of the right hand, contracted, signified an hundred.—B.

Methuselah: who lived 969 years. Gen. 5:27.

three conquests: Anglo-Saxon, Danish, and Norman—assuming the urns to be Roman.

diuturnity: longlastingness.

Sic ego: Thus let me be placed when I am turned to bones. Tibullus, 3.2.26.—B.

conservatories: places of preservation.

propension: attachment.

indistinction: state of being indistinguishable.

Archimedes: who in his *Arenarius* calculated the number of grains of sand in the universe.

Moses: in the Psalm of Moses, Ps. 90:10.—B.

when avarice makes us the sport of death; when even David grew
politicly cruel, and Solomon could hardly be said to be the wisest of
men. But many are too early old, and before the date of age: adversity stretcheth our days, misery makes Alcmena's nights, and time
hath no wings unto it. But the most tedious being is that which can
unwish itself, content to be nothing, or never to have been; which was
beyond the malcontent of Job, who cursed, not the day of his life,
but his nativity: content to have so far been as to have a title to
future being, although he had lived here but in an hidden state of
life, and, as it were, an abortion.

What song the sirens sang, or what name Achilles assumed when
he hid himself among women, though puzzling questions, are not
beyond all conjecture. What time the persons of these ossuaries
entered the famous nations of the dead, and slept with princes and
counsellors, might admit a wide solution. But who were the proprietaries of these bones, or what bodies these ashes made up, were
a question above antiquarism, not to be resolved by man—nor
easily perhaps by spirits, except we consult the provincial guardians,
or tutelary observators. Had they made as good provision for their
names as they have done for their relics, they had not so grossly
erred in the art of perpetuation; but to subsist in bones, and be but
pyramidally extant, is a fallacy in duration. Vain ashes, which, in
the oblivion of names, persons, times, and sexes, have found unto
themselves a fruitless continuation, and only arise unto late posterity
as emblems of mortal vanities, antidotes against pride, vainglory,
and madding vices! Pagan vainglories which thought the world
might last for ever had encouragement for ambition, and, finding no
Atropos unto the immortality of their names, were never damped
with the necessity of oblivion. Even old ambitions had the advantage
of ours in the attempts of their vainglories, who, acting early, and
before the probable meridian of time, have by this time found

David: 2 Sam. 8:2. *Solomon*: 1 Kgs. 11:1–8.
Alcmena's nights: one night made as long as three by Zeus for his pleasures with
  Hercules' mother. Lucian, *Dialogues of the Gods*, 14(10), 'Hermes and Helios'.
Job: Job 3:1–16.
puzzling questions: of Tiberius unto grammarians. Suetonius, *Tiberius*, 70.—*B.*
nations of the dead: Odyssey, 10.526.—*B.*
princes and counsellors: Job 3:13–15.—*B.* *proprietaries*: owners.
provincial . . . observators: guardian angels of provinces or persons.
pyramidally: as a merely physical relic.
Atropos: the Fate who cut the thread of life.
meridian of time: 1000 B.C., assuming the world to have been created in 4000 B.C.,
  and to last 6,000 years.

great accomplishment of their designs, whereby the ancient heroes
have already outlasted their monuments and mechanical preservations. But in this latter scene of time we cannot expect such mummies
unto our memories, when ambition may fear the prophecy of
Elias, and Charles V can never hope to live within two Methuselahs
of Hector.

And, therefore, restless inquietude for the diuturnity of our
memories, unto present considerations, seems a vanity almost out
of date, and superannuated piece of folly. We cannot hope to live so
long in our names as some have done in their persons ; one face of
Janus holds no proportion unto the other. 'Tis too late to be ambitious : the great mutations of the world are acted, or time may be
too short for our designs. To extend our memories by monuments,
whose death we daily pray for (and whose duration we cannot hope
without injury to our expectations) in the advent of the last day, were
a contradiction to our beliefs. We whose generations are ordained
in this setting part of time are providentially taken off from such
imaginations ; and, being necessitated to eye the remaining particle
of futurity, are naturally constituted unto thoughts of the next
world, and cannot excusably decline the consideration of that duration which maketh pyramids pillars of snow, and all that's past a
moment.

Circles and right lines limit and close all bodies, and the mortal
right-lined circle must conclude and shut up all. There is no antidote
against the opium of time, which temporally considereth all things :
our fathers find their graves in our short memories, and sadly tell
us how we may be buried in our survivors'. Gravestones tell truth
scarce forty years ; generations pass while some trees stand, and old
families last not three oaks. To be read by bare inscriptions like
many in Gruter ; to hope for eternity by enigmatical epithets, or

---

mechanical: artificial.
prophecy of Elias: that the world may last but six thousand years.—B. See above,
    p. 48.
Charles V: born in 1500, with only 500 years left before the supposed end of the
    world.
two Methuselahs: twice 969, i.e. 1,938.
Hector: Hector's fame lasting above two lives of Methuselah before that famous
    prince was extant.—B. The traditional date of the fall of Troy is 1184 B.C.
diuturnity: long duration.
Janus: the Roman god with two faces, regarding time past and time to come.
daily pray for: in the Lord's Prayer: Thy kingdom come.
right-lined circle: θ, the initial of the Greek word for death, θάνατος.—B.
forty years: old ones being taken up, and other bodies laid under them.—B.
Gruter: J. Gruterus, *Inscriptiones Antiquae* (1603).

first letters of our names : to be studied by antiquaries, who we were, and have new names given us, like many of the mummies—are cold consolations unto the students of perpetuity, even by everlasting languages.

To be content that times to come should only know there was such a man, not caring whether they knew more of him, was a frigid ambition in Cardan, disparaging his horoscopal inclination and judgement of himself. Who cares to subsist like Hippocrates' patients, or Achilles' horses in Homer, under naked nominations, without deserts and noble acts, which are the balsam of our memories, the *entelechia* and soul of our subsistences? To be nameless in worthy deeds exceeds an infamous history : the Canaanitish woman lives more happily without a name than Herodias with one. And who had not rather have been the good thief than Pilate?

But the iniquity of oblivion blindly scattereth her poppy, and deals with the memory of men without distinction to merit of perpetuity. Who can but pity the founder of the pyramids? Herostratus lives, that burnt the temple of Diana : he is almost lost that built it. Time hath spared the epitaph of Adrian's horse, confounded that of himself. In vain we compute our felicities by the advantage of our good names, since bad have equal durations, and Thersites is like to live as long as Agamemnon. Who knows whether the best of men be known, or whether there be not more remarkable persons forgot than any that stand remembered in the known account of time? Without the favour of the everlasting register, the first man had been as unknown as the last, and Methuselah's long life had been his only chronicle.

Oblivion is not to be hired : the greater part must be content to be as though they had not been, to be found in the register of God,

---

mummies: which men show in several countries, giving them what names they please, and unto some the names of old Egyptian kings out of Herodotus.—B.

Cardan: G. Cardano (1501–76), *De Propria Vita*, 9 (1614, p. 42).—*B*.

judgement of himself: given in *In Ptolemaeum De Astrorum Iudiciis* (1578, pp. 629–680).

Achilles' horses: *Iliad*, 16.149–52. *entelechia*: informing spirit.

Canaanitish woman: Matt. 15:22–8.

Herodias: Matt. 14:3–11, Mark 6:17–28.

Herostratus: who fired the temple to immortalize himself, by coincidence on the night in 356 B.C. when Alexander the Great was born.

that built it: Chersiphron. Pliny, 36.21(95).

Adrian's horse: Dio Cassius, 69.10.2, records that the Emperor Hadrian had an epitaph inscribed for his horse Borysthenes; one of doubtful authenticity was published in the sixteenth century.

Agamemnon: Horace, *Odes*, 4.9.25–30.

not in the record of man. Twenty-seven names make up the first
story, and the recorded names ever since contain not one living
century. The number of the dead long exceedeth all that shall live ;
the night of time far surpasseth the day—and who knows when was
the equinox ? Every hour adds unto that current arithmetic, which
scarce stands one moment. And since death must be the Lucina of
life, and even pagans could doubt whether thus to live were to die ;
since our longest sun sets at right descensions, and makes but winter
arches, and therefore it cannot be long before we lie down in darkness,
and have our light in ashes ; since the brother of death daily haunts us
with dying mementoes, and time, that grows old itself, bids us hope
no long duration—diuturnity is a dream and folly of expectation.

Darkness and light divide the course of time, and oblivion shares
with memory a great part even of our living beings ; we slightly
remember our felicities, and the smartest strokes of affliction leave
but short smart upon us. Sense endureth no extremities, and sorrows
destroy us or themselves. To weep into stones are fables : afflictions
induce callosities, miseries are slippery, or fall like snow upon
us ; which, notwithstanding, is no unhappy stupidity. To be ignorant
of evils to come, and forgetful of evils past, is a merciful provision
in nature, whereby we digest the mixture of our few and evil days ;
and, our delivered senses not relapsing into cutting remembrances,
our sorrows are not kept raw by the edge of repetitions. A great
part of antiquity contented their hopes of subsistency with a transmigration of their souls : a good way to continue their memories,
while, having the advantage of plural successions, they could not
but act something remarkable in such variety of beings, and, en-
joying the fame of their past selves, make accumulation of glory
unto their last durations. Others, rather than be lost in the uncomfortable night of nothing, were content to recede into the common
being, and make one particle of the public soul of all things—which
was no more than to return into their unknown and divine original
again. Egyptian ingenuity was more unsatisfied, contriving their
bodies in sweet consistences to attend the return of their souls. But

---

first story: before the Flood.—B.
Lucina: Roman goddess of childbirth, and thence birth itself.
pagans: e.g. Euripides, quoted by Plato, *Gorgias*, 492e.—B.
winter arches: our longest possible life is but as a winter's day.
light in ashes: according to the custom of the Jews, who place a lighted wax
    candle in a pot of ashes by the corpse.—B.
brother of death: sleep.   *diuturnity*: longlastingness.
weep into stones: as did Niobe. Ovid, *Metamorphoses*, 6.304–12.

all was vanity, feeding the wind, and folly: the Egyptian mummies which Cambyses or time hath spared, avarice now consumeth. Mummy is become merchandise, Mizraim cures wounds, and Pharaoh is sold for balsams.

In vain do individuals hope for immortality, or any patent from oblivion, in preservations below the moon. Men have been deceived even in their flatteries above the sun, and studied conceits to perpetuate their names in heaven: the various cosmography of that part hath already varied the names of contrived constellations— Nimrod is lost in Orion, and Osiris in the Dog-star. While we look for incorruption in the heavens, we find they are but like the earth, durable in their main bodies, alterable in their parts—whereof, beside comets and new stars, perspectives begin to tell tales; and the spots that wander about the sun, with Phaeton's favour, would make clear conviction.

There is nothing strictly immortal but immortality: whatever hath no beginning may be confident of no end. All others have a dependent being, and within the reach of destruction; which is the peculiar of that necessary essence that cannot destroy itself, and the highest strain of omnipotency, to be so powerfully constituted as not to suffer even from the power of itself. But the sufficiency of Christian immortality frustrates all earthly glory, and the quality of either state after death, makes a folly of posthumous memory. God, who can only destroy our souls, and hath assured our resurrection, either of our bodies or names hath directly promised no duration—wherein there is so much of chance that the boldest expectants have found unhappy frustration; and to hold long subsistence seems but a scape in oblivion. But man is a noble animal, splendid in ashes and pompous in the grave, solemnizing nativities and deaths with equal lustre, nor omitting ceremonies of bravery in the infamy of his nature.

Life is a pure flame, and we live by an invisible sun within us. A small fire sufficeth for life: great flames seemed too little after death, while men vainly affected precious pyres, and to burn like

---

feeding the wind: Eccles. 1:14, etc.—*B.*
Cambyses: a son of Cyrus the Great who conquered Egypt in the sixth century
B.C.   *mummy*: as a drug.
Mizraim: son of Ham, typifying an Egyptian. Gen. 10:6.
patent: concession.   *conceits*: devices.
incorruption in the heavens: Aristotle, *De Caelo*, 2.1.
perspectives: telescopes.   *no end*: Aristotle, *De Caelo*, 1.12.
peculiar: exclusive privilege.   *expectants*: those who expect.
a scape in: an oversight on the part of.

Sardanapalus. But the wisdom of funeral laws found the folly of prodigal blazes, and reduced undoing fires unto the rule of sober obsequies, wherein few could be so mean as not to provide wood, pitch, a mourner, and an urn.

Five languages secured not the epitaph of Gordianus. The man of God lives longer without a tomb than any by one, invisibly interred by angels, and adjudged to obscurity, though not without some marks directing human discovery. Enoch and Elias, without either tomb or burial, in an anomalous state of being, are the great examples of perpetuity in their long and living memory—in strict account being still on this side death, and having a late part yet to act upon this stage of earth. If in the decretory term of the world we shall not all die, but be changed, according to received translation, the last day will make but few graves; at least, quick resurrections will anticipate lasting sepultures: some graves will be opened before they be quite closed, and Lazarus be no wonder. When many that feared to die shall groan that they can die but once, the dismal state is the second and living death—when life puts despair on the damned; when men shall wish the coverings of mountains, not of monuments, and annihilation shall be courted.

While some have studied monuments, others have studiously declined them; and some have been so vainly boisterous that they durst not acknowledge their graves—wherein Alaricus seems most subtle, who had a river turned to hide his bones at the bottom. Even Sylla, that thought himself safe in his urn, could not prevent revenging tongues, and stones thrown at his monument. Happy are they whom privacy makes innocent; who deal so with men in this

---

Sardanapalus: who, hopelessly besieged, burnt with himself all his treasures, concubines, and wives. Athenaeus, 12.38(529).

funeral laws: Cicero, *Laws*, 2.23(59).

an urn: according to the epitaph of Rufus and Beronica in Gruter, *Inscriptiones Antiquae* (1603, p. xiv.8): No more was found of their goods than sufficed to buy a pyre, and pitch with which the bodies might be burnt, and a woman hired to weep at the head of the cortège, and an urn bought.—*B.*

Gordianus: In Greek, Latin, Persian, Hebrew, and Egyptian characters, defaced by Licinius the Emperor.—*B. Augustan History*, 'The Three Gordians', 34.2–5.

angels: Jude 9.

Enoch and Elias: taken up to heaven. Gen. 5:24, 2 Kgs. 2:11.

yet to act: as the two witnesses of Rev. 11:3 ff.

decretory term: final judgement.   *changed*: 1 Cor. 15:51.

living death: Rev. 21:8.   *mountains*: Rev. 6:16.

studied: sought, devised.   *Alaricus*: King of the Goths, died in 410.

Sylla: Dio Cassius, 78(77).13.7, records how Caracalla searched out Sulla's tomb and repaired it.

world that they are not afraid to meet them in the next; who, when
they die, make no commotion among the dead, and are not touched
with that poetical taunt of Isaiah.

Pyramids, arches, obelisks, were but the irregularities of vainglory, and wild enormities of ancient magnanimity. But the most
magnanimous resolution rests in the Christian religion, which
trampleth upon pride, and sets on the neck of ambition, humbly
pursuing that infallible perpetuity unto which all others must
diminish their diameters, and be poorly seen in angles of contingency.

Pious spirits who passed their days in raptures of futurity made
little more of this world than the world that was before it—while
they lay obscure in the chaos of preordination, and night of their
fore-beings. And if any have been so happy as truly to understand
Christian annihilation, extasis, exolution, liquefaction, transforma-
tion, the kiss of the Spouse, gustation of God, and ingression into
the divine shadow—they have already had an handsome anticipa-
tion of heaven: the glory of the world is surely over, and the earth
in ashes unto them.

To subsist in lasting monuments; to live in their productions;
to exist in their names, and predicament of chimeras, was large
satisfaction unto old expectations, and made one part of their
Elysiums. But all this is nothing in the metaphysics of true belief.
To live indeed is to be again ourselves, which being not only an
hope but an evidence in noble believers, 'tis all one to lie in St.
Innocent's Churchyard as in the sands of Egypt: ready to be anything, in the ecstasy of being ever, and as content with six foot as
the moles of Adrianus.

Lucan:
. . . Tabesne cadavera solvat
An rogus haud refert. . . .

Isaiah: Isa. 14:4–17.—*B.*   *contingency*: the least of angles.—*B.*
chaos of preordination: see above, p. 42.   *extasis*: ecstasy.
exolution: release of the soul.   *Spouse*: God.
ingression: entry.   *divine shadow*: see above, p. 11.
predicament of chimeras: state of existing only in name or legend.
St. Innocent's Churchyard: in Paris, where bodies soon consume.—*B.*
moles of Adrianus: a stately mausoleum or sepulchral pile built by Hadrian in
   Rome, where now standeth the Castle of St. Angelo.—*B.*
Lucan: *Pharsalia*, 7.809–10: Whether corruption dissolves corpses or a pyre does
   not matter.

The Garden of Cyrus

To my worthy and honoured friend
Nicholas Bacon of Gillingham, Esquire[n]

Had I not observed that purblind men have discoursed well of sight,
and some without issue excellently of generation, I, that was never
master of any considerable garden, had not attempted this subject.
But the earth is the garden of nature, and each fruitful country a
paradise. Dioscorides made most of his observations in his march
about with Antonius, and Theophrastus raised his generalities
chiefly from the field.

Beside, we write no herbal, nor can this volume deceive you who
have handled the massiest thereof; who know that three folios are yet
too little, and how new herbals fly from America upon us.[n] From
persevering enquirers, and old in those singularities, we expect such
descriptions; wherein England is now so exact that it yields not to
other countries.

We pretend not to multiply vegetable divisions by quincuncial and
reticulate plants, or erect a new phytology. The field of knowledge
hath been so traced, it is hard to spring anything new. Of old things
we write something new—if truth may receive addition, or envy will
have anything new, since the ancients knew the late anatomical
discoveries, and Hippocrates the circulation.[n]

You have been so long out of trite learning that 'tis hard to find a
subject proper for you; and if you have met with a sheet upon this,
we have missed our intention. In this multiplicity of writing, bye and
barren themes are best fitted for invention: subjects so often discoursed confine the imagination, and fix our conceptions unto the

---

purblind men: V. F. Plempius, *Ophthalmographia* (1632), N. Cabeus on Aristotle's
    Meteorologica (1646).—*B.*
without issue: W. Harvey, *De Generatione Animalium* (1651).—*B.*
Dioscorides: first-century A.D. author of *De Materia Medica*, here confused with
    a doctor in Mark Antony's army.
Theophrastus: (*c.* 370–288/5 B.C.), author of *On Plants* and *On the Causes of
    Plants*.
massiest: B. Besler, *Hortus Eystetensis* (1613).—*B.*
three folios: J. Bauhin and J. Cherler, *Historia Plantarum* (1650–1).—*B.*
old: my worthy friend Mr. Goodyer, an ancient and learned botanist.—*B.*
singularities: remarkable things.
England: as in London and divers parts, whereof we mention none lest we seem
    to omit any.—*B.*

notions of fore-writers. Beside, such discourses allow excursions, and venially admit of collateral truths, though at some distance from their principals. Wherein, if we sometimes take wide liberty, we are not single, but err by great example.

He that will illustrate the excellency of this order may easily fail upon so spruce a subject, wherein we have not affrighted the common reader with any other diagrams than of itself, and have industriously declined illustrations from rare and unknown plants.

Your discerning judgement, so well acquainted with that study, will expect herein no mathematical truths, as well understanding, how few generalities and *u finita's* there are in nature; how Scaliger hath found exceptions in most universals of Aristotle and Theophrastus; how botanical maxims must have fair allowance, and are tolerably current if not intolerably overbalanced by exceptions.

You have wisely ordered your vegetable delights, beyond the reach of exception. The Turks, who pass their days in gardens here, will have gardens also hereafter; and delighting in flowers on earth, must have lilies and roses in heaven. In garden delights 'tis not easy to hold a mediocrity: that insinuating pleasure is seldom without some extremity. The ancients venially delighted in flourishing gardens: many were florists that knew not the true use of a flower (and in Pliny's days none had directly treated of that subject). Some commendably affected plantations of venomous vegetables; some confined their delights unto single plants; and Cato seemed to dote upon cabbage—while the ingenuous delight of tulipists stands saluted with hard language even by their own professors.

That in this garden discourse we range into extraneous things and many parts of art and nature, we follow herein the example of old and new plantations, wherein noble spirits contented not themselves with trees, but, by the attendance of aviaries, fish-ponds, and all variety of animals, they made their gardens the epitome of the earth, and some resemblance of the secular shows of old.

great example: Hippocrates *On Superfetation* and *On Dentition* digresses on sexual intercourse and tonsillitis.—*B.*
u finita's: rules without exceptions.—*B.*, referring to the rule in Latin grammar that all final *u*'s are long.
Scaliger: J. C. Scaliger in his commentaries on Theophrastus' *Causes of Plants* and the work *On Plants* attributed to Aristotle.
current: valid.
venomous vegetables: King Attalus in Plutarch, *Demetrius*, 20.2.
Cato: *On Agriculture*, 156–8.   *tulipists*: tulip enthusiasts.
professors: who termed the seventeenth-century panic speculation in tulip bulbs 'tulipomania', and the bulb 'fool's-plant'.—*B.*
secular shows: spectacles once in a hundred years.

That we conjoin these parts of different subjects, or that this should succeed the other, your judgement will admit without impute of incongruity, since the delightful world comes after death, and paradise succeeds the grave; since the verdant state of things is the symbol of the Resurrection, and to flourish in the state of glory we must first be sown in corruption—beside the ancient practice of noble persons, to conclude in garden-graves, and urns themselves of old to be wrapped up in flowers and garlands.

Nullum sine venia placuisse eloquium is more sensibly understood by writers than by readers, nor well apprehended by either till works have hanged out like Apelles his pictures, wherein even common eyes will find something for emendation.

To wish all readers of your abilities, were unreasonably to multiply the number of scholars beyond the temper of these times; but unto this ill-judging age we charitably desire a portion of your equity, judgement, candour, and ingenuity—wherein you are so rich as not to lose by diffusion. And being a flourishing branch of that noble family unto which we owe so much observance, you are not new set, but long rooted in such perfection; whereof having had so lasting confirmation in your worthy conversation, constant amity, and expression; and knowing you a serious student in the highest arcanas of nature; with much excuse we bring these low delights and poor maniples to your treasure.

Norwich.
May 1.   Your affectionate friend and servant,
                                          Thomas Browne.

---

impute: accusation.   *corruption*: 1 Cor. 15:42.
garlands: like that of Philopoemen in Plutarch, *Philopoemen*, 21.3.
Nullum sine: No eloquence has pleased without some allowance being made.
Apelles: Pliny, *Natural History*, 35.36(84–5), tells how the Greek painter would hide behind his works to overhear the comments of passers-by.
noble family: of the most worthy Sir Edmund Bacon, prime baronet, my true and noble friend.—B.
maniples: handfuls.

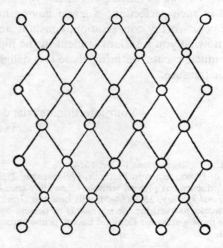

*Quid Quincunce speciosius, qui, in
quam cunq3 partem spectaueris,
rectus est: Quintilian:*

Quid Quincunce: What is more handsome than the quincunx, which, in whatsoever direction you look, is straight? Quintilian, 8.3.9.

The Garden of Cyrus

or

the quincuncial, lozenge, or network plantations of the ancients, artificially, naturally, mystically considered

CHAPTER I

That Vulcan gave arrows unto Apollo and Diana the fourth day after their nativities, according to Gentile theology, may pass for no blind apprehension of the creation of the sun and moon in the work of the fourth day, when the diffused light contracted into orbs and shooting rays of those luminaries. Plainer descriptions there are from pagan pens of the creatures of the fourth day, while the divine philosopher unhappily omitteth the noblest part of the third, and Ovid (whom many conceive to have borrowed his description from Moses), coldly deserting the remarkable account of the text, in three words describeth this work of the third day: the vegetable creation and first ornamental scene of nature; the primitive food of animals; and first story of physic, in dietetical conservation.

For though physic may plead high from that medical act of God in casting so deep a sleep upon our first parent, and chirurgery find its whole art in that one passage concerning the rib of Adam, yet is there no rivality with garden contrivance and herbary. For if paradise were planted the third day of the Creation, as wiser divinity concludeth, the nativity thereof was too early for horoscopy: gardens were before gardeners, and but some hours after the earth.

Of deeper doubt is its topography and local designation; yet being the primitive garden, and without much controversy seated in the East, it is more than probable the first curiosity and cultivation of plants most flourished in those quarters. And since the Ark of Noah

---

Gentile theology: Hyginus, *Fabulae*, 140 (a dubious reading).
diffused light: created before its local sources, sun, moon, and stars. Gen. 1:3–5, 14–19.
divine philosopher: Plato, in his *Timaeus.—B.*
Ovid: *Metamorphoses*, 1.44: He ordered the woods to be covered with foliage.— *B.*
dietetical conservation: creation of a guaranteed food supply. Gen. 1:11–12.
plead high: claim an ancient origin.   *chirurgery*: surgery.
Adam: Gen. 2:21. Diaeresis, in opening the flesh; exaeresis, in taking out the rib; synthesis, in closing up the part again.—*B.*
rivality: competition.   *herbary*: the science of herbs.
paradise: Gen. 2:8ff.
controversy: For some there is from the ambiguity of the word *mikedem*: whether 'from the east' or 'from the beginning'.—*B.*

first touched upon some mountains of Armenia, the planting art arose again in the East, and found its revolution not far from the place of its nativity, about the plains of those regions. And if Zoroaster were either Ham, Cush, or Mizraim, they were early proficients therein who left (as Pliny delivereth) a work of agriculture.

However, the account of the pensile or hanging gardens of Babylon, if made by Semiramis, the third or fourth from Nimrod, is of no slender antiquity; which, being not framed upon ordinary level of ground, but raised upon pillars, admitting under-passages, we cannot accept as the first Babylonian gardens, but a more eminent progress and advancement in that art than any that went before it—somewhat answering or hinting the old opinion concerning paradise itself, with many conceptions elevated above the plane of the earth.

Nebuchadnezzar (whom some will have to be the famous Syrian king of Diodorus) beautifully repaired that city, and so magnificently built his hanging gardens that from succeeding writers he had the honour of the first. From whence overlooking Babylon and all the region about it, he found no circumscription to the eye of his ambition, till, over-delighted with the bravery of this paradise, in his melancholy metamorphosis he found the folly of that delight, and a proper punishment in the contrary habitation, in wild plantations and wanderings of the fields.

The Persian gallants who destroyed this monarchy maintained their botanical bravery. Unto whom we owe the very name of paradise, wherewith we meet not in Scripture before the time of Solomon, and conceived originally Persian—the word for that disputed garden expressing in the Hebrew no more than a field enclosed, which from the same root is content to derive a garden and a buckler.

Cyrus the Elder, brought up in woods and mountains, when time and power enabled, pursued the dictate of his education, and brought the treasures of the field into rule and circumscription; so

---

Armenia: Gen. 8:4.
Zoroaster: traditionally the sixth-century B.C. founder of the Persian magi.
Mizraim: Gen. 10:6.
Pliny: *Nat. Hist.*, 18.5(22), mentions Mago of Carthage, mistaken here for a magus.
Nimrod: Gen. 10:8–12.   *with many conceptions*: in the opinion of many.
Diodorus: Diodorus Siculus, 2.10.
succeeding writers: e.g. Josephus, *Jewish Antiquities*, 10.11.1(226).
over-delighted: Dan. 4:30.   *fields*: Dan. 4:33.
Cyrus the Elder: sixth-century B.C. founder of the Persian empire.
mountains: Herodotus, 1.110.

nobly beautifying the hanging gardens of Babylon that he was also thought to be the author thereof.

Ahasuerus (whom many conceive to have been Artaxerxes Longimanus) in the country and city of flowers, and in an open garden, entertained his princes and people, while Vashti more modestly treated the ladies within the palace thereof.

But if (as some opinion) King Ahasuerus were Artaxerxes Mnemon, that found a life and reign answerable unto his great memory, our magnified Cyrus was his second brother, who gave the occasion of that memorable work and almost miraculous retreat of Xenophon. A person of high spirit and honour, naturally a king, though fatally prevented by the harmless chance of postgeniture; not only a lord of gardens, but a manual planter thereof, disposing his trees like his armies in regular ordination: so that, while old Laertes hath found a name in Homer for pruning hedges, and clearing away thorns and briars; while King Attalus lives for his poisonous plantations of aconites, henbane, hellebore, and plants hardly admitted within the walls of paradise; while many of the ancients do poorly live in the single names of vegetables—all stories do look upon Cyrus as the splendid and regular planter.

According whereto Xenophon describeth his gallant plantation at Sardis, thus rendered by Strebaeus: *Arbores pari intervallo sitas, rectos ordines, & omnia perpulchre in quincuncem directa.* Which we shall take for granted as being accordingly rendered by the most elegant of the Latins; and by no made term, but in use before by Varro: that is, the rows and orders so handsomely disposed, or five trees so set together, that a regular angularity and through prospect was left on every side; owing this name not only unto the quintuple number of trees, but the figure declaring that number; which, being doubled at the angle, makes up the letter χ, that is the emphatical decussation, or fundamental figure.

Artaxerxes Longimanus: who became King Artaxerxes I of Persia in 464 B.C.
city of flowers: Shushan in Shushiana. Esther 1:5–9.—*B.*
Artaxerxes Mnemon: grandson of Artaxerxes I.
second brother: next younger brother. Plutarch, *Artaxerxes*, 1.
retreat of Xenophon: his *Anabasis*.   *postgeniture*: being born later.
Homer: Odyssey, 24.226–31, 244–7.   *Attalus*: Plutarch, *Demetrius*, 20.2.
names of vegetables: e.g. *Aristolochia, Lysimachia, Oenanthe, Phalaris.*
Xenophon: *Oeconomicus*, 4.21: The trees are beautiful and planted at regular
    intervals, the rows straight, and everything most beautifully arranged quin-
    cuncially.
Latins: Cicero, *De Senectute*, 17(59).   *Varro*: *De Re Rustica*, 1.7.2.
doubled at the angle: in Roman numerals two V's making an X.
emphatical: clear.

Now though in some ancient and modern practice the area or decussated plot might be a perfect square, answerable to a Tuscan pedestal, and the quinquernio or cinquepoint of a die—wherein by diagonal lines the intersection was rectangular, accommodable unto plantations of large growing trees—and we must not deny ourselves the advantage of this order; yet shall we chiefly insist upon that of Curtius and Porta in their brief description hereof. Wherein the *decussis* is made within a longilateral square, with opposite angles acute and obtuse at the intersection; and so upon progression making a rhombus or lozenge figuration, which seemeth very agreeable unto the original figure. Answerable whereunto we observe the decussated characters in many consulary coins, and even in those of Constantine and his sons, which pretend their pattern in the sky. The crucigerous ensign carried this figure, not transversely or rectangularly intersected, but in a decussation, after the form of an Andrean or Burgundian cross, which answereth this description.

Where by the way we shall decline the old theme, so traced by antiquity, of crosses and crucifixion; whereof some being right, and of one single piece without traversion, or transom, do little advantage our subject. Nor shall we take in the mystical tau, or the cross of our blessed Saviour, which, having in some descriptions an *empedon* or crossing foot-stay, made not one single transversion. And since the learned Lipsius hath made some doubt even of the cross of St. Andrew; since some martyrological histories deliver his death by the general name of a cross, and Hippolytus will have him suffer by the sword; we should have enough to make out the received cross of that martyr. Nor shall we urge the labarum and famous standard of Constantine; or make further use thereof than as the first letters in the name of our Saviour Christ, in use among Christians before the days of Constantine: to be observed in sepulchral monuments of

Tuscan: the fourth order of classical architecture.
quinquernio or cinquepoint: face with five dots.
Curtius and Porta: B. Curtius, *Horti* (1560); G. B. della Porta, *Villa* (1592).
decussis: X shape.   *longilateral square*: rectangle.
consulary: of the Roman republic.
Constantine: who claimed to have seen the cross in a vision while marching
    against Rome in 312.
crucigerous: cross-bearing.   *Andrean or Burgundian*: X-shaped.
right: consisting of an upright piece only.   *traversion*: cross-piece.
empedon: footrest.   *Lipsius*: J. Lipsius, *De Cruce*, 1.7 (*Opera*, 1637, iii.649).
Hippolytus: In *The Twelve Apostles* he in fact says that Andrew was crucified on
    an olive-wood upright.
first letters: in Greek *X* and *P*, commonly combined in a cipher ☧.
sepulchral monuments: of Marius under Hadrian, and of Alexander under one of
    the Antonines.—*B.*

martyrs in the reign of Adrian and Antoninus; and to be found in the antiquities of the Gentiles before the advent of Christ, as in the medal of King Ptolemy, signed with the same characters (and might be the beginning of some word or name which antiquaries have not hit on).

We will not revive the mysterious crosses of Egypt, with circles on their heads, in the breast of Serapis, and the hands of their genial spirits (not unlike the character of Venus, and looked on by ancient Christians with relation unto Christ), since, however they first began, the Egyptians thereby expressed the process and motion of the spirit of the world, and the diffusion thereof upon the celestial and elemental nature, implied by a circle and a right-lined intersection—a secret in their telesms and magical characters among them. Though he that considereth the plain cross upon the head of the owl in the Lateran obelisk, or the cross erected upon a pitcher diffusing streams of water into two basins with sprinkling branches in them, and all described upon a two-footed altar,[n] as in the hieroglyphics of the brazen Table of Bembus, will hardly decline all thought of Christian signality in them.

We shall not call in the Hebrew *tenupha*, or ceremony of their oblations, waved by the priest unto the four quarters of the world after the form of a cross, as in the peace-offerings. And if it were clearly made out what is remarkably delivered from the traditions of the rabbins, that, as the oil was poured coronally or circularly upon the head of kings, so the High Priest was anointed decussatively or in the form of a X; though it could not escape a typical thought of Christ from mystical considerators, yet, being the conceit is Hebrew, we should rather expect its verification from analogy in that language, than to confine the same unto the unconcerned letters of Greece, or make it out by the characters of Cadmus or Palamedes.

Of this quincuncial ordination the ancients practised much, discoursed little; and the moderns have nothing enlarged: which he that more nearly considereth in the form of its square rhombus and decussation, with the several commodities, mysteries, parallelisms,

Ptolemy: king of Egypt.   *Serapis*: a Graeco-Egyptian deity.
character of Venus: the symbol ♀.   *telesms*: talismans.
plain cross: wherein the lower part is somewhat longer.—B.
Table of Bembus: a first-century A.D. collection of hieroglyphs.
signality: significance.   *tenupha*: Ezek. 48:10.
typical: symbolic.   *considerators*: men who consider.
Cadmus: Phoenician founder of Thebes who taught letters to the Boeotians.
Palamedes: Greek hero in the Trojan War, said to have invented some letters of the alphabet.

and resemblances, both in art and nature, shall easily discern the elegancy of this order.

That this was in some ways of practice in diverse and distant nations, hints or deliveries there are from no slender antiquity. In the hanging gardens of Babylon, from Abydenus, Eusebius, and others, Curtius describeth this rule of decussation. In the memorable garden of Alcinous, anciently conceived an original fancy from paradise, mention there is of well-contrived order: for so hath Didymus (and Eustathius) expounded the emphatical word. Diomedes, describing the rural possessions of his father, gives account in the same language of trees orderly planted. And Ulysses, being a boy, was promised by his father forty fig-trees, and fifty rows of vines producing all kind of grapes.

That the eastern inhabitants of India made use of such order, even in open plantations, is deducible from Theophrastus; who, describing the trees whereof they made their garments, plainly delivereth that they were planted κατ᾽ ὄρχους, and in such order that at a distance men would mistake them for vineyards. The same seems confirmed in Greece from a singular expression in Aristotle concerning the order of vines, delivered by a military term representing the orders of soldiers, which also confirmeth the antiquity of this form yet used in vineal plantations.

That the same was used in Latin plantations is plainly confirmed from the commending pen of Varro, Quintilian, and handsome description of Virgil.

That the first plantations not long after the Flood were disposed after this manner, the generality and antiquity of this order, observed in vineyards and wine plantations, affordeth some conjecture. And since, from judicious enquiry, Saturn, who divided the world between his three sons; who beareth a sickle in his hand; who taught

---

Curtius: Horti, 6.12 (1560, p. 149), cites the statement of Abydenus, derived from Eusebius, that Nebuchadnezzar built the hanging gardens.
rule of decussation: Curtius, p. 150: 'The decussation itself presented a highly pleasing and most enjoyable sight.'—*B.*
Alcinous: Homer, *Odyssey*, 7.112–31.
Didymus and Eustathius: commentators on Homer.
Diomedes: *Iliad*, 14.123.
Ulysses: Odyssey, 24.341–2; the plants being drawn up in ranks, according to the interpretations of Phavorinus and Philoxenus in their lexicons.—*B.*
Theophrastus: On Plants, 4.4.8, 4.7.7–8.   κατ᾽ ὄρχους: in rows.
Aristotle: Politics, 7.10.5: Vines standing in close order.—*B.*
Varro: De Re Rustica, 1.7.2.   *Quintilian*: 8.3.9.
Virgil: Georgics, 2.277–8: Space them out in rows, and when the trees are planted let every path likewise exactly square in a clear-cut arrangement.—*B.*

the plantations of vines, the setting, grafting of trees, and the best part of agriculture; is discovered to be Noah—[n]whether this early dispersed husbandry in vineyards had not its original in that patriarch is no such paralogical doubt.

And if it were clear that this was used by Noah after the Flood, I could easily believe it was in use before it: not willing to fix to such ancient inventions no higher original than Noah; nor readily conceiving those aged heroes, whose diet was vegetable, and only or chiefly consisted in the fruits of the earth, were much deficient in their splendid cultivations; or, after the experience of fifteen hundred years, left much for future discovery in botanical agriculture. Nor fully persuaded that wine was the invention of Noah; that fermented liquors, which often make themselves, so long escaped their luxury or experience; that the first sin of the new world was no sin of the old. That Cain and Abel were the first that offered sacrifice; or, because the Scripture is silent, that Adam or Isaac offered none at all.

Whether Abraham, brought up in the first planting country, observed not some rule hereof when he planted a grove at Beersheba; or whether, at least, a like ordination were not in the garden of Solomon, probability may contest—answerably unto the wisdom of that eminent botanologer and orderly disposer of all his other works. Especially since this was one piece of gallantry wherein he pursued the specious part of felicity, according to his own description: 'I made me gardens and orchards, and planted trees in them of all kinds of fruit. I made me pools of water, to water therewith the wood that bringeth forth trees'—which was no ordinary plantation if, according to the Targum or Chaldee paraphrase, it contained all kinds of plants, and some fetched as far as India; and the extent thereof were from the wall of Jerusalem unto the water of Siloah.

And if Jordan were but *Jaar Eden*, that is, the River of Eden, Genesar but *Gansar* or the Prince of Gardens; and it could be made out that the plain of Jordan were watered not comparatively but causally, and because it was the paradise of God, as the learned Abramas hinteth—he was not far from the prototype and original of plantations. And since even in paradise itself the tree of knowledge

paralogical: unreasonable. *higher original*: more ancient origin.
first sin: Gen. 9:21. *Cain and Abel*: Gen. 4:3–5.
Beersheba: Gen. 21:33. *Solomon*: in the Song of Songs.
botanologer: botanist. *specious*: visual.
description: Eccles. 2:5–6.—*B.* *Siloah*: Neh. 3:15.
comparatively: by the way. *causally*: as the main purpose.
Abramas: N. Abram, *Vetus Testamenti Pharus*, 2.16 (1648, p. 56).—*B.*

was placed in the middle of the garden, whatever was the ambient figure, there wanted not a centre and rule of decussation.

Whether the groves and sacred plantations of antiquity were not thus orderly placed, either by quaternios or quintuple ordinations, may favourably be doubted. For since they were so methodical in the constitutions of their temples as to observe the due situation, aspect, manner, form, and order in architectonical relations, whether they were not as distinct in their groves and plantations about them, in form and species respectively unto their deities, is not without probability of conjecture. And in their groves of the sun this was a fit number, by multiplication, to denote the days of the year, and might hieroglyphically speak as much as the mystical statua of Janus in the language of his fingers. And since they were so critical in the number of his horses, the strings of his harp, and rays about his head, denoting the orbs of heaven, the seasons and months of the year, witty idolatry would hardly be flat in other appropriations.

CHAP. II

Nor was this only a form of practice in plantations, but found imitation from high antiquity in sundry artificial contrivances and manual operations. For (to omit the position of squared stones *cuneatim* or wedgewise in the walls of Roman and Gothic buildings, and the *lithostrata* or figured pavements of the ancients, which consisted not all of square stones, but were divided into triquetrous segments, honeycombs, and sexangular figures, according to Vitruvius), the squared stones and bricks in ancient fabrics were placed after this order, and two above or below conjoined by a middle stone or plinthus—observable in the ruins of *Forum Nervae*, the mausoleum of Augustus, the Pyramid of Cestius, and the sculpture draughts of the larger pyramids of Egypt. And, therefore, in the draughts of eminent fabrics, painters do commonly imitate this order in the lines of their description.

In the laureate draughts of sculpture and picture, the leaves and foliate works are commonly thus contrived, which is but in imitation

---

quaternios: sets of four.   *species*: appearance.
statua: statue.
Janus: which King Numa set up with his fingers so disposed that they numerically denoted 365. Pliny, 34.16(33).—*B.*
horses: four, for the seasons.   *strings*: seven, for the known planets.
rays: twelve, for the months.   *witty*: ingenious.
flat: unimaginative.   *appropriations*: correspondences.
Vitruvius: in his first-century B.C. *Architecture*, 7.1.3–4.
Forum . . . Cestius: in Rome.   *sculpture draughts*: engravings.

of the *pulvinaria* and ancient pillow-work observable in Ionic pieces, about columns, temples, and altars; to omit many other analogies in architectonical draughts, which art itself is founded upon fives, as having its subject, and most graceful pieces, divided by this number.

The triumphal oval, and civical crowns of laurel, oak, and myrtle, when fully made, were plaited after this order. And—to omit the crossed crowns of Christian princes; what figure that was which Anastasius described upon the head of Leo III; or who first brought in the arched crown—that of Charles the Great (which seems the first remarkably closed crown) was framed after this manner, with an intersection in the middle from the main crossing bars, and the interspaces unto the frontal circle continued by handsome network-plates much after this order. Whereon we shall not insist, because from greater antiquity, and practice of consecration, we meet with the radiated and starry crown upon the head of Augustus and many succeeding emperors; since the Armenians and Parthians had a peculiar royal cap; and the Grecians, from Alexander, another kind of diadem. And even diadems themselves were but fasciations and handsome ligatures about the heads of princes; nor wholly omitted in the mitral crown (which common picture seems to set too upright and forward upon the head of Aaron), worn sometimes singly or doubly by princes, according to their kingdoms, and no more to be expected from two crowns at once upon the head of Ptolemy; and so easily made out, when historians tell us some bound up wounds, some hanged themselves with diadems.

The beds of the ancients were corded somewhat after this fashion; that is, not directly, as ours at present, but obliquely from side to side, and after the manner of network; whereby they strengthened the *spondae* or bedsides, and spent less cord in the work, as is demonstrated by Blancanus.

laureate draughts: laurel patterns.

founded upon fives: of a structure five parts: foundations, walls, openings, internal divisions, roof; five columns: Tuscan, Doric, Ionic, Corinthian, Composite; five different intercolumniations (spacings of columns): pycnostyle, distyle, systyle, araeostyle, eustyle.—*B.*

Anastasius: author of a history of the popes.   *Leo III*: pope (795–816).

Charles the Great: Charlemagne, King of the Franks (768–814), crowned Emperor of the West in 800.

continued: contained.   *fasciations*: bands.

common picture: in the Geneva Bible, Exod. 28.

Ptolemy: I Macc. 11:13.—*B.* Ptolemy VI, Philometor, King of Egypt, 181–146 B.C., and of Syria.

wounds: Justinus, 15.3.13.   *hanged*: Plutarch, *Lucullus*, 18.4.

Blancanus: J. Blancanus, *Aristotelis Loca Mathematica* (1615, p. 190).—*B.*

And as they lay in crossed beds, so they sat upon seeming cross-legged seats, in which form the noblest thereof were framed; observable in the triumphal seats, the *sella curulis* or aedile chairs, in the coins of Cestius, Sylla, and Julius. That they sat also cross-legged many noble draughts declare, and in this figure the sitting gods and goddesses are drawn in medals and medallions. And, beside this kind of work in retiary and hanging textures, in embroideries and eminent needleworks, the like is obvious unto every eye in glass windows; nor only in glassy contrivances, but also in lattice and stonework, conceived in the Temple of Solomon: wherein the windows are termed *fenestrae reticulatae*, or lights framed like nets; and agreeable unto the Greek expression concerning Christ in the Canticles, 'looking through the nets', which ours hath rendered, 'He looketh forth at the windows, showing himself through the lattice' —that is, partly seen and unseen, according to the visible and invisible side of his nature. To omit the noble reticulate work in the chapiters of the pillars of Solomon, with lilies and pomegranates upon a network ground; and the *craticula* or grate through which the ashes fell in the altar of burnt offerings.

That the networks and nets of antiquity were little different in the form from ours at present, is confirmable from the nets in the hands of the retiary gladiators, the proper combatants with the *secutores*; to omit the ancient *conopeion* or gnat-net of the Egyptians, the inventors of that artifice; the rushy labyrinths of Theocritus; the nosegay nets which hung from the head under the nostrils of princes; and that uneasy metaphor of *reticulum jecoris*, which some expound the lobe, we the caul, above the liver. As for that famous network of Vulcan which enclosed Mars and Venus, and caused that unextinguishable laugh in heaven, since the gods themselves could not discern it, we shall not pry into it (although why Vulcan bound them, Neptune loosed them, and Apollo should first discover them, might afford no vulgar mythology). Heralds have not omitted this order, or imitation thereof, whiles they symbolically adorn their scutcheons

Cestius: Gaius Cestius Epulo, a Roman official of the first century B.C.
Sylla: Lucius Cornelius Sulla (138–78 B.C.), Roman dictator.
Julius: Caesar.
retiary: network.
fenestrae: a Latin rendering of the Septuagint Greek of Ezek. 41:16.
Canticles: S. of S. 2:9.—*B.*
burnt offerings: Exod. 27:4.
conopeion: mosquito-net.
Theocritus: *Idylls*, 21.11.
reticulum: Lev. 3:4, etc.—*B.*
medallions: the larger sort of medals.—*B.*
glass-windows: then commonly diamond-paned.
network ground: 1 Kgs. 7:17–20.
secutores: pursuers.
labyrinths: nets.
nosegay nets: Cicero, *Against Verres*, 2.5.11(27).
unextinguishable: Homer, *Odyssey*, 8.326.—*B.*

with mascles, fusils, and saltires, and while they disposed the figures of ermines and vaired coats in this quincuncial method.

The same is not forgot by lapidaries, while they cut their gems pyramidally, or by equicrural triangles; perspective picturers, in their base, horizon, and lines of distances, cannot escape these rhomboidal decussations: sculptors, in their strongest shadows, after this order do draw their double hatches; and the very Americans do naturally fall upon it in their neat and curious textures, which is also observed in the elegant artifices of Europe. But this is no law unto the woof of the neat retiary spider, which seems to weave without transversion, and by the union of right lines to make out a continued surface; which is beyond the common art of textury, and may still nettle Minerva, the goddess of that mystery: and he that shall hatch the little seeds, either found in small webs, or white round eggs carried under the bellies of some spiders, and behold how, at their first production in boxes, they will presently fill the same with their webs, may observe the early and untaught finger of nature, and how they are natively provided with a stock sufficient for such texture.

The rural charm against dodder, tetter, and strangling weeds, was contrived after this order, while they placed a chalked tile at the four corners, and one in the middle of their fields; which, though ridiculous in the intention, was rational in the contrivance, and a good way to diffuse the magic through all parts of the area.

Somewhat after this manner they ordered the little stones in the old game of *pentalithismus*, or casting up five stones to catch them on the back of their hand. And with some resemblance hereof the *proci* or prodigal paramours disposed their men, when they played at Penelope: for, being themselves an hundred and eight, they set fifty-four stones on either side, and one in the middle which they called Penelope, which he that hit was master of the game.

In chess-boards and tables we yet find pyramids and squares. I

---

mascles: lozenge-shaped devices with central lozenge-shaped apertures.
fusils: elongated lozenges.   *saltires*: diagonal crosses.
pyramidally: A square-based pyramid seen from above shows its upper edges in an X shape.
equicrural: isosceles.   *sculptors*: engravers.
double hatches: cross-shading.
right lines: lines crossing each other at right-angles.   *textury*: weaving.
Minerva: as in the contention between Minerva and Arachne. Ovid, *Metamorphoses*, 6.5–145.—*B.*
tetter: *Bryonia dioica*, white bryony or tetterberry.
pentalithismus: fivestones, knucklebones.
Penelope: in Eustathius his *Comment upon Homer, Odyssey*, 1.401.—*B.*
tables: backgammon.

wish we had their true and ancient description (far different from ours), or the *chet mat* of the Persians; which might continue some elegant remarkables, as being an invention as high as Hermes the secretary of Osiris, figuring the whole world, the motion of the planets, with eclipses of sun and moon.

Physicians are not without the use of this decussation in several operations, in ligatures and union of dissolved continuities. Mechanics make use hereof in forcical organs, and instruments of incision; wherein who can but magnify the power of decussation, inservient to contrary ends: solution and consolidation, union and division; illustrable from Aristotle in the old *nucifragium* or nutcracker, and the instruments of evulsion, compression or incision—which, consisting of two *vectes* or arms converted towards each other, the innitency and stress being made upon the *hypomochlion* or fulciment in the decussation, the greater compression is made by the union of two impulsors.

The Roman battalia was ordered after this manner, whereof (as sufficiently known) Virgil hath left but an hint and obscure intimation. For thus were the maniples and cohorts of the *hastati*, *principes*, and *triarii* placed in their bodies, wherein consisted the strength of the Roman battle. By this ordination they readily fell into each other:

hast.   ▭ ▭ ▭ ▭ ▭

pr.   ▭ ▭ ▭ ▭

tr.   ▭ ▭ ▭ ▭ ▭

the *hastati*, being pressed, handsomely retired into the intervals of the *principes*, these into that of the *triarii*; which making as it were a new body, might jointly renew the battle, wherein consisted the secret of their successes. And therefore it was remarkably singular in the

continue: contain.   high: ancient.   Hermes: Plato, *Phaedrus*, 274c–d.—*B*.
forcical organs: pincers and pliers.   inservient to: serving.
Aristotle: in the spurious *Quaestiones Mechanicae*, illustrated by Blancanus (1615, p. 185).
vectes: levers.   innitency: pressure.
hypomochlion or fulciment: fulcrum.   impulsors: levers.
Roman battalia: in the disposure of the legions in the wars of the Republic, before the division of the legion into ten cohorts by the emperors.—*B*.
Virgil: *Georgics*, 2.279–81.   hastati: spearmen, front line.
principes: second line.   triarii: third-line reserve of veterans.

battle of Africa that Scipio, fearing a rout from the elephants of the enemy, left not the *principes* in their alternate distances—whereby the elephants, passing the vacuities of the *hastati*, might have run upon them—but drew his battle into right order, and, leaving the passages bare, defeated the mischief intended by the elephants. Out of this figure were made two remarkable forms of battle, the *cuneus* and *forceps*, or the shear and wedge battles, each made of half a rhombus, and but differenced by position. The wedge invented to break or work into a body, the *forceps* to environ and defeat the power thereof, composed out of the selectest soldiery, and disposed into the form of a V, wherein receiving the wedge, it enclosed it on both sides. After this form the famous Narses ordered his battle against the Franks, and by this figure the Almans were enclosed, and cut in pieces.

The rhombus or lozenge figure so visible in this order was also a remarkable form of battle in the Grecian cavalry, observed by the Thessalians, and Philip, King of Macedon, and frequently by the Parthians, as being most ready to turn every way, and best to be commanded, as having its ductors or commanders at each angle.

The Macedonian phalanx (a long time thought invincible) consisted of a long square: for though they might be sixteen in rank and file, yet when they shut close, so that the sixth pike advanced before the first rank, though the number might be square, the figure was oblong, answerable unto the quincuncial quadrate of Curtius. According to this square, Thucydides delivers, the Athenians disposed their battle against the Lacedaemonians—brickwise—and by the same word the learned Guellius expoundeth the quadrate of Virgil, after the form of a brick or tile.

And as the first station and position of trees, so was the first habitation of men, not in round cities, as of later foundation; for the form of Babylon, the first city, was square, and so shall also be the last, according to the description of the Holy City in the Apocalypse. The famous pillars of Seth, before the Flood, had also the like

---

Scipio: Scipio Africanus Major, at the Battle of Zama against the Carthaginians in 202 B.C. Livy, 30.32.10–33.1.

Narses: general of the Emperor Justinian who defeated the Franks and Alemanni in 553 and 563.

Almans: Germans defeated by Julian in 357 near Strasbourg.

long square: rectangle.   *quadrate*: quadrilateral.

Curtius: B. Curtius, *Horti*, 10.13 (1560, pp. 267–8).

Thucydides: *Peloponnesian War*, 6.67.1,

Guellius: V. Guellius on Virgil, *Georgics*, 2.278.   *Apocalypse*: Rev. 21:16.

Seth: Josephus, *Jewish Antiquities*, 1.2.3 (70–71).

foundation, if they were but antediluvian obelisks, and such as Ham and his Egyptian race imitated after the Flood.

But Nineveh, which authors acknowledge to have exceeded Babylon, was of a longilateral figure, ninety-five furlongs broad and an hundred and fifty long, and so making about sixty miles in circuit, which is the measure of three days journey according unto military marches or castrensial mansions. So that if Jonas entered at the narrower side, he found enough for one day's walk to attain the heart of the city to make his proclamation. And if we imagine a city extending from Ware to London, the expression will be moderate of six score thousand infants, although we allow vacuities, fields, and intervals of habitation, as there needs must be when the monument of Ninus took up no less than ten furlongs.

And, though none of the seven wonders, yet a noble piece of antiquity, and made by a copy exceeding all the rest, had its principal parts disposed after this manner: that is, the labyrinth of Crete, built upon a long quadrate, containing five large squares communicating by right inflections, terminating in the centre of the middle square and lodging of the Minotaur, if we conform unto the description of the elegant medal thereof in Agostino. And though in many accounts we reckon grossly by the square, yet is that very often to be accepted as a long-sided quadrate; which was the figure of the Ark of the Covenant, the table of the shewbread, and the stone wherein the names of the twelve tribes were engraved, that is, three in a row, naturally making a longilateral figure, the perfect quadrate being made by nine.

What figure the stones themselves maintained, tradition and Scripture are silent; yet lapidaries in precious stones affect a table or long square, and in such proportion that the two lateral, and also the three inferior tables, are equal unto the superior, and the angles of the lateral tables contain and constitute the *hypotenusae*, or broader sides subtending.

---

obelisks: being erected upon a square base.—B.
Egyptian race: That the Egyptians were descended from Ham the son of Noah was assumed from Pss. 78:51, 105:23, 27.
castrensial mansions: intervals between camps.   *one day's walk*: Jonah 3:4.
Ware: in Hertfordshire, 24 miles from London.
six score thousand: Jonah 4:11.   *Ninus*: legendary founder of Nineveh.
Agostino: A. Agostino, *Dialoghi intorno alle Medaglie*, 3 (1650, p. 85).
Covenant: Gen. 6:15.   *shewbread*: Exod. 25:23.
twelve tribes: Exod. 28:17–21.   *longilateral*: long-sided, rectangular.
maintained: presented.

That the Tables of the Law were of this figure, general imitation
and tradition hath confirmed; yet are we unwilling to load the shoulders of Moses with such massy stones as some pictures lay upon
them, since 'tis plainly delivered that he came down with them in his
hand; since the word strictly taken implies no such massy hewing, but
cutting and fashioning of them into shape and surface; since some
will have them emeralds, and if they were made of the materials of
Mount Sinai, not improbable that they were marble—since the words
were not many, the letters short of seven hundred, and the Tables,
written on both sides, required no such capacity.

The beds of the ancients were different from ours at present
(which are almost square), being framed oblong, and about a double
unto their breadth; not much unlike the area or bed of this quincuncial
quadrate. The single beds of Greece were six foot and a little more in
length, three in breadth; the giantlike bed of Og, which had four
cubits of breadth, nine and a half in length, varied not much from this
proportion. The funeral bed of King Cheops in the greater pyramid,
which holds seven in length and four foot in breadth, had no great
difformity from this measure; and whatsoever were the breadth, the
length could hardly be less, of the tyrannical bed of Procrustes, since
in a shorter measure he had not been fitted with persons for his
cruelty of extension. But the old sepulchral bed or Amazonian tomb
in the market-place of Megara was in the form of a lozenge, readily
made out by the composure of the body: for the arms not lying
fasciated or wrapped up after the Grecian manner, but in a middle
distension, the including lines will strictly make out that figure.

CHAP. III

Now although this elegant ordination of vegetables hath found
coincidence or imitation in sundry works of art, yet is it not also
destitute of natural examples; and, though overlooked by all, was
elegantly observable in several works of nature.

Could we satisfy ourselves in the position of the lights above, or
discover the wisdom of that order so invariably maintained in the
fixed stars of heaven; could we have any light why the stellar part

Moses: Exod. 32:15–16.
beds of Greece: Aristotle, *Mechanica.*—B. See not above, p. 147.
bed of Og: Deut. 3:11.   *difformity*: difference in shape.
Procrustes: the legendary brigand of ancient Greece who laid travellers on a bed:
    if shorter, they were stretched; if longer, amputated.
extension: stretching.   *Amazonian tomb*: Plutarch, *Theseus*, 27.6.—B.
fasciated: swathed.   *in a middle distension*: half-extended.

of the first mass separated into this order, that the girdle of Orion should ever maintain its line, and the two stars in Charles's Wain never leave pointing at the pole-star—we might abate the Pythagorical music of the spheres, the sevenfold pipe of Pan, and the strange cryptography of Gaffarel in his starry book of heaven.

But not to look so high as heaven—or the single quincunx of the Hyades upon the head of Taurus, the triangle and remarkable *crusero* about the foot of the Centaur—observable rudiments there are hereof in subterraneous concretions and bodies in the earth: in the gypsum or talcum rhomboides, in the *favaginites* or honey-comb-stone, in the asteria and astroites, and in the crucigerous stone of St. Iago of Galicia.

The same is observably effected in the iulus, catkins, or pendulous excrescences of several trees, of walnuts, alders, and hazels; which, hanging all the winter, and maintaining their network close, by the expansion thereof are the early foretellers of the spring: discoverable also in long pepper, and elegantly in the iulus of *Calamus aromaticus*, so plentifully growing with us; in the first palms of willows, and in the flowers of sycamore, *Petasites*, *Asphodelus*, and *blattaria*, before explication. After such order stand the flowery branches in our best spread *Verbascum*, and the seeds about the spicous head or torch of *Tapsus barbatus*, in as fair a regularity as the circular and wreathed order will admit, which advanceth one side of the square, and makes the same rhomboidal: in the squamous heads of scabious, knapweed, and the elegant *Jacea pinea*; and in the scaly composure of the oak-rose, which some years most aboundeth.

After this order hath nature planted the leaves in the head of the common and prickled artichoke (wherein the black and shining

---

music of the spheres: see note above, p. 76.
pipe of Pan: Virgil, *Eclogues*, 2.36–7.
Gaffarel: J. Gaffarel, *Unheard-of Curiosities*, 4.13 (1650, p. 382).
crusero: the Southern Cross.   *honeycomb-stone*: fossilized honeycomb coral.
asteria and astroites: certain star-shaped gems, minerals or fossils.
crucigerous: cross-bearing.   *iulus*: catkin.
Calamus aromaticus: not the true Oriental *Calamus aromaticus* but the British *Acorus calamus*, sweet flag.
Petasites: butterbur.   *blattaria*: *Verbascum blattaria*, moth mullein.
spread Verbascum: seemingly *ethiopis*, Ethiopian mullein.   *spicous*: spiky.
Tapsus barbatus: *Verbascum thapsus*, common mullein.   *squamous*: scaly.
Jacea pinea: a species of knapweed.
oak-rose: the artichoke gall, *Capitula squammata quercuum* of Bauhin, *Historia Plantarum*, 7 (1650, I.ii.86), whereof, though he saith 'They are very seldom found—we have only found them twice', yet we find them commonly with us, and in great numbers.—*B.*

flies do shelter themselves when they retire from the purple flower about it); the same is also found in the pricks, sockets, and impressions of the seeds in the pulp or bottom thereof, wherein do elegantly stick the fathers of their mother: to omit the quincuncial specks on the top of the mistle-berry, especially that which grows upon the *tilia* or lime-tree; and the remarkable disposure of those yellow fringes about the purple pistil of arum, and elegant clusters of dragons, so peculiarly secured by nature with an umbrella or screening leaf about them.

The spongy leaves of some seawracks, fucus, oaks, in their several kinds, found about the shore with ejectments of the sea, are overwrought with network elegantly containing this order; which plainly declareth the naturality of this texture, and how the needle of nature delighteth to work even in low and doubtful vegetations.

The *arbustetum* or thicket on the head of the teasel may be observed in this order; and he that considereth that fabric, so regularly palisadoed, and stemmed with flowers of the royal colour, in the house of the solitary maggot may find the seraglio of Solomon; and contemplating the calycular shafts, and uncous disposure of their extremities, so accommodable unto the office of abstersion, not condemn as wholly improbable the conceit of those who accept it for the herb *borith*. Where, by the way, we could with much inquiry never discover any transfiguration in this abstemious insect, although we have kept them long in their proper houses, and boxes; where some, wrapped up in their webs, have lived upon their own bowels from September unto July.

In such a grove do walk the little creepers about the head of the burr. And such an order is observed in the aculeous, prickly plantation upon the heads of several common thistles, remarkably in the notable palisadoes about the flower of the milk thistle; and he that inquireth into the little bottom of the globe thistle may find that gallant bush arise from a scalp of like disposure.

---

fathers of their mother: seeds. *Greek Anthology*, 14.58.—*B.*
arum: cuckoo-pint.   *dragons*: *Dracunculus vulgaris*, dragonwort.
seawracks: seaweeds.   *oaks*: species of seaweed with oak-leaf-like fronds.
ejectments: jetsam.   *palisadoed*: spiked.
maggot: there being a single maggot found in almost every head.—*B.*
seraglio of Solomon: room for a thousand. 1 Kgs. 11:3.
uncous: hooked.   *abstersion*: scouring.
conceit: idea.   *borith*: a cleansing herb. Jer. 2:22.—*B.*
palisadoes: rows of spikes.   *milk thistle*: *Silybum marianum*.
bottom: clew, ball on which thread is wound.
globe thistle: a species of *Echinops*.   *disposure*: arrangement.

The white umbrella or medical bush of elder is an epitome of this order, arising from five main stems quincuncially disposed, and tolerably maintained in their subdivisions—to omit the lower observations in the seminal spike of mercury, weld, and plantain.

Thus hath nature ranged the flowers of sainfoin and French honeysuckle, and somewhat after this manner hath ordered the bush in Jupiter's beard or houseleek (which old superstition set on the tops of houses as a defensative aginst lightning and thunder); the like in fenny sengreen or the water soldier, which, though a military name from Greece, makes out the Roman order.

A like ordination there is in the favaginous sockets and lozenge seeds of the noble flower of the sun, wherein in lozenge-figured boxes nature shuts up the seeds, and balsam which is about them.

But the fir and pine-tree from their fruits do naturally dictate this position, the rhomboidal protuberances in pineapples maintaining this quincuncial order unto each other, and each rhombus in itself. Thus are also disposed the triangular foliations in the conical fruit of the fir-tree, orderly shadowing and protecting the winged seeds below them.

The like so often occurreth to the curiosity of observers, especially in spicated seeds and flowers, that we shall not need to take in the single quincunx of Fuchsius in the growth of the male fern, the seedy disposure of *Gramen ischaemon*, and the trunk or neat reticulate work in the cod of the satchel palm.

For even in very many round-stalk plants the leaves are set after a quintuple ordination, the first leaf answering the fifth in lateral disposition; wherein the leaves successively rounding the stalk, in four at the furthest the compass is absolved, and the fifth leaf or sprout returns to the position of the other fifth before it: as, in accounting upward, is often observable in furze, pellitory, ragweed, the sprouts of oaks and thorns upon pollards; and very remarkably

mercury: *Chenopodium bonus-henricus*, Good King Henry.
weld: *Reseda luteola*, dyer's greenweed.
French honeysuckle: *Hedysarum coronarium*, found in Italy.
fenny sengreen: *Stratiotes aloides*.   *favaginous*: honeycombed.
flower of the sun: *Helianthus*, sunflower.
Fuchsius: L. Fuchs, *Historia Plantarum*, 225 (1542, p. 595).
Gramen ischaemon: *Digitaria ischaemum*, smooth finger grass.
satchel palm: *Manicaria saccifera*.
compass is absolved: circuit is completed.
ragweed: *Senecio jacobaea*, ragwort.
pollards: upon pollard oaks and thorns.—B.

in the regular disposure of the rugged excrescences in the yearly shoots of the pine.

But in square-stalked plants the leaves stand respectively unto each other, either in cross or decussation to those above or below them, arising at cross positions; whereby they shadow not each other, and better resist the force of winds, which, in a parallel situation, and upon square stalks, would more forcibly bear upon them.

And, to omit how leaves and sprouts which compass not the stalk are often set in a rhomboides, and, making long and short diagonals, do stand like the legs of quadrupeds when they go; nor to urge the thwart enclosure and furdling of flowers and blossoms before explication, as in the multiplied leaves of peony: and the chiasmus in five-leaved flowers, while one lies wrapped about the staminous beards, the other four obliquely shutting and closing upon each other; and how even flowers which consist of four leaves stand not ordinarily in three and one, but two and two, crosswise unto the stylus—even the autumnal buds, which await the return of the sun, do (after the winter solstice) multiply their calycular leaves, making little rhombuses and network figures, as in the sycamore and lilac.

The like is discoverable in the original production of plants, which first putting forth two leaves, those which succeed bear not over each other, but shoot obliquely or crosswise until the stalk appeareth, which sendeth not forth its first leaves without all order unto them— and he that from hence can discover in what position the two first leaves did arise is no ordinary observator.

Where, by the way, he that observeth the rudimental spring of seeds shall find strict rule, although not after this order. How little is required unto effectual generation, and in what diminutives the plastic principle lodgeth, is exemplified in seeds, wherein the greater mass affords so little comproduction. In beans the leaf and root sprout from the germen, the main sides split and lie by; and in some pulled up near the time of blooming, we have found the pulpous sides entire or little wasted. In acorns the neb dilating splitteth the two sides, which sometimes lie whole when the oak is sprouted two handfuls. In lupins these pulpy sides do sometimes arise with the stalk in a resemblance of two fat leaves. Wheat and rye will grow up if, after they have shot some tender roots, the adhering pulp be taken from them. Beans will prosper though a part be cut away and so much

---

furdling: furling.   *explication*: unfolding
chiasmus: cross-wise arrangement.   *plastic*: formative.
comproduction: participation in growth.

set as sufficeth to contain and keep the germen close. From this superfluous pulp, in unkindly and wet years, may arise that multiplicity of little insects which infest the roots and sprouts of tender grains and pulses.

In the little neb, or fructifying principle, the motion is regular, and not transvertible as to make that ever the leaf which nature intendeth the root; observable from their conversion until they attain their right position, if seeds be set inversedly.

In vain we expect the production of plants from different parts of the seed: from the same *corculum* or little original proceed both germinations; and in the power of this slender particle lie many roots and sprouts, that though the same be pulled away, the generative particle will renew them again and proceed to a perfect plant; and malt may be observed to grow though the comes be fallen from it.

The seminal neb hath a defined and single place, and not extended unto both extremes. And therefore many too vulgarly conceive that barley and oats grow at both ends; for they arise from one punctilio or generative neb, and the spear, sliding under the husk, first appeareth nigh the top. But in wheat and rye, being bare, the sprouts are seen together. If barley unhulled would grow, both would appear at once. But in this and oatmeal the neb is broken away, which makes them the milder food, and less apt to raise fermentation in decoctions.

Men, taking notice of what is outwardly visible, conceive a sensible priority in the root; but as they begin from one part, so they seem to start and set out upon one signal of nature. In beans yet soft, in peas while they adhere unto the cod, the rudimental leaf and root are discoverable. In the seeds of rocket and mustard sprouting in glasses of water, when the one is manifest the other is also perceptible. In muddy waters apt to breed duckweed and periwinkles, if the first and rudimental strokes of duckweed be observed, the leaves and root anticipate not each other. But in the date-stone the first sprout is neither root nor leaf distinctly, but both together; for the germination being to pass through the narrow navel and hole about the midst of the stone, the generative germ is fain to enlengthen itself, and, shooting out about an inch, at that distance divideth into the ascending and descending portion.

And though it be generally thought that seeds will root at that end where they adhere to their originals, and observable it is that

transvertible: convertible.	*conversion*: turning.
corculum: heart.	*comes*: sprouts on malted barley.
punctilio: small point.	*unhulled*: with the husk removed.
cod: pod.	*strokes*: thin lines.

the neb sets most often next the stalk, as in grains, pulses, and most small seeds, yet is it hardly made out in many greater plants. For in acorns, almonds, pistachios, walnuts, and acuminated shells, the germ puts forth at the remotest part of the pulp. And therefore, to set seeds in that posture wherein the leaf and roots may shoot right without contortion or forced circumvolution, which might render them strongly rooted and straighter, were a criticism in agriculture. And nature seems to have made some provision hereof in many from their figure, that as they fall from the tree they may lie in positions agreeable to such advantages.

Beside the open and visible testicles of plants, the seminal powers lie in great part invisible; while the sun finds polypody in stone walls, the little stinging-nettle and nightshade in barren, sandy highways, scurvy-grass in Greenland, and unknown plants in earth brought from remote countries. Beside the known longevity of some trees, what is the most lasting herb or seed seems not easily determinable. Mandrakes, upon known account, have lived near an hundred years. Seeds found in wildfowls' gizzards have sprouted in the earth. The seeds of marjoram and stramonium, carelessly kept, have grown after seven years. Even in garden-plots long fallow and digged up, the seeds of *blattaria* and yellow henbane, after twelve years' burial, have produced themselves again.

That bodies are first spirits Paracelsus could affirm, which, in the maturation of seeds and fruits, seems obscurely implied by Aristotle when he delivereth that the spirituous parts are converted into water, and the water into earth; and attested by observation in the maturative progress of seeds, wherein at first may be discerned a flatuous distension of the husk, afterwards a thin liquor, which longer time digesteth into a pulp or kernel, observable in almonds and large nuts; and some way answered in the progressional perfection of animal semination, in its spermatical maturation from crude pubescency unto perfection. And even that seeds themselves, in their rudimental discoveries, appear in foliaceous surcles or sprouts within their coverings, in a diaphanous jelly before deeper incrassation, is also visibly verified in cherries, acorns, plums.

right: straight.   *criticism*: nice point.
stramonium: *Datura stramonium*, thorn-apple.
blattaria: *Verbascum blattaria*, moth mullein.
Paracelsus: *Philosophia Sagax*, 1.3 (*Opera*, 1603–5, x.123).
Aristotle: *Meteorologica*, 4.3.   *flatuous*: inflated.
surcles: small shoots.
incrassation: thickening.

From seminal considerations, either in reference unto one another or distinction from animal production, the Holy Scripture describeth the vegetable creation; and while it divideth plants but into herb and tree, though it seemeth to make but an accidental division from magnitude, it tacitly containeth the natural distinction of vegetables observed by herbarists, and comprehending the four kinds. For, since the most natural distinction is made from the production of leaf or stalk, and plants after the two first seminal leaves do either proceed to send forth more leaves or a stalk, and the folious and stalky emission distinguisheth herbs and trees, in a large acception it compriseth all vegetables; for the frutex and suffrutex are under the progression of trees, and stand authentically differenced but from the accidents of the stalk.

The equivocal production of things under undiscerned principles makes a large part of generation; though they seem to hold a wide univocacy in their set and certain originals, while almost every plant breeds its peculiar insect, most a butterfly, moth or fly: wherein the oak seems to contain the largest seminality, while the iulus, oak-apple, pill, woolly tuft, foraminous roundels upon the leaf, and grapes under ground, make a fly with some difference. The great variety of flies lies in the variety of their originals: in the seeds of caterpillars or cankers there lieth not only a butterfly or moth, but, if they be sterile or untimely cast, their production is often a fly; which we have also observed from corrupted and mouldered eggs, both of hens and fishes—to omit the generation of bees out of the bodies of dead heifers, or (what is strange yet well attested), the production of eels in the backs of living cods and perches.

The exiguity and smallness of some seeds extending to large productions is one of the magnalities of nature, somewhat illustrating the work of the Creation, and vast production from nothing. The true seeds of cypress and rampions are indistinguishable by old eyes. Of the seeds of tobacco a thousand make not one grain; the disputed

---

Scripture: Gen. 1:11.   *four kinds*: trees, shrubs, woody-based herbs, herbs.
folious: foliar.   *large acception*: broad interpretation.
suffrutex: plant with woody base and herbaceous annual growth above.
under the progression of: of the same sequence of development as.
equivocal production: the alleged hatching of parasites from their hosts.
univocacy: agreement, correspondence.
iulus: catkin gall.   *pill*: spangle gall.
woolly tuft: wool-sower gall.   *foraminous roundels*: silk-button spangle galls.
grapes: oak truffle galls.   *bees*: in fact the fly *Eristalis tenax*, drone-fly.
magnalities: wonders.   *one grain*: 60 milligrams.
disputed seeds: spores, whose existence was argued against until shown incontrovertibly by magnifying-glasses.

seeds of hart's-tongue and maidenhair require a greater number. From such undiscernible seminalities arise spontaneous productions. He that would discern the rudimental stroke of a plant may behold it in the original of duckweed, at the bigness of a pin's point, from convenient water in glasses, wherein a watchful eye may also discover the puncticular originals of periwinkles and gnats.

That seeds of some plants are less than any animal's, seems of no clear decision; that the biggest of vegetables exceedeth the biggest of animals, in full bulk and all dimensions, admits exception in the whale, which in length and above-ground measure will also contend with tall oaks. That the richest odour of plants surpasseth that of animals may seem of some doubt, since animal musk seems to excel the vegetable, and we find so noble a scent in the tulip-fly and goat-beetle.

Now, whether seminal nebs hold any sure proportion unto seminal enclosures; why the form of the germ doth not answer the figure of the enclosing pulp; why the neb is seated upon the solid and not the channelled side of the seed as in grains; why, since we often meet with two yolks in one shell, and sometimes one egg within another, we do not oftener meet with two nebs in one distinct seed; why, since the eggs of a hen laid at one course do commonly outweigh the bird, and some moths coming out of their cases, without assistance of food, will lay so many eggs as to outweigh their bodies, trees rarely bear their fruit in that gravity or proportion; whether in the germination of seeds, according to Hippocrates, the lighter part ascendeth and maketh the sprout, the heaviest tending downward frameth the root, since we observe that the first shoot of seeds in water will sink or bow down at the upper and leafing end; whether it be not more rational epicurism to contrive whole dishes out of the nebs and spirited particles of plants, than from the gallatures and treadles of eggs, since that part is found to hold no seminal share in oval generation—are queries which might enlarge but must conclude this digression.

And though not in this order, yet how nature delighteth in this number, and what consent and co-ordination there is in the leaves

---

spontaneous production: the 'equivocal generation' referred to above.
puncticular: point-sized.   *tulip-fly*: not identified.
goat-beetle: the long and tender green *capricornus*, rarely found—we could never meet with but two.—B., possibly meaning the musk beetle, *Cerambyx aromia moschata*, rather than the ordinary goat-chafer.
Hippocrates: *De Natura Pueri*, 22.   *gallatures and treadles*: germs.
oval generation: the development of the egg.

and parts of flowers, it cannot escape our observation in no small number of plants. For the calycular or supporting and closing leaves do answer the number of the flowers, especially in such as exceed not the number of swallows' eggs, as in violets, stitchwort blossoms; and flowers of one leaf have often five divisions, answered by a like number of calycular leaves, as *Gentianella*, convolvulus, bell-flowers. In many the flowers, blades, or staminous shoots and leaves, are all equally five, as in cockle, mullein, and *blattaria*—wherein the flowers before explication are pentagonally wrapped up, with some resemblance of the *blatta* or moth from whence it hath its name. But the contrivance of nature is singular in the opening and shutting of bindweeds, performed by five inflexures, distinguishable by pyramidal figures, and also different colours.

The rose at first is thought to have been of five leaves, as it yet groweth wild among us; but in the most luxuriant, the calycular leaves do still maintain that number. But nothing is more admired than the five brethren of the rose, and the strange disposure of the appendices or beards in the calycular leaves thereof; which, in despair of resolution, is tolerably salved from this contrivance, best ordered and suited for the free closure of them before explication: for those two which are smooth and of no beard are contrived to lie undermost, as without prominent parts, and fit to be smoothly covered; the other two, which are beset with beards on either side, stand outward and uncovered; but the fifth or half-bearded leaf is covered on the bare side, but on the open side stands free, and bearded like the other.

Besides, a large number of leaves have five divisions, and may be circumscribed by a pentagon, or figure of five angles, made by right lines from the extremity of their leaves, as in maple, vine, fig-tree. But five-leaved flowers are commonly disposed circularly about the stylus, according to the higher geometry of nature, dividing a circle by five radii which concur not to make diameters as in quadrilateral and sexangular intersections.

Now the number of five is remarkable in every circle, not only as the first spherical number, but the measure of spherical motion. For spherical bodies move by fives, and every globular figure placed

---

swallows' eggs: which exceed not five.—B.   *Gentianella*: felwort.
blattaria: *Verbascum blattaria*, moth mullein.   *inflexures*: inward folds.
five brethren: five leaves of the calyx.   *explication*: unfolding.
right: straight.   *sexangular*: hexagonal.
spherical number: in that when multiplied by itself the product's final digit is 5.

upon a plane, in direct volutation returns to the first point of contaction in the fifth touch, accounting by the axes of the diameters, or cardinal points of the four quarters thereof. And before it arriveth unto the same point again, it maketh five circles equal unto itself, in each progress from those quarters absolving an equal circle.

By the same number doth nature divide the circle of the sea-star, and in that order and number disposeth those elegant semicircles or dental sockets and eggs in the sea hedgehog. And no mean observations hereof there is in the mathematics of the neatest retiary spider which, concluding in forty-four circles, from five semidiameters beginneth that elegant texture.

And after this manner doth lay the foundation of the circular branches of the oak, which being five-cornered in the tender annual sprouts, and manifesting upon incision the signature of a star, is after made circular and swelled into a round body—which practice of nature is become a point of art, and makes two problems in Euclid. But the bramble, which sends forth shoots and prickles from its angles, maintains its pentagonal figure, and the unobserved signature of a handsome porch within it; to omit the five small buttons dividing the circle of the ivy-berry, and the five characters in the winter stalk of the walnut, with many other observables which cannot escape the eyes of signal discerners such as know where to find Ajax his name in delphinium, or Aaron's mitre in henbane.

Quincuncial forms and ordinations are also observable in animal figurations. For (to omit the *hyoides* or throat-bone of animals; the *furcula* or merrythought in birds, which supporteth the *scapulae*, affording a passage for the windpipe and the gullet; the wings of flies, and disposure of their legs in their first formation from maggots, and the position of their horns, wings, and legs in their aurelian cases and swaddling clouts), the back of the *Cimex arboreus*, found

direct volutation: rolling along a straight line.
contaction: contact (on its own surface).
maketh five circles: covers five times its own area.
absolving: covering the area of. *sea-star*: starfish.
semidiameters: radial threads. *Euclid*: *Elements*, 4.11, 14.
signature: figure. *signal discerners*: perceivers of significances.
Ajax: Ovid, *Metamorphoses*, 13.397–8.
delphinium: *Delphinium ambiguum*, larkspur.
Aaron's mitre: Exod. 28:36–9.
henbane: Josephus, *Jewish Antiquities*, 3.7.6 (172–8), well illustrated in the Loeb edition.
Cimex arboreus: several species of capsid or plant bug show this marking.

often upon trees and lesser plants, doth elegantly discover the Burgundian decussation. And the like is observable in the belly of the *Notonecton* or water-beetle, which swimmeth on its back, and the handsome rhombuses of the sea-poult or weasel, on either side the spine.

The sexangular cells in the honeycombs of bees are disposed after this order. Much there is not of wonder in the confused houses of pismires, though much in their busy life and actions: more in the edificial palaces of bees and monarchical spirits, who make their combs six-cornered, declining a circle (whereof many stand not close together and completely fill the area of the place), but rather affecting a six-sided figure, whereby every cell affords a common side unto six more, and also a fit receptacle for the bee itself, which, gathering into a cylindrical figure, aptly enters its sexangular house, more nearly approaching a circular figure than either doth the square or triangle; and the combs themselves so regularly contrived that their mutual intersections make three lozenges at the bottom of every cell—which, severally regarded, make three rows of neat rhomboidal figures connected at the angles, and so continue three several chains throughout the whole comb.

As for the *favago* found commonly on the sea-shore, though named from an honeycomb, it but rudely makes out the resemblance, and better agrees with the round cells of humble-bees. He that would exactly discern the shop of a bee's mouth need observing eyes and good augmenting glasses; wherein is discoverable one of the neatest pieces in nature: and must have a more piercing eye than mine, who finds out the shape of bulls' heads in the guts of drones pressed out behind, according to the experiment of Gomesius; wherein notwithstanding there seemeth somewhat which might incline a pliant fancy to credulity of similitude.

A resemblance hereof there is in the orderly and rarely disposed cells made by flies and insects, which we have often found fastened about small sprigs; and in those cottonary and woolly pillows which sometimes we meet with fastened unto leaves there is included an

---

Notonecton: *Notonecton glauca*, water boatman.
sea-poult or weasel: *Gadus lota*, sea-cat, sea-loach, rockling, weasel fish.
sexangular: hexagonal.
edificial: of the nature of a (large and stately) building.
favago: presumably the structure made in sand by *Sabellaria alveolata*, the honeycomb worm.
Gomesius: B. Gomesius, *Diascepseon de Sale*, 1.20 (1605, p. 80).—*B*.
cottonary: white, downy, and fibrous; cottony.

elegant network texture out of which come many small flies. And
some resemblance there is of this order in the eggs of some butterflies and moths, as they stick upon leaves and other substances;
which, being dropped from behind, nor directed by the eye, doth
neatly declare how nature geometrizeth, and observeth order in all
things.

A like correspondency in figure is found in the skins and outward teguments of animals, whereof a regardable part are beautiful by this texture, as the backs of several snakes and serpents:
elegantly remarkable in the *aspis* and the dart-snake, in the
chiasmus and larger decussations upon the back of the rattlesnake,
and in the close and finer texture of the *mater formicarum* or
snake that delights in ant-hills; whereby, upon approach of outward injuries, they can raise a thicker phalanx on their backs,
and handsomely contrive themselves into all kinds of flexures—
whereas their bellies are commonly covered with smooth semi-
circular divisions, as best accommodable unto their quick and gliding
motion.

This way is followed by nature in the peculiar and remarkable
tail of the beaver, wherein the scaly particles are disposed somewhat after this order, which is the plainest resolution of the wonder
of Bellonius while he saith 'with incredible artifice' hath nature
framed the tail or oar of the beaver—where, by the way, we cannot
but wish a model of their houses, so much extolled by some de-
scribers; wherein, since they are so bold as to venture upon three
stages, we might examine their artifice in the contignations, the
rule and order in the compartitions; or whether that magnified
structure be any more than a rude rectangular pile or mere hovel-
building.

Thus works the hand of nature in the feathery plantation about
birds, observable in the skins of the breast, legs, and pinions of
turkeys, geese, and ducks, and the oars or finny feet of waterfowl.
And such a natural net is the scaly covering of fishes, of mullets,
carps, tenches, &c., even in such as are excoriable and consist of

geometrizeth: cf. note above, p. 17.   *aspis*: asp.
dart-snake: snake-like lizard of the genus *Acontias*.
chiasmus: cross-patterning.   *mater formicarum*: lit. 'mother of ants'.
resolution: explanation.   *Bellonius*: P. Belon, *De Aquatilibus* (1553, p. 29).
contignations: structure of the storeys.
compartitions: divisions into compartments.   *magnified*: much praised.
waterfowl: elegantly conspicuous on the inside of the stripped skins of dive-fowl
     (divers), of the cormorant, goosander, weasel (smew), loon, etc.—*B*.
excoriable: capable of being skinned.

smaller scales, as bretts, soles, and flounders. The like reticulate grain is observable in some Russia leather—to omit the ruder figures of the ostracion, the triangular or cunny fish, or the pricks of the sea porcupine.

The same is also observable in some part of the skin of man, in habits of neat texture, and therefore not unaptly compared unto a net. We shall not affirm that from such grounds the Egyptian embalmers imitated this texture, yet in their linen folds the same is still observable among their neatest mummies, in the figures of Isis and Osiris, and the tutelary spirits in the Bembine Table. Nor is it to be overlooked how Orus, the hieroglyphic of the world, is described in a network covering from the shoulder to the foot. And (not to enlarge upon the cruciated character of Trismegistus, or handed crosses, so often occurring in the needles of Pharaoh, and obelisks of antiquity) the *statuae Isiacae*, teraphims, and little idols found about the mummies, do make a decussation or Jacob's cross with their arms, like that on the head of Ephraim and Manasses, and this *decussis* is also graphically described between them.

This reticulate or network was also considerable in the inward parts of man, not only from the first *subtegmen* or warp of his formation, but in the netty fibres of the veins and vessels of life; wherein, according to common anatomy, the right and transverse fibres are decussated by the oblique fibres, and so must frame a reticulate and quincuncial figure by their obliquations—emphatically extending that elegant expression of Scripture, 'Thou hast curiously embroidered me': 'Thou hast wrought me up after the finest way of texture, and as it were with a needle.'

Nor is the same observable only in some parts, but in the whole body of man, which, upon the extension of arms and legs, doth make out a square whose intersection is at the genitals (to omit the fantastical quincunx in Plato, of the first hermaph-

---

bretts: young herring or sprats.   *ostracion*: trunk- or coffer-fish.
cunny fish: presumably a species of ray or skate.
sea porcupine: *Diodon hystrix*, porcupine-fish.
Bembine Table: first-century A.D. collection of hieroglyphs in bronze.
Orus: Horus, Egyptian god of the sun.
cruciated character: the letter X, supposed to have been invented by Hermes (Mercurius) Trismegistus.
handed crosses: crosses with handles, being held by a finger in the circle.—*B.*
statuae Isiacae: statues pertaining to the cult of Isis.
Jacob's cross: Gen. 48:13–14.   *decussis*: figure X.
subtegmen: weft, web.   *obliquations*: oblique intersections.
Scripture: Ps. 139:14.   *Plato*: *Symposium*, 189–93.

rodite or double man, united at the loins, which Jupiter after divided).

A rudimental resemblance hereof there is in the cruciated and rugged folds of the reticulum or net-like ventricle of ruminating horned animals, which is the second in order, and culinarily called the honeycomb. For many divisions there are in the stomach of several animals; what number they maintain in the scarus and ruminating fish, common description or our own experiment hath made no discovery: but in the ventricle of porpoises there are three divisions; in many birds a crop, gizzard, and little receptacle before it—but in cornigerous animals which chew the cud there are no less than four of distinct position and office.

The reticulum, by these crossed cells, makes a further digestion in the dry and exsuccous part of the aliment received from the first ventricle. For at the bottom of the gullet there is a double orifice. What is first received at the mouth descendeth into the first and greater stomach, from whence it is returned into the mouth again; and after a fuller mastication and salivous mixture, what part thereof descendeth again, in a moist and succulent body, it slides down the softer and more permeable orifice into the omasus or third stomach; and from thence conveyed into the fourth, receives its last digestion. The other dry and exsuccous part, after rumination by the larger and stronger orifice, beareth into the first stomach, from thence into the reticulum, and so progressively into the other divisions. And therefore in calves newly calved there is little or no use of the two first ventricles, for the milk and liquid aliment slippeth down the softer orifice into the third stomach; where making little or no stay, it passeth into the fourth, the seat of the coagulum or runnet, or that division of stomach which seems to bear the name of the whole in the Greek translation of the priest's fee in the sacrifice of peace-offerings.

As for those rhomboidal figures made by the cartilaginous parts of the weasand in the lungs of great fishes and other animals, as Rondeletius discovered, we have not found them so to answer our figure as to be drawn into illustration. Something we expected in the

---

cornigerous: horned.
four of distinctive position: stomach, reticulum, omasum, abomasum.—*B*.
exsuccous: juiceless.   *coagulum or runnet*: rennet.
Greek translation: The Septuagint version of Lev. 7:31 ('breast' in A.V.) means 'breastlet' or 'part of the breast'.
Rondeletius: G. Rondelet, *De Piscibus Marinis*, 3.11 (1554, p. 62).

more discernible texture of the lungs of frogs, which, notwithstanding, being but two curious bladders not weighing above a grain, we found interwoven with veins not observing any just order. More orderly situated are those cretaceous and chalky concretions found sometimes in the bigness of a small vetch on either side their spine; which, being not agreeable unto our order, not yet observed by any, we shall not here discourse on.

But had we found a better account and tolerable anatomy of that prominent jowl of the spermaceti whale than quaestuary operation (or the stench of the last cast upon our shore) permitted, we might have perhaps discovered some handsome order in those net-like sesses and sockets made like honeycombs, containing that medical matter.

Lastly, the incession or local motion of animals is made with analogy unto this figure, by decussative diametrals, quincuncial lines and angles. For (to omit the enquiry how butterflies and breezes move their four wings, how birds and fishes in air and water move by joint strokes of opposite wings and fins, and how salient animals in jumping forward seem to arise and fall upon a square base), as the station of most quadrupeds is made upon a long square, so in their motion they make a rhomboides; their common progression being performed diametrally, by decussation and cross advancement of their legs—which not observed begot that remarkable absurdity in the position of the legs of Castor's horse in the Capitol. The snake, which moveth circularly, makes his spires in like order, the convex and concave spirals answering each other at alternate distances. In the motion of man, the arms and legs observe this thwarting position, but the legs alone do move quincuncially by single angles, with some resemblance of a V measured by successive advancement from each foot, and the angle of indenture great or less according to the extent or brevity of the stride.

Studious observators may discover more analogies in the orderly book of nature, and cannot escape the elegancy of her hand in other correspondences. The figures of nails and crucifying appurtenances are but precariously made out in the granadilla or

small vetch: i.e. seed or pod of a small species of vetch.
quaestuary operation: labour for gain.
upon our shore: 1652, described in *Pseudodoxia Epidemica*, 3.26 (3rd ed., 1658, pp. 143–4).—*B.*
sesses: containers.   *incession or local motion*: movement.
diametrals: diametrical lines.   *breezes*: gad-flies.
salient: leaping.   *station*: standing position.
Castor's horse: standing on its two left legs.   *indenture*: intersection.

flower of Christ's passion, and we despair to behold in these parts that handsome draught of crucifixion in the fruit of the Barbado pine. The seminal spike of *phalaris* or great shaking-grass more nearly answers the tail of a rattlesnake than many resemblances in Porta; and if the man orchis of Columna be well made out, it excelleth all analogies. In young walnuts cut athwart, it is not hard to apprehend strange characters; and in those of somewhat elder growth, handsome ornamental draughts about a plain cross. In the root of osmund or water-fern, every eye may discern the form of a half-moon, rainbow, or half the character of Pisces. Some find Hebrew, Arabic, Greek, and Latin characters in plants: in a common one among us we seem to read *aiaia, viviu, lilil.*

Right lines and circles make out the bulk of plants. In the parts thereof we find helical or spiral roundels, volutas, conical sections, circular pyramids, and frustums of Archimedes; and cannot overlook the orderly hand of nature in the alternate succession of the flat and narrower sides in the tender shoots of the ash, or the regular inequality of bigness in the five-leaved flowers of henbane, and something like in the calycular leaves of tutsan; how the spots of persicaria do manifest themselves between the sixth and tenth rib; how the triangular cap in the stem or stylus of tulips doth constantly point at three outward leaves; that spicated flowers do open first at the stalk; that white flowers have yellow thrums or knops; that the neb of beans and peas do all look downward, and so press not upon each other—and how the seeds of many pappose or downy flowers, locked up in sockets after a gomphosis or mortise-articulation, diffuse themselves circularly into branches of rare order, observable in *tragopogon* or goat's-beard, conformable to the spider's web, and the radii in like manner telarily interwoven.

And how in animal natures even colours hold correspondences

Barbado pine: pineapple, though the banana is meant.
phalaris: *Briza media*, common quaking grass.
Porta: G. B. della Porta, *Phytognomonica* (1588).
man orchis: *Aceras anthropophorum*.
Columna: F. Colonna, *Minus Cogitae Stirpes*, 146 (1616, pp. 318–19).—*B.*
osmund or water-fern: *Osmunda regalis*.
character of Pisces: the zodiacal sign ♓.
a common one: apparently some kind of sedge.
volutas: scrolls.
Archimedes: who wrote about conic sections.
persicaria: *Polygonum persicaria*, common persicaria.
spicated: spiked.   *first at the stalk*: i.e. the lower ones first.—*B.*
gomphosis or mortise-articulation: immovable fixation in cavities.
goat's-beard: *Tragopogon pratensis*.   *telarily*: like a spider's web.

and mutual correlations. That the colour of the caterpillar will show again in the butterfly, with some latitude is allowable: though the regular spots in their wings seem but a mealy adhesion and such as may be wiped away, yet, since they come in this variety out of their cases, there must be regular pores in those parts and membranes, defining such exudations.

That Augustus had native notes on his body and belly, after the order and number in the stars of Charles's Wain, will not seem strange unto astral physiognomy, which accordingly considereth moles in the body of man, or physical observators who, from the position of moles in the face, reduce them to rule and correspondency in other parts. Whether after the like method medical conjecture may not be raised upon parts inwardly affected, since parts about the lips are the critical seats of pustules discharged in agues, and scrofulous tumours about the neck do so often speak the like about the mesentery, may also be considered.

The russet neck in young lambs seems but adventitious, and may owe its tincture to some contaction in the womb. But that if sheep have any black or deep russet in their faces, they want not the same about their legs and feet; that black hounds have mealy mouths and feet; that black cows which have any white in their tails should not miss of some in their bellies, and if all white in their bodies, yet if black-mouthed their ears and feet maintain the same colour—are correspondent tinctures not ordinarily failing in nature, which easily unites the accidents of extremities, since in some generations she transmutes the parts themselves, while in the aurelian metamorphosis the head of the canker becomes the tail of the butterfly. Which is, in some way, not beyond the contrivance of art in submersions and inlays, inverting the extremes of the plant, and fetching the root from the top; and also imitated in handsome columnary work, in the inversion of the extremes, wherein the capital and the base hold such near correspondency.

In the motive parts of animals may be discovered mutual proportions: not only in those of quadrupeds, but in the thigh-bone, leg, foot-bone, and claws of birds. The legs of spiders are made after a sesquitertian proportion, and the long legs of some locusts double unto some others. But the internodial parts of vegetables,

---

Augustus: Suetonius, *Augustus*, 80.—*B.*   *native notes*: birthmarks.
russet neck: to be observed in white young lambs, which afterward vanisheth.—*B.*
contaction: contact.   *canker*: caterpillar.
submersions and inlays: layering of plants.   *internodial*: between nodes.

or spaces between the joints, are contrived with more uncertainty; though the joints themselves in many plants maintain a regular number.

In vegetable composure, the unition of prominent parts seems most to answer the apophyses or processes of animal bones, whereof they are the produced parts or prominent explantations. And though in the parts of plants, which are not ordained for motion, we do not expect correspondent articulations, yet in the setting-on of some flowers, and seeds in their sockets, and the lineal commissure of the pulp of several seeds, may be observed some shadow of the harmony, some show of the gomphosis or mortise-articulation.

As for the diarthrosis or motive articulation, there is expected little analogy: though long-stalked leaves do move by long lines, and have observable motions, yet are they made by outward impulsion, like the motion of pendulous bodies, while the parts themselves are united by some kind of symphysis unto the stock.

But standing vegetables, void of motive articulations, are not without many motions. For beside the motion of vegetation upward, and of radiation unto all quarters, that of contraction, dilatation, inclination, and contortion, is discoverable in many plants (to omit the rose of Jericho, the ear of rye which moves with change of weather, and the magical spit—made of no rare plants—which winds before the fire, and roasts the bird without turning).

Even animals near the classis of plants seem to have the most restless motions: the summer-worm of ponds and plashes makes a long waving motion; the hair-worm seldom lies still. He that would behold a very anomalous motion may observe it in the tortile and tiring strokes of gnat-worms.

CHAP. IIII

As for the delights, commodities, mysteries, with other concernments of this order, we are unwilling to fly them over in the short deliveries of Virgil, Varro, or others, and shall therefore enlarge with additional ampliations.

unition: joining.
produced parts: swellings.
gomphosis or mortise-articulation: fixation in sockets.
diarthrosis: mobile jointing.   *symphysis*: fusion.
summer-worm: larva of mosquito, etc.
hair-worm: nematoid worm, *Gordius aquaticus*.   *tiring*: pulling.
gnat-worms: found often in some form of red maggot in the standing water of cisterns in the summer.—B.

apophyses: natural growing processes.
explantations: outgrowths.

By this position they had a just proportion of earth to supply an equality of nourishment, the distance being ordered thick or thin according to the magnitude or vigorous attraction of the plant, the goodness, leanness, or propriety of the soil; and therefore the rule of Solon concerning the territory of Athens not extendible unto all, allowing the distance of six foot unto common trees, and nine for the fig and olive.

They had a due diffusion of their roots on all or both sides, whereby they maintained some proportion to their height in trees of large radication. For, that they strictly make good their profundeur or depth unto their height, according to common conceit and that expression of Virgil, though confirmable from the plane-tree in Pliny, and some few examples, is not to be expected from the generality of trees almost in any kind, either of side-spreading or tap-roots, except we measure them by lateral and opposite diffusions; nor commonly to be found in minor or herby plants, if we except sea holly, liquorice, sea rush, and some others.

They had a commodious radiation in their growth, and a due expansion of their branches for shadow or delight. For trees thickly planted do run up in height and branch with no expansion, shooting unequally, or short and thin upon the neighbouring side. And therefore trees are inwardly bare, and spring and leaf from the outward and sunny side of their branches.

Whereby they also avoided the peril of συνολεθρία, or one tree perishing with another, as it happeneth oft-times from the sick effluviums, or entanglements of the roots falling foul with each other—observable in elms set in hedges where if one dieth the neighbouring tree prospereth not long after.

In this situation, divided into many intervals and open unto six passages, they had the advantage of a fair perflation from winds, brushing and cleansing their surfaces, relaxing and closing their pores unto due perspiration. For, that they afford large effluviums, perceptible from odours diffused at great distances, is observable from onions out of the earth, which, though dry, and kept until the spring, as they shoot forth large and many leaves, do notably abate of their weight. And mint growing in glasses of water, until it arriveth

Solon: Plutarch, *Solon*, 23.6.   *large radication*: widespread roots.
conceit: conception.
Virgil: *Aeneid*, 4.445–6: It stretched its roots as far towards hell as its top towards
    heaven.
Pliny: *Natural History*, 12.5(9).   *sea holly*: *Eryngium maritimum*.
sea rush: *Juncus maritimus*.
συνολεθρία: shared disease or infestation.   *perflation*: ventilation.

unto the weight of an ounce, in a shady place, will sometimes exhaust a pound of water.

And as they send forth much, so may they receive somewhat in. For, beside the common way and road of reception by the root, there may be a refection and imbibition from without: for gentle showers refresh plants, though they enter not their roots, and the good and bad effluviums of vegetables promote or debilitate each other. So *epithymum* and dodder, rootless and out of the ground, maintain themselves upon thyme, savory, and plants whereon they hang; and ivy, divided from the root, we have observed to live some years by the cirrous parts commonly conceived but as tenacles and holdfasts unto it. The stalks of mint cropped from the root, stripped from the leaves and set in glasses, with the root end upward and out of the water, we have observed to send forth sprouts and leaves without the aid of roots, and *scordium* to grow in like manner, the leaves set downward in water (to omit several sea-plants which grown on single roots from stones, although in very many there are side-shoots and fibres beside the fastening root).

By this open position they were fairly exposed unto the rays of moon and sun, so considerable in the growth of vegetables. For though poplars, willows, and several trees be made to grow about the brinks of Acheron and dark habitations of the dead; though some plants are content to grow in obscure wells, wherein also old elm pumps afford sometimes long bushy sprouts not observable in any above ground; and large fields of vegetables are able to maintain their verdure at the bottom and shady part of the sea; yet the greatest number are not content without the actual rays of the sun, but bend, incline, and follow them, as large lists of solisequious and sun-following plants. And some observe the method of its motion in their own growth and conversion, twining towards the west by the south, as bryony, hops, woodbine, and several kinds of bindweed; which we shall more admire when any can tell us they observe another motion and twist by the north at the antipodes. The same plants rooted against an erect north wall full of holes will find a way through them to look upon the sun. And in tender plants from mustard-seed, sown in the winter, and in a pot of earth placed inwardly in a chamber against a south window, the tender stalks of two leaves arose not

---

epithymum: *Cuscuta epithymum*, lesser dodder.
tenacles: organs of attachment.
scordium: *Teucrium scordium*, water germander.
Acheron: Homer, *Odyssey*, 10.509–10.   *solisequious*: sun-following.

erect but bending towards the window, nor looking much higher
than the meridian sun. And if the pot were turned, they would work
themselves into their former declinations, making their conversion
by the east. That the leaves of the olive and some other trees solsti-
tially turn, and precisely tell us when the sun is entered Cancer, is
scarce expectable in any climate (and Theophrastus warily observes
it); yet somewhat thereof is observable in our own, in the leaves of
willows and sallows some weeks after the solstice. But the great
convolvulus, or white-flowered bindweed, observes both motions of
the sun: while the flower twists equinoctionally from the left hand to
the right, according to the daily revolution, the stalk twineth ecliptically from the right to the left, according to the annual conversion.

Some commend the exposure of these orders unto the western
gales, as the most generative and fructifying breath of heaven; but
we applaud the husbandry of Solomon (whereto agreeth the doctrine of Theophrastus): 'Arise, O north wind; and blow thou south
upon my garden, that the spices thereof may flow out'. For the
north wind closing the pores and shutting up the effluviums, when
the south doth after open and relax them, the aromatical gums do
drop, and sweet odours fly actively from them. And if his garden had
the same situation which maps and charts afford it, on the east side
of Jerusalem and having the wall on the west, these were the winds
unto which it was well exposed.

By this way of plantation they increased the number of their trees,
which they lost in quaternios and square orders; which is a commodity insisted on by Varro, and one great intent of nature in this
position of flowers and seeds in the elegant formation of plants, and
the former rules observed in natural and artificial figurations.

Whether in this order, and one tree in some measure breaking the
cold and pinching gusts of winds from the other, trees will not better
maintain their inward circles, and either escape or moderate their
eccentricities, may also be considered. For the circles in trees are

declinations: directions.
Cancer: the sign of the zodiac entered by the sun on Midsummer Day.
Theophrastus warily observes: *On Plants*, 1.10.1.
equinoctionally: according to the revolution of the celestial sphere.
ecliptically: in the same direction as that in which the sun seems to move during
    the year relative to the celestial sphere.
Solomon: S. of S. 4:16.
doctrine of Theophrastus: *On Plants*, 4.1.4.
quaternios: four-square plantations, with adjacent rows not staggered.
commodity: convenience.   *Varro*: *De Re Rustica*, 1.7.2.

naturally concentrical, parallel unto the bark and unto each other, till frost and piercing winds contract and close them on the weather side, the opposite semicircle widely enlarging, and at a comely distance; which hindereth oft-times the beauty and roundness of trees, and makes the timber less serviceable; whiles the ascending juice, not readily passing, settles in knots and inequalities. And therefore it is no new course of agriculture to observe the native position of trees according to north and south in their transplantations.

The same is also observable underground in the circinations and spherical rounds of onions, wherein the circles of the orbs are oft-times larger, and the meridional lines stand wider upon one side than the other; and where the largeness will make up the number of planetical orbs, that of Luna and the lower planets exceed the dimensions of Saturn and the higher. Whether the like be not verified in the circles of the large roots of bryony and mandrakes, or why in the knots of deal or fir the circles are often eccentrical, although not in a plane but vertical and right position, deserves a further enquiry.

Whether there be not some irregularity of roundness in most plants according to their position—whether some small compression of pores be not perceptible in parts which stand against the current of waters, as in reeds, bullrushes, and other vegetables, toward the streaming quarter, may also be observed; and therefore such as are long and weak are commonly contrived into a roundness of figure, whereby the water presseth less, and slippeth more smoothly from them; and even in flags of flat-figured leaves, the greater part obvert their sharper sides unto the current in ditches.

But whether plants which float upon the surface of the water be for the most part of cooling qualities, those which shoot above it of heating virtues, and why; whether sargasso, for many miles floating upon the western ocean, or sea-lettuce and *phasganium* at the bottom of our seas, make good the like qualities; why fenny waters afford the hottest and sweetest plants, as calamus, cyperus, and crowfoot, and mud cast out of ditches most naturally produceth arsesmart; why

---

circinations: spherical layers.
planetical orbs: then thought to be seven: those of the moon, the sun, Mercury, Venus, Mars, Jupiter, and Saturn.
streaming: upstream.   *obvert*: turn.
sea-lettuce: the seaweeds *Ulva lactuca* and *Ulva latissima*.
phasganium: *Lobelia dortmanna*, water lobelia.
calamus: *Acorus calamus*, sweet flag.
cyperus: *Cyperus longus*, sweet galingale.
arsesmart: *Polygonum hydropiper*, water pepper, biting persicaria.

plants so greedy of water so little regard oil; why, since many seeds contain much oil within them, they endure it not well without, either in their growth or production; why, since seeds shoot commonly underground and out of the air, those which are let fall in shallow glasses upon the surface of the water will sooner sprout than those at the bottom (and if the water be covered with oil, those at the bottom will hardly sprout at all)—we have not room to conjecture.

Whether ivy would not less offend the trees in this clean ordination, and well-kept paths, might perhaps deserve the question. But this were a query only unto some habitations, and little concerning Cyrus or the Babylonian territory: wherein by no industry Harpalus could make ivy grow, and Alexander hardly found it about those parts to imitate the pomp of Bacchus. And though in these northern regions we are too much acquainted with one ivy, we know too little of another; whereby we apprehend not the expressions of antiquity— the splenetic medicine of Galen, and the emphasis of the poet in the beauty of the white ivy.

The like concerning the growth of mistletoe, which dependeth not only of the species or kind of tree, but much also of the soil; and therefore common in some places, not readily found in others: frequent in France, not so common in Spain, and scarce at all in the territory of Ferrara; nor easily to be found where it is most required —upon oaks—, less on trees continually verdant, although in some places the olive escapeth it not, requiting its detriment in the delightful view of its red berries, as Clusius observed in Spain, and Bellonius about Jerusalem. But this parasitical plant suffers nothing to grow upon it by any way of art; nor could we ever make it grow where nature had not planted it, as we have in vain attempted by inoculation and insition upon its native or foreign stock. And though there seem nothing improbable in the seed, it hath not succeeded by sation in any manner of ground—wherein we had no reason to despair, since we read of vegetable horns, and how rams' horns will root about Goa.[n]

But besides these rural commodities, it cannot be meanly delectable in the variety of figures which these orders, open and closed, do make: whilst every enclosure makes a rhombus, the figures obliquely

---

Bacchus: Theophrastus, *On Plants*, 4.4.1.
Galen: *De Simplicium Medicamentorum Temperamentis ac Facultatibus*, 7(29).
emphasis: implied meaning.
the poet: Virgil, *Eclogues*, 7.38: lovelier than white ivy.—*B*.
Clusius: C. de l'Écluse, *Rariorum Plantarum Historia*, 1.17 (1601, p. 26), who also
    gives Belon's observation.
insition: engrafting.   *sation*: sowing.

taken a rhomboides, the intervals bounded with parallel lines, and each intersection built upon a square, affording two triangles or pyramids vertically conjoined; which, in the strict quincuncial order, do oppositely make acute and blunt angles.

And though therein we meet not with right angles, yet, every rhombus containing four angles equal unto four right, it virtually contains four right. Nor is this strange unto such as observe the natural lines of trees, and parts disposed in them. For neither in the root doth nature affect this angle, which, shooting downward for the stability of the plant, doth best effect the same by figures of inclination; nor in the branches and stalky leaves, which grow most at acute angles, as declining from their head the root, and diminishing their angles with their altitude—verified also in lesser plants, whereby they better support themselves, and bear not so heavily upon the stalk; so that while, near the root, they often make an angle of seventy parts, the sprouts near the top will often come short of thirty. Even in the nerves and master veins of the leaves, the acute angle ruleth; the obtuse but seldom found, and in the backward part of the leaf, reflecting and arching about the stalk. But why oft-times one side of the leaf is unequal unto the other, as in hazel and oaks; why on either side the master vein the lesser and derivative channels stand not directly opposite, nor at equal angles respectively unto the adverse side, but those of one part do often exceed the other, as the walnut and many more, deserves another enquiry.

Now if for this order we affect coniferous and tapering trees—particularly the cypress, which grows in a conical figure—we have found a tree not only of great ornament, but in its essentials of affinity unto this order: a solid rhombus being made by the conversion of two equicrural cones, as Archimedes hath defined. And these were the common trees about Babylon and the East, whereof the Ark was made; and Alexander found no trees so accommodable to build his navy; and this we rather think to be the tree mentioned in the Canticles, which stricter botanology will hardly allow to be camphor.

And if delight or ornamental view invite a comely disposure by circular amputations, as is elegantly performed in hawthorns, then

---

vertically: by their apexes.
seventy parts: 70°.
equicrural: isosceles.
Ark: Gen. 6:14.
Canticles: S. of S. 1:14, 4:13. The Hebrew *copher* is now translated 'henna'.
botanology: botany.
circular amputations: pruning and clipping to form cylindrical stages.

blunt: obtuse.
conversion: turning base to base.
Archimedes: in his work on conic sections.
Alexander: Arrian, *Anabasis*, 7.19.4.

will they answer the figures made by the conversion of a rhombus, which maketh two concentrical circles; the greater circumference being made by the lesser angles, the lesser by the greater.

The cylindrical figure of trees is virtually contained and latent in this order, a cylinder, or long round, being made by the conversion or turning of a parallelogram, and most handsomely by a long square; which makes an equal, strong, and lasting figure in trees, agreeable unto the body and motive parts of animals, the greatest number of plants, and almost all roots; though their stalks be angular, and of many corners, which seem not to follow the figure of their seeds, since many angular seeds send forth round stalks, and spherical seeds arise from angular spindles, and many rather conform unto their roots, as the round stalks of bulbous roots, and in tuberous roots stems of like figure. But why, since the largest number of plants maintain a circular figure, there are so few with teretous or long round leaves; why coniferous trees are tenuifolious or narrow leafed; why plants of few or no joints have commonly round stalks; why the greatest number of hollow stalks are round stalks; or why in this variety of angular stalks the quadrangular most exceedeth— were too long a speculation. Meanwhile, obvious experience may find that, in plants of divided leaves above, nature often beginneth circularly in the two first leaves below; while in the singular plant of ivy she exerciseth a contrary geometry, and beginning with angular leaves below, rounds them in the upper branches.

Nor can the rows in this order want delight, as carrying an aspect answerable unto the *dipteros hypaethros*, or double order of columns open above; the opposite ranks of trees standing like pillars in the *cavaedia* of the courts of famous buildings, and the *porticos* of the *templa subdialia* of old; somewhat imitating the *peristylia* (or cloister buildings) and the *exedrae* of the ancients, wherein men discoursed, walked, and exercised. For, that they derived the rule of columns from trees, especially in their proportional diminutions, is illustrated by Vitruvius from the shafts of fir and pine. And though the inter-arborations do imitate the *araeostylos* or thin order, not strictly

---

conversion of a rhombus: the describing of two concentric circles each touching a
    pair of opposite angles of a rhombus.
spindles: stalks.
dipteros hypaethros: building with two unroofed wings of columns.
cavaedia: inner courts of Roman buildings.
templa subdialia: open-air temples.   *exedrae*: arcades with recesses.
Vitruvius: *Architecture*, 5.1.3.   *araeostylos*: thin spacing of columns.

answering the proportion of intercolumniations, yet in many trees they will not exceed the intermission of the columns in the court of the tabernacle: which, being an hundred cubits long and made up by twenty pillars, will afford no less than intervals of five cubits.

Beside, in this kind of aspect, the sight being not diffused, but circumscribed between long parallels and the ἐπισκιασμός and adumbration from the branches, it frameth a penthouse over the eye, and maketh a quiet vision. And therefore, in diffused and open aspects, men hollow their hand above their eye, and make an artificial brow whereby they direct the dispersed rays of sight, and by this shade preserve a moderate light in the chamber of the eye; keeping the *pupilla* plump and fair, and not contracted or shrunk as in light and vagrant vision.

And therefore Providence hath arched and paved the great house of the world with colours of mediocrity, that is, blue and green above and below the sight, moderately terminating the *acies* of the eye. For most plants, though green above ground, maintain their original white below it, according to the candour of their seminal pulp; and the rudimental leaves do first appear in that colour (observable in seeds sprouting in water, upon their first foliation): green seeming to be the first supervenient or above-ground complexion of vegetables, separable in many upon ligature or inhumation— as succory, endive, artichokes—and which is also lost upon fading in the autumn.

And this is also agreeable unto water itself, the alimental vehicle of plants, which first altereth into this colour; and, containing many vegetable seminalities, revealeth their seeds by greenness: and therefore soonest expected in rain or standing water, not easily found in distilled or water strongly boiled, wherein the seeds are extinguished by fire and decoction, and therefore last long and pure without such alteration, affording neither uliginous coats, gnat-worms, acari, hair-worms, like crude and common water—and

---

intercolumniations: spacings of columns. See note above, p. 147.
intermission: spacing.
ἐπισκιασμός *and adumbration*: shade.
vagrant: unshaded.
candour: whiteness.
supervenient: occurring above.
ligature or inhumation: blanching by tying outer leaves over the heart or by earthing-up.
seminalities: principles of growth.
gnat-worms: gnat larvae.
hair-worms: Gordius aquaticus.

tabernacle: Exod. 27:9–11.
pupilla: pupil.
acies: vision.
foliation: formation of leaves.

uliginous coats: slimy scums.
acari: mites.

therefore most fit for wholesome beverage, and with malt makes ale and beer without boiling. What large water-drinkers some plants are, the Canary tree, and birches—in some northern countries drenching the fields about them—do sufficiently demonstrate. How water itself is able to maintain the growth of vegetables, and without extinction of their generative or medical virtues, beside the experiment of Helmont's tree, we have found in some which have lived six years in glasses. The seeds of scurvy-grass growing in waterpots have been fruitful in the land; and *Asarum*, after a year's space (and once casting its leaves) in water, in the second leaves hath handsomely performed its vomiting operation.

Nor are only dark and green colours but shades and shadows contrived through the great volume of nature, and trees ordained not only to protect and shadow others, but by their shades and shadowing parts to preserve and cherish themselves: the whole radiation or branchings shadowing the stock and the root, the leaves, the branches and fruit, too much exposed to the winds and scorching sun. The calycular leaves enclose the tender flowers, and the flowers themselves lie wrapped about the seeds in their rudiment and first formations; which being advanced, the flowers fall away, and are therefore contrived in variety of figures best satisfying the intention: handsomely observable in hooded and gaping flowers, and the butterfly blooms of leguminous plants, the lower leaf closely involving the rudimental cod, and the alary or wingy divisions embracing or hanging over it.

But seeds themselves do lie in perpetual shades, either under the leaf or shut up in coverings; and such as lie barest have their husks, skins, and pulps about them, wherein the neb and generative particle lieth moist, and secured from the injury of air and sun. Darkness and light hold interchangeable dominions, and alternately rule the seminal state of things: light unto Pluto is darkness unto Jupiter. Legions of seminal ideas lie in their second chaos and Orcus of Hippocrates till, putting on the habits of their forms, they show themselves upon the

Canary tree: a til tree, *Oreodaphne fetens*, reputed to supply water to the islanders of Hierro in the Canaries.
Helmont's tree: J. B. van Helmont, *Complexionum atque Mistionum Elementalium Figmentum*, 30 (*Ortus Medicinae*, 1648, p. 109), described how a stem of willow, rooted in sterile earth and watered only with rain or distilled water, grew for five years till over thirty times its initial weight.
Asarum: *Asarum europaeum*, asarabacca, a well-known emetic.   *cod*: pod.
seminal ideas: See note above, p. 42.   *Orcus*: underworld.
Hippocrates: *Regimen*, 1.5.

stage of the world and open dominion of Jove. They that held the stars of heaven were but rays and flashing glimpses of the empyreal light through holes and perforations of the upper heaven, took off the natural shadows of stars; while, according to better discovery, the poor inhabitants of the moon have but a polary life, and must pass half their days in the shadow of that luminary.

Light, that makes things seen, makes some things invisible: were it not for darkness and the shadow of the earth, the noblest part of the creation had remained unseen, and the stars in heaven as invisible as on the fourth day, when they were created above the horizon with the sun, or there was not an eye to behold them. The greatest mystery of religion is expressed by adumbration, and in the noblest part of Jewish types we find the cherubims shadowing the mercy-seat. Life itself is but the shadow of death, and souls departed but the shadows of the living. All things fall under this name: the sun itself is but the dark simulacrum, and light but the shadow of God.

Lastly, it is no wonder that this quincuncial order was first—and still—affected as grateful unto the eye, for all things are seen quincuncially: for at the eye, the pyramidal rays from the object receive a decussation, and so strike a second base upon the retina or hinder coat, the proper organ of vision wherein the pictures from objects are represented (answerable to the paper or wall in the dark chamber), after the decussation of the rays at the hole of the horny coat, and their refraction upon the crystalline humour (answering the foramen of the window, and the convex or burning-glasses which refract the rays that enter it). And if ancient anatomy would hold, a like disposure there was of the optic or visual nerves in the brain, wherein antiquity conceived a concurrence by decussation. And this not only observable in the laws of direct vision, but in some part also verified in the reflected rays of sight: for, making the angle of incidence equal to that of reflection, the visual ray returneth quincuncially and after the form of a V; and the line of reflection being

took off: dispensed with.
fourth day: Gen. 1:14–19.
mercy-seat: Heb. 9:5.
shadows of stars: eclipses and occultations.
adumbration: overshadowing. Luke 1:35.
shadow of God: See above, p. 11.
pyramidal rays: the reflected rays subtended by a visible object at the eye, diagrammatically represented.
dark chamber: camera obscura.   *horny coat*: cornea.
humour: lens of the eye.
concurrence by decussation: linking of the left eye to the right side of the brain, and vice versa.
visual ray: The phrase evinces a belief that sight depended on rays emitted by the eyes.

continued unto the place of vision, there ariseth a semi-decussation,[n] which makes the object seen in a perpendicular unto itself, and as far below the reflectent as it is from it above—observable in the sun and moon beheld in water.

And this is also the law of reflection in moved bodies and sounds, which, though not made by decussation, observe the rule of equality between incidence and reflection; whereby whispering places are framed by elliptical arches laid sidewise, where, the voice being delivered at the focus of one extremity, observing an equality unto the angle of incidence, it will reflect unto the focus of the other end, and so escape the ears of the standers in the middle.

A like rule is observed in the reflection of the vocal and sonorous line in echoes, which cannot therefore be heard in all stations; but happening in woody plantations by waters, and able to return some words, if reached by a pleasant and well-dividing voice there may be heard the softest notes in nature.

And this not only verified in the way of sense, but in animal and intellectual receptions, things entering upon the intellect by a pyramid from without, and thence into the memory by another from within—the common decussation being in the understanding, as is delivered by Bovillus.[n] Whether the intellectual and fantastical lines be not thus rightly disposed, but magnified, diminished, distorted, and ill-placed in the mathematics of some brains, whereby they have irregular apprehensions of things, perverted notions, conceptions, and incurable hallucinations, were no unpleasant speculation.

And if Egyptian philosophy may obtain, the scale of influences was thus disposed, and the genial spirits of both worlds do trace their way in ascending and descending pyramids: mystically apprehended in the letter X, and the open bill and straddling legs of a stork, which was imitated by that character.

Of this figure Plato made choice to illustrate the motion of the soul, both of the world and man; while he delivereth that God divided the whole conjunction lengthwise, according to the figure of a Greek X, and then, turning it about, reflected it into a circle—by the circle implying the uniform motion of the first orb, and by the right lines, the planetical and various motions within it. And this also with

---

reflectent: reflecting surface.   *moved bodies*: when they bounce.
well-dividing: well-tuned.   *animal*: mental, spiritual.
genial: guardian.   *Plato*: *Timaeus*, 36b–d.
first orb: *primum mobile*.   *right*: straight.

application unto the soul of man, which hath a double aspect: one right, whereby it beholdeth the body and objects without; another circular and reciprocal, whereby it beholdeth itself. The circle declaring the motion of the indivisible soul, simple, according to the divinity of its nature, and returning into itself; the right lines respecting the motion pertaining unto sense and vegetation; and the central decussation, the wondrous connection of the several faculties conjointly in one substance. And so conjoined the unity and duality of the soul, and made out the three substances so much considered by him; that is, the indivisible or divine, the divisible or corporeal, and that third, which was the systasis or harmony of those two, in the mystical decussation.

And if that were clearly made out which Justin Martyr took for granted, this figure hath had the honour to characterize and notify our blessed Saviour, as he delivereth in that borrowed expression from Plato: *Decussavit eum in universo*. The hint whereof he would have Plato derive from the figure of the brazen serpent, and to have mistaken the letter X for T; whereas it is not improbable he learned these and other mystical expressions in his learned observations of Egypt, where he might obviously behold the Mercurial characters, the handed crosses, and other mysteries (not thoroughly understood) in the sacred letter X; which, being derivative from the stork, one of the ten sacred animals, might be originally Egyptian, and brought into Greece by Cadmus of that country.

CHAP. V

To enlarge this contemplation unto all the mysteries and secrets accommodable unto this number were inexcusable Pythagorism; yet cannot omit the ancient conceit of five, surnamed the number of justice, as justly dividing between the digits, and hanging in the centre of nine described by square numeration (which, angularly

---

considered by him: *Timaeus*, 35, 37.   *systasis*: union.
Justin Martyr: *First Apology*, 60 (78–9) alluding to *Timaeus*, 36, as a foreshadowing of the Crucifixion.
notify: signify.   *Decussavit*: He placed him cross-wise in the universe.
brazen serpent: Num. 21.8–9.
Mercurial characters: possibly the symbol (☿) of the planet Mercury, as well as the handed cross of Hermes (Mercurius) Trismegistus.
Cadmus: the legendary Phoenician founder of Thebes, supposed to have taught the Boeotians letters.
Pythagorism: indulgence in Pythagorean ideas of the mystical significances of numbers.
square numeration: 1 2 3
                       4 5 6
                       7 8 9

divided, will make the decussated number, and so agreeable unto the quincuncial ordination, and rows divided by equality and just decorum in the whole complantation); and might be the original of that common game among us wherein the fifth place is sovereign and carrieth the chief intention—the ancients wisely instructing youth, even in their recreations, unto virtue, that is, early to drive at the middle point and central seat of justice.

Nor can we omit how, agreeable unto this number, an handsome division is made in trees and plants, since Plutarch and the ancients have named it the divisive number, justly dividing the entities of the world, many remarkable things in it, and also comprehending the general division of vegetables. And he that considers how most blossoms of trees, and greatest number of flowers, consist of five leaves—and therein doth rest the settled rule of nature, so that in those which exceed there is often found, or easily made, a variety—may readily discover how nature rests in this number, which is indeed the first rest and pause of numeration in the fingers, the natural organs thereof. Nor in the division of the feet of perfect animals doth nature exceed this account; and even in the joints of feet—which in birds are most multiplied—surpasseth not this number, so progressionally making them out in many that from five in the fore-claw she descendeth unto two in the hindmost, and so in four feet makes up the number of joints in the five fingers or toes of man.

Not to omit the quintuple section of a cone, of handsome practice in ornamental garden-plots, and in some way discoverable in so many works of nature: in the leaves, fruits, and seeds of vegetables, and scales of some fishes—so much considerable in glasses and the optic doctrine, wherein the learned may consider the crystalline humour of the eye in the cuttle-fish and *lolligo*.

He that forgets not how antiquity named this the conjugal or wedding number, and made it the emblem of the most remarkable conjunction, will conceive it duly appliable unto this handsome

---

common game: dutch-pins, a form of kayles, skittles, or nine-pins, in which the game is won if the central king-pin alone is knocked down.
Plutarch: *The E at Delphi*, 13–15.
entities of the world: the ether, and fire, air, water, and earth.
division of vegetables: tree, shrub, woody herb, herb, and that fifth which comprehendeth the fungi and *tubera.*—*B.*
hindmost: as herons, bitterns, and long-clawed fowls.—*B.*
feet: toes or claws.　　　　　　　　　　*number of joints*: fourteen.
section of a cone: ellipse, parabola, hyperbola, circle, triangle.—*B.*
glasses: telescopes and microscopes.　　*crystalline humour*: lens.
lolligo: cuttle-fish.　　*wedding number*: Plutarch, *The E at Delphi*, 8.

economy and vegetable combination; may hence apprehend the allegorical sense of that obscure expression of Hesiod; and afford no improbable reason why Plato admitted his nuptial guests by fives in the kindred of the married couple.

And though a sharper mystery might be implied in the number of the five wise and foolish virgins which were to meet the bridegroom, yet was the same agreeable unto the conjugal number, which ancient numerists made out by two and three: the first parity and imparity, the active and passive digits, the material and formal principles in generative societies; and not discordant even from the customs of the Romans, who admitted but five torches in their nuptial solemnities. Whether there were any mystery or not implied, the most generative animals were created on this day, and had accordingly the largest benediction; and under a quintuple consideration wanton antiquity considered the circumstances of generation, while by this number of five they naturally divided the nectar of the fifth planet.

The same number in the Hebrew mysteries and cabalistical accounts was the character of generation, declared by the letter *he*, the fifth in their alphabet; according to that cabalistical dogma, if Abram had not had this letter added unto his name, he had remained fruitless and without the power of generation: not only because hereby the number of his name attained two hundred and forty-eight, the number of the affirmative precepts, but because, as in created natures there is a male and female, so in divine and intelligent productions the mother of life and fountain of souls in cabalistical technology is called *binah*, whose seal and character was *he*. So that, being sterile before, he received the power of generation from that measure and mansion in the archetype, and was made conformable unto *binah*. And upon such involved considerations the ten of Sarai was exchanged into five.

If any shall look upon this as a stable number, and fitly appropriable unto trees as bodies of rest and station, he hath herein a

economy: organization.
Plato: *Laws*, 6 (775).
this day: Gen. 1:20–3.
Hesiod: the fifth days: *Works and Days*, 802.
virgins: Matt. 25:1.
fifth planet: Horace, *Odes*, 1.13.15–16: The lips which Venus has imbued with the quintessence of her nectar.—*B.*
precepts: in Mosaic law, which Abraham could then observe to perfection. Gen. 17:5.
technology: technical terminology.
ten of Sarai: The last letter of her name, *iod*, was the tenth of the alphabet, and was changed to *he*. Gen. 17:15.—*B.*
station: immobility.

great foundation in nature who, observing much variety in legs and motive organs of animals—as two, four, six, eight, twelve, fourteen, and more—hath passed over five and ten, and assigned them unto none. And for the stability of this number he shall not want the sphericity of its nature, which, multiplied in itself, will return into its own denomination, and bring up the rear of the account. Which is also one of the numbers that makes up the mystical name of God, which, consisting of letters denoting all the spherical numbers—ten, five, and six—emphatically sets forth the notion of Trismegistus, and that intelligible sphere which is the nature of God.

Many expressions by this number occur in Holy Scripture, perhaps unjustly laden with mystical expositions, and little concerning our order. That the Israelites were forbidden to eat the fruit of their new-planted trees before the fifth year was very agreeable unto the natural rules of husbandry, fruits being unwholesome and lash before the fourth or fifth year. In the second day, or feminine part of five, there was added no approbation; for in the third or masculine day the same is twice repeated, and a double benediction enclosed both creations—whereof the one, in some part, was but an accomplishment of the other. That the trespasser was to pay a fifth part above the head or principal makes no secret in this number, and implied no more than one part above the principal; which being considered in four parts, the additional forfeit must bear the name of a fifth. The five golden mice had plainly their determination from the number of the princes. That five should put to flight an hundred might have nothing mystically implied, considering a rank of soldiers could scarce consist of a lesser number. Saint Paul had rather speak five words in a known than ten thousand in an unknown tongue: that is as little as could well be spoken, a simple proposition consisting of three words, and a complexed one not ordinarily short of five.

unto none: or very few, as the *Phalangium monstrosum Brasilianum*, or ten-legged spider.—*B.*, referring to a species of spider with two pedipalps, or leg-like organs of touch, as well as eight legs.
rear of the account: See note above, p. 163.
ten, five, and six: The Hebrew letters in the name Yahweh also denoted these numbers.   *emphatically*: implicitly.
Trismegistus: God is a sphere whose centre is everywhere and circumference nowhere.
Israelites: Lev. 19:23–5.   *lash*: watery.
no approbation: Gen. 1:6–8.   *double benediction*: Gen. 1:10, 12.
trespasser: Lev. 6:5.   *golden mice*: 1 Sam. 6:4, 18.
an hundred: Lev. 26:8.   *Saint Paul*: 1 Cor. 14:19.

More considerable there are in this mystical account which we must not insist on. And therefore, why the radical letters in the Pentateuch should equal the number of the soldiery of the tribes; why our Saviour in the wilderness fed five thousand persons with five barley loaves, and again, but four thousand with no less than seven of wheat; why Joseph designed five changes of raiment unto Benjamin, and David took just five pebbles out of the brook against the pagan champion—we leave it unto arithmetical divinity and theological explanation.

Yet if any delight in new problems, or think it worth the enquiry, whether the critical physician hath rightly hit the nominal notation of *quinque*; why the ancients mixed five or three but not four parts of water unto their wine, and Hippocrates observed a fifth proportion in the mixture of water with milk, as in dysenteries and bloody fluxes; under what abstruse foundation astrologers do figure the good or bad fate from our children in Good Fortune, or the fifth house of their celestial schemes; whether the Egyptians described a star by a figure of five points with reference unto the five capital aspects whereby they transmit their influences, or abstruser considerations; why the cabalistical doctors, who conceive the whole sephiroth or divine emanations to have guided the ten-stringed harp of David whereby he pacified the evil spirit of Saul, in strict numeration do begin with the perihypate meson or si fa ut, and so place the *tiphereth*, answering C (sol fa ut), upon the fifth string; or whether this number be oftener applied unto bad things and ends than good in Holy Scripture, and why—he may meet with abstrusities of no ready resolution.

If any shall question the rationality of that magic in the cure of the

radical letters: consonants in the roots of Hebrew words.
Pentateuch: alleged to contain 600,045 radical letters.
soldiery of the tribes: 603,550, according to Num. 1:46, 2:32.
barley loaves: John 6:9–10.   *seven of wheat*: Matt. 15:34–8; Mark 8:5–9.
Benjamin: Gen. 45:22.   *David*: 1 Sam. 17:40.
critical physician: literary doctor—J. C. Scaliger, who, in *De Causis Linguae Latinae*, alleged for the Latin word for five a Greek etymology signifying four plus one.
nominal notation: substantive meaning.
ancients: Plutarch, *Symposiacs*, 3.9.   *Hippocrates*: *Epidemics*, 7.3.
capital aspects: the positional relationships among planets: conjunct, opposite, sextile, trigonal, tetragonal.—*B.*
Saul: 1 Sam. 16:23.   *perihypate meson*: the note F.
tiphereth: the fifth from the lowest of the ten sephiroth, or divine emanations; associated with beauty.

blind man by Serapis commanded to place five fingers on his altar, and then his hand on his eyes; why since the whole comedy is primarily and naturally comprised in four parts, and antiquity permitted not so many persons to speak in one scene, yet would not comprehend the same in more or less than five acts; why amongst sea-stars nature chiefly delighteth in five points, and since there are found some of no fewer than twelve, and some of seven and nine, there are few or none discovered of six or eight: if any shall enquire why the flowers of rue properly consisting of four leaves, the first and third flower have five; why since many flowers have one leaf, or none as Scaliger will have it, divers three, and the greatest number consist of five, divided from their bottoms, there are yet so few of two; or why nature generally beginning or setting out with two opposite leaves at the root, doth so seldom conclude with that order and number at the flower—he shall not pass his hours in vulgar speculations.

If any shall further query, why magnetical philosophy excludeth decussations, and needles transversely placed do naturally distract their verticities; why geomancers do imitate the quintuple figure in their mother characters of acquisition and amission, etc., somewhat answering the figures in the lady or speckled beetle; with what equity chiromantical conjecturers decry these decussations in the lines and mounts of the hand; what that decussated figure intendeth in the medal of Alexander the Great; why the goddesses sit commonly cross-legged in ancient draughts, since Juno is described in the same as a veneficial posture to hinder the birth of Hercules: if any shall doubt why, at the amphidromical feasts on the fifth day after the child was born, presents were sent from friends, of polypuses and cuttlefishes; why five must be only left in that symbolical mutiny among the men of Cadmus; why Proteus in Homer, the symbol of

---

Serapis: In fact the cure is supposed to have taken place in a temple of the god of healing, Aesculapius, on an island in the Tiber in the second century A.D.
four parts: protasis (exposition), epitasis (development), catastasis (intensification), catastrophe (dénouement).—*B*.
five acts: Horace, *Ars Poetica*, 189–90.   *sea-stars*: starfish.
Scaliger: J. C. Scaliger. *Exercitationes*, 178.2, rejects the idea of single-leaved plants, while pointing out that some have none at all.
magnetical philosophy: the science of magnetism.
distract their verticities: turn their points.   *amission*: loss.
lady: ladybird.   *Alexander the Great*: referring to a control-mark.
draughts: drawings.   *veneficial*: supernaturally malignant.
Hercules: Ovid, *Metamorphoses*, 9.298–300.
amphidromical: at which the child was carried round the hearth.
Cadmus: Ovid, 3.126.   *Homer*: *Odyssey*, 4.412.

the first matter, before he settled himself in the midst of his sea monsters doth place them out by fives; why the fifth year's ox was acceptable sacrifice unto Jupiter; or why the noble Antoninus in some sense doth call the soul itself a rhombus—he shall not fall on trite or trivial disquisitions.

And these we invent and propose unto acuter enquirers, nauseating crambe verities and questions overqueried. Flat and flexible truths are beat out by every hammer, but Vulcan and his whole forge sweat to work out Achilles his armour. A large field is yet left unto sharper discerners to enlarge upon this order, to search out the quaternios and figured draughts of this nature; and, moderating the study of names and mere nomenclature of plants, to erect generalities, disclose unobserved proprieties: not only in the vegetable shop, but the whole volume of nature; affording delightful truths confirmable by sense and ocular observation—which seems to me the surest path to trace the labyrinth of truth. For though discursive enquiry and rational conjecture may leave handsome gashes and flesh-wounds, yet, without conjunction of this, expect no mortal or dispatching blows unto error.

But the quincunx of heaven runs low, and 'tis time to close the five ports of knowledge. We are unwilling to spin out our awaking thoughts into the phantasms of sleep, which too often continueth precogitations—making cables of cobwebs, and wildernesses of handsome groves. Beside, Hippocrates hath spoke so little, and the oneirocritical masters have left such frigid interpretations from plants, that there is little encouragement to dream of paradise itself. Nor will the sweetest delight of gardens afford much comfort in sleep, wherein the dullness of that sense shakes hands with delectable odours; and, though in the bed of Cleopatra, can hardly with any delight raise up the ghost of a rose.

Jupiter: *Iliad*, 2.403, 7.315.
Antoninus: Marcus Aurelius, *Meditations*, 8.41, 11.12, 12.3.
nauseating: nauseated by.　　　*crambe*: stale.
Vulcan: *Iliad*, 18.468–613.　　*quaternios*: mystic numbers.
proprieties: properties.
quincunx of heaven: the Hyades, near the horizon about midnight at the beginning of March.—*B*.
ports: gates, i.e. senses.　　*precogitations*: earlier thoughts.
Hippocrates: *De Insomniis*.—*B*.
oneirocritical masters: Artemidorus and Achmet (Apomazar), *Oneirocritica* (1603).—*B*.
bed of Cleopatra: strewed with roses.—*B*.

Night, which pagan theology could make the daughter of Chaos,
affords no advantage to the description of order. Although no lower
than that mass can we derive its genealogy, all things began in
order: so shall they end, and so shall they begin again, according to
the ordainer of order, and mystical mathematics of the City of
Heaven.

Though Somnus in Homer be sent to rouse up Agamemnon, I find
no such effects in the drowsy approaches of sleep. To keep our eyes
open longer were but to act our antipodes: the huntsmen are up in
America, and they are already past their first sleep in Persia. But
who can be drowsy at that hour which freed us from everlasting
sleep, or have slumbering thoughts at that time when sleep itself must
end, and—as some conjecture—all shall awake again?

FINIS

pagan theology: Hesiod, *Theogony*, 123.   *lower*: more recently.
Somnus: sleep.   *Homer*: *Iliad*, 2.6, where it is in fact a dream.

Notes

Religio Medici

p. 1   In December 1643 appeared a forged commission, purporting to issue from the Court at Edinburgh, inciting the Catholics in Ireland to rise on behalf of Charles I.

p. 11   The sentence quoted in Browne's footnote has been traced back as far as the twelfth century. In his next sentence he contrasts imaginative metaphorical descriptions by Neoplatonic or Hermetic philosophers such as Ficino and Paracelsus with the defined terms of Aristotle, *De Anima*, 2.1, 7.

p. 13   The disciples of Pythagoras, detecting numerical relations or analogies among all the phenomena of the universe, taught that its origin lay in number, which was either the basic substance or inherent pattern of all things, and alone gave absolutely certain principles of knowledge. Out of a combination of these mathematical metaphysics with their musical ideas arose the concept of cosmic harmony. See Aristotle, *Metaphysica*, 1.5.

p. 13   The doctrine of signatures taught that the appearances of plants, stones, and so on, symbolized their hidden medical and magical properties, as, for instance, the lichen *Lobaria pulmonaria* was called lungwort, on account of its lung-shaped lobes, and supposed to cure diseases of the lung.

p. 13   A favourite Neoplatonic idea, to be found in the Hermetic *Smaragdine Table*.

p. 16   Vives, elaborating slightly on Pliny, *Natural History*, 11.1 (1, 4), writes in his commentary on Augustine, *City of God*, 11.22 (tr. J. Healey, 1620, p. 405): 'Nature is in the least creatures, pismires, gnats, bees, and spiders, as potent as in horses, oxen, whales, or elephants, and as admirable.'

p. 16   According to scholastic philosophers there were three souls, the vegetative, the sensitive, and the rational. Plants possessed only the first, with the powers of growth and reproduction; animals had as well the second, being capable of movement and feeling, while man alone had all three.

p. 17   This idea was promulgated most notably by Raymond of Sabunde in his *Theologia Naturalis* (c. 1435).

p. 18   Forms were the essential inward characters which, according to scholastic philosophy, determined the outward shapes.

p. 18   The doctrine arose of course from the Creation myth, being typically expressed by Augustine, *City of God*, 11.22 (1620, p. 404): 'God the great workman'. Cf. also 5.11, 7.29.

p. 19   Scholastic philosophy taught that the celestial orbs of Ptolemaic theory were revolved by angels.

p. 22   Diogenes Laertius, 10.139.1 (tr. R. D. Hicks, Loeb edition, 1925, ii.663): 'A blessed and eternal being has no trouble himself and brings no trouble upon any other being; hence he is exempt from movements of anger and partiality, for every such movement implies weakness.'

p. 24   Expounded in *Pseudodoxia Epidemica*, 4.5.

p. 24   This sentence partly reappears, and its subject is treated at length, in *Pseudodoxia Epidemica*, 6.2.

p. 25   According to Aristotelean physics, the heavier always naturally sought and found its place beneath the lighter, so that earth, being the heavier, might be expected always to be under water.

p. 25   See *Pseudodoxia*, 6.6.

p. 25   See *Pseudodoxia*, 7.3.

p. 25   See also *Pseudodoxia*, 7.11.

p. 25   See also *Pseudodoxia*, 7.6.

p. 26   On the advice of his librarian, Ptolemy II (King of Egypt 283–246 B.C.) commissioned from six elders of each of the twelve tribes of Israel a translation of the Old Testament into Greek, thence known as the Septuagint, or work of the seventy. See Josephus, *Jewish Antiquities*, 12.2.1, 4–7, 11–14 (11–16, 34–9, 48–9, 56–7, 86–118).

p. 26   Browne's derogatory opinions about the Koran are probably second-hand: cf. G. Sandys, *Relation of a Journey*, I (2nd ed., 1621, pp. 53–4): 'The Alcoran . . . is written in Arabic rhyme, without due proportion of numbers: . . . it is farced with fables, visions, legends, and relations.'

p. 27   Most of Cicero's verse mentioned in his letters has perished. See W. W. Ewbank, *The Poems of Cicero* (1933, pp. 10–26).

p. 27   The great library of the Museum, assembled by the Ptolemies, was destroyed during the siege by Julius Caesar in 47 B.C.; the lesser library of the Serapeion by Christians in the fourth century, and by Muslims in 640.

p. 27   The Samaritan version of the Pentateuch, not printed till 1645, was known to differ slightly from the standard Massoretic version of the Jews.

p. 29   Christians based their claim to Socrates as a monotheist on his citations of a singular deity in Plato's *Apology* (e.g. 29d, 30a, e, 31a, 33c). In his defence against the charge of atheism (26c), however, he implies belief in gods in the plural (28a). Xenophon, *Memorabilia*, 1.1, substantiates this, and explains Socrates' 'God' as his presiding genius or inspiration. He was condemned for the political corruption of youth; his acceptance of death may have been due, according to Xenophon, *Apology*, 6–7, 27, 32, to fear of senility.

p. 29   Virgilius, an eighth-century bishop of Salzburg, was denounced to Pope Zacharias by Boniface, Bishop of Mainz, who took Virgilius's theory of antipodes to imply another world complete with its own sun and moon. However, the latter's clarification seems to have been accepted since he occupied his see for thirty years after the martyrdom of Boniface.

p. 30   Cf. Augustine, *City of God*, 10.12 (1620, p. 359): 'All the miracles done in this world are less than the world itself.'

p. 31   L. Alberti, *Descrittione di Tutta l'Italia* (Venice, 1596, f. 16^r). The Genoese were, all the same, rewarded also with territory, revenue, and trading rights.

p. 31 Treated at length in *Pseudodoxia Epidemica*, 7.12.

p. 32 Browne testified at Bury St. Edmunds Assizes in 1664 that two girls were possessed by means of witchcraft.

p. 39 The Lutherans opted for the 'Traducian' doctrine that souls were transmitted by parents to children, as opposed to the 'Creationist' theory that each soul was a new creation infused by God.

p. 39 The practically universal belief in these hybrids was fostered by such imaginatively illustrated accounts as Conrad Lycosthenes, *Prodigiorum ac Ostentorum Chronicon* (Basle, 1557, pp. 664–70).

p. 39 The Greek physician Galen, *Of the Use of the Parts*, 3.10, professes to have written it to show the wisdom, power, and goodness of the Creator.

p. 40 According to Thomas Aquinas, *Summa Theologiae*, 1.75.6, discussing whether the soul could decay, corruption only existed where there existed also some contrary force or quality.

p. 42 'In our chaos' we are only potentially existent as matter (material cause) as yet unmanufactured (by efficient cause) according to that pattern (formal cause) in which we are to carry out our purpose (final cause). In so far as God is omnipresent, we may be said to sleep in the bosom of the great first cause before birth, as we rest awake in it after death.

p. 44 Excepting Christian IV of Denmark, Browne had survived Henri IV of France, Charles IX and Gustavus Adolphus of Sweden, the Tsar Basil IV, Philip III of Spain, James I of England, Maurice of Nassau, and Sigismund III of Poland. The three contemporary emperors were Rodolph II, Mathias, and Ferdinand II; the Turkish Sultans, Achmet I, Mustapha I, Osman II, and Amurath IV; the popes, Leo XI, Paul V, Gregory XV, and Urban VIII.

p. 48 Whether the world and its creatures had deteriorated was a much debated question, Browne's opinion being notably forwarded by G. Hakewill, *An Apology . . . or an Examination and Censure of the Common Error touching Nature's perpetual and Universal Decay* (3rd ed., augmented, Oxford, 1635).

p. 53 In *Pseudodoxia*, 3.14, Browne discusses asbestos, sometimes known as 'salamander's wool'.

p. 57 Aristotle had been accused of a 'shameful and dirty relationship' with his patron Hermias. For this and other criticisms, see I. Düring, *Aristotle in the Biographical Tradition* (Göteborg, 1957, pp. 277, 373–95).

p. 57 This ceremonial act by the Doge, which took place annually on Ascension Day, signified the marriage to the sea rather of Venice itself, symbolizing the maritime basis of her prosperity and power.

p. 60 Dionysius the Pseudo-Areopagite (c. A.D. 500), a Neoplatonist, formulated the doctrine of nine choirs of angels, arranged in three hierarchies, in his *Celestial Hierarchy*, 6–8.

p. 63   A climate was originally a division of the Earth's surface made by ancient geographers, consisting of a latitudinal belt limited by two parallels on which the length of their longest days differed by half an hour. Beyond the seventh climates either side of the Equator, early maps are vague: with a Midsummer Day of over 16½ hours, Browne's birthplace, London, may more accurately be said to lie in the tenth climate.

p. 71   Browne married in 1641, about six years after this was written, but two years before he authorized its publication.

p. 76   Cf. *The Merchant of Venice*, V.i.83–8.

p. 83   According to Cicero, *Academic Questions*, 2.31 (100), Anaxagoras asserted that ice, since it is the product of standing water which appears black, must itself be of that colour.

p. 83   Aristotle, *De Anima*, 1.2, quotes Democritus (fire), Diogenes (air), and Hippon (water).

p. 83   See *Pseudodoxia Epidemica*, 2.5.

Hydriotaphia

p. 91   Thomas Le Gros was the son of Sir Charles Le Gros, a patient of Browne's, of Crostwick Hall, near Norwich.

p. 96   Though widely read himself in the classics and history, Browne is, from this point on throughout *Hydriotaphia*, frequently indebted for his examples to previous specialists such as Johannes Kirchmann, *De Funeribus Romanorum* (1625); Lilio G. Giraldi, *De Sepulchris* (1539); and Francesco Perucci, *Pompe Funebri di Tutte le Nationi del Mondo* (1639).

p. 106   The direct authority for this and the next paragraph, O. Wormius, *Danica Monumenta*, 1.7, quotes in fact A. Guagninus, *Sarmatiae Europeae Descriptio* (1578).

p. 117   Browne's own skull was stolen from his grave in the church of St. Peter Mancroft, Norwich, in 1840, and reburied in 1922.

p. 117   The first known mention of adipocire, as the substance was termed on its rediscovery in a Paris cemetery in the eighteenth century by A. F. Fourcroy.

p. 118   By Jacobus Tirinus, annotating Ezekiel 37 in the *Biblia Magna* (Paris, 1644).

The Garden of Cyrus

p. 135   This Nicholas Bacon was a grandson of the first premier baronet, who was half-brother to the famous Francis.

p. 135   e.g. F. Hernandez, *Nova Plantarum . . . Mexicanorum Historia* (1651).

p. 135   Asserted by J. van der Linden, *Selecta Medica*, 13.232, 16.53 (1656, pp. 536, 715).

p. 143 Illustrated by J. B. Casalius, *De Veteribus Christianorum Ritibus*, 2 (1645, pp. 10, 7):

p. 145 The identification had been made by, e.g., H. Bochart, *Geographia Sacra*, 1.1(1646).

p. 176 The sprouting of rams' horns stuck into the earth was described by E. Linschoten, *Discourse of Voyages*, 1.61 (1598, p. 110).

p. 182 A Y on its side may be seen in the diagrammatic representation of the actual and apparent positions of a reflected image in relation to the eye:

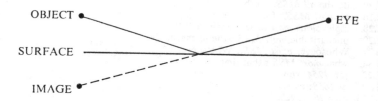

p. 182 C. de Bouelles, *De Intellectu*, 14.8 (1510, f. 18), gives this diagram:

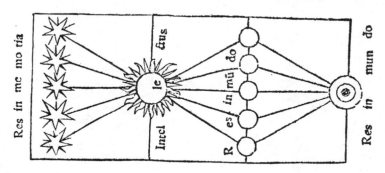

Textual Notes

In the cases recorded below, the present editor has seen fit, for reasons of comprehensibility, to depart from the readings of Professor Martin's text. Readings in *Religio Medici*, from the eight manuscripts (listed by Martin, p. xii), the editions of 1645 to 1685, and the Edinburgh edition of 1754, have been taken from Martin's textual notes and the apparatuses of Denonain and Sanna, and, in the case of the printed versions, checked against the editions themselves. In this list the readings chosen for the present edition are given first, with page and line numbers; those of Martin, second. The manuscripts are not particularized, except for that belonging to Pembroke College, Oxford (*P*), edited by Denonain as *Une Version Primitive de Religio Medici* (Algiers, 1958). Editions are symbolized by their dates.

16.15.   sets *two MSS. 1642, 1669 etc.*: set
17.21.   sweetened . . . preserved *most MSS.*: sweeteneth . . . preserveth
19.22.   and they *some MSS.*: and
21.18.   no *most MSS.*: not
24.6.   nor *two MSS.*: not
30.11.   do *1754*: done
34.17.   heat *all MSS. and eds.*: beat
34.17.   that *most MSS.*: the
36.26.   nearer *most MSS.*: near
48.12.   fire *most MSS.*: force
49.23.   that *most MSS.*: the
54.10.   they do *P*: it doth
57.19.   all passion *most MSS.*: passion
59.5.   do *1645 etc.*: doth
64.12.   him *1672, 1685*: them
65.6.   consideration *all MSS.*: considerations
67.26.   remain *Wilkin 1835*: remains
67.29.   do the *all MSS.*: doth
72.16.   of *most MSS.*: for
72.28.   malevolous *most MSS.*: uncharitable
72.29.   uncharitable *most MSS.*: the uncharitable
76.27.   Whosoever *most MSS.*: Whatsoever
80.34.   what *most MSS.*: that that
86.22.   ran *1754*: run
151.7.   of *1658*: by
167.13. cells *1658*: eels

Index

Corrections and Additions

p. x, l. 8 *for* planted *read* confirmed
p. xi, l. 21 *for* treatises *read* essays
p. xi, l. 23 *for* religious *read* specifically Christian
p. xi, l. 33 *for* also shows a taste *read* shows a taste, too,
p. xiii, l. 29 *for* plausibility *read* credibility
p. xvii, 5th l. from foot *for* preface *read* peroration
p. xxi Reading List 3. *Important Books: add*
  C. A. PATRIDES, ed., *Approaches to Sir Thomas Browne.* University of Missouri
  Press, 1982.
p. xxii *Important Articles: add*
  BREINER, Laurence A., 'The Generation of Metaphor in Thomas Browne',
  Modern Language Quarterly, 38 (1977), 261–75.
p. 2 n. before *ingenuous* insert *declared*: below, p. 61.
p. 4 n. before *resolutions* insert *pagans*: countrymen, villagers—Mark 6: 1–6.
p. 5 n. *for* of the host. *read* exaltation of feeling.
p. 7, l. 21 *for* say), *read* say)
p. 14 n. add as final note *industrious fly*: the bee.
p. 15 n. for *Lord.*: read *Lord*:
p. 16 n. before *expansed* insert *Africa*: proverbial source of novelties and wonders.
p. 17, penult. l. *for* of species or *read* or species of
p. 21 n. before *advisoes* insert *second causes*: nature and fortune.
p. 23, l. 16 *for* scripture *read* Scripture
p. 23 n. add as final note *finger*: Exod. 8:19, Luke 11:20.
p. 27 n. *three great inventions*: *for* compass. *read* compass (or clocks).
p. 36 n. *similitude of God*: *for* Gen. 2:7; *read* Gen. 1:26–7, 2:7;
p. 42 n. before *not yet* insert *have a being*: Acts 17:28.
p. 59 n. before *little flock* insert two notes *needle*: Matt. 19:24, etc.
            compellation: collective designation.
p. 60 n. before *zeals* insert 2 notes *decree*: Gen. 1:26.
            synod: the Trinity.
p. 63 n. above *constellated* insert *grasshoppers*: Lev. 11:22.
p. 66 n. add as final note *Lazarus*: a beggar, typified in Luke 16:20.
p. 73 n. *Battle of Lepanto*: *for* 1570, *read* 1571,
p. 75 n. *flux and reflux . . .*: *for* Boeotoia *read* Boeotia
p. 79, l. 24 *for* point *read* point^n
p. 81 n. *Themistocles*: for *Strategematon* read *Strategemata*
pp. 87–8 Collation of the text of Digby's letter printed in 1643 with the original manuscript in the Bodleian Library, Oxford (MS. Rawl. D 391, f. 60^r), has produced
  the following substantive corrections:
    p. 87, l. 8 *for* the receipt *read* receipt
    p. 87, l. 21 *for* subject *read* subjects
    p. 87, l. 22 *for* writ *read* wrote
    p. 87, l. 31 *for* something *read* in some things
    p. 88, l. 16 *for* hand *read* hands
    p. 88, l. 18 *for* of March *read* March
p. 91 n. before *direct* insert *relics of many*: dispersed bones of saints.
p. 92 n. before *Venus* insert *centos*: patchwork.
p. 98 n. *Chinois*: *for* Chinsor. *read* Chinese.
p. 98 n. add as final note *sentence of God*: Gen. 3:19.
p. 99 n. *hair . . .*: *for* Luke. *read* Luke
p. 102 n. before *Caesar* insert *emphatical*: allusive.
p. 105 n. before *Propertius* insert *exility*: slenderness.
p. 107 n. before *Ludovicus Pius* insert *Ansgarius*: St. Anskar (801–65).
p. 113 n. *golden urn*: *for* ibid. . . . 24.2. *read* Trajan.—*B.*
p. 124 n. *corporal animosity*: *for* loathing . . . existence. *read* physical high-spiritedness.
p. 126 n. *one little . . .* hundred.—*B. transpose to foot of page*
p. 129 n. add as final note *hired*: bought off.
p. 131 n. before *expectants* insert *can only*: alone can.
p. 133, l. 15, & n. *for* extasis *read* ecstasis
p. 143, 2 ll. from foot *for* square *read* square,
p. 144 n. *Ulysses*: *for* Phavorinus *read* Favorinus
p. 147 n. *laureate . . .* patterns. *should be final note on p. 146*
p. 147 n. above *founded upon fives* insert *pulvinaria*: couches of the gods.
p. 152 n. *longilateral . . .* rectangular. transpose to above *castrensial mansions*
p. 156, l. 9 *for* aginst *read* against
p. 164 n. insert as first note *Burgundian*: X-shaped.
p. 164 n. *favago*: *for* presumably . . . worm. *read* sponge-like mass of empty egg-cases
  of the common whelk.
p. 165 n. *mater formicarum*: *before* lit. *insert* tzicatlinan,
p. 166 n. *cunny fish*: *for* presumably . . . skate. *read* Mullus surmuletus, red mullet.

p. 166 n. *Scripture: for* Ps. 139:14. *read* adapted from Ps. 139:14–15.
p. 168, l. 6 *for* not yet *read* nor yet
p. 170 n. before *internodial* insert *sesquitertian proportion:* ratio of 4 to 3.
p. 171 n. before *summer-worm* insert *no rare plants:* hazel-wands.
p. 173 n. add as final note *inwardly:* indoors.
p. 185 n. before *fifth planet* insert *quintuple consideration:* seeing, talking, touching, kissing, coupling.
p. 194: Notes *above* p. 83 *insert* p. 79 See *Pseudodoxia Epidemica,* 6.14.
p. 194: Notes p. 118 *for* 1644 *read* 1643
p. 196 Textual Notes *add*

In 1976 the editor discovered Browne's autograph corrections of the text of the seventh edition of *Religio Medici* (1672) in Norwich Central Library. The most important changes, located by the page and line numbers of the present edition, are as follows (agreements with other texts are indicated in parentheses):

    22.6.   Elias *replaced with* Eliiah
    24.26. successive *emended to* successively (*1642, 1678, 1682, four MSS.*)
    34.2.   common *deleted*
    36.31. on *replaced with* ouer (*P*)
    41.22. not *expanded to* not care to
    42.1.   out of *changed to* out in (*P*)
    43.27. nearest (*1672*) *corrected to* neatest (nearest way *MSS.,* 1642: neatest
             way 1643–1645a, 1678, 1682)
    46.3.   understand *expanded to* understand them (*MSS.*)
    46.8.   cunningly *replaced with* purposely
    56.35. they (they that *MSS., 1642*) *expanded to* they who (*1678, 1682*)
    65.1.   passion (to passion *all other eds.*) *corrected to* vnto passion
    81.12. soul begins *emended to* soul beginning (*some MSS., 1678, 1682*)
    81.26. take *emended to* taking (*presumably intending also the deletion of the
             preceding* and)
    84.6.   God (Gods *1672*) *emended to* from God

The appearance of the emendations at 24.26, 43.27, 56.35, and 81.12 in *1678* endows that edition with authority. The following readings of *1678* (here modernized) were rejected by Martin, while the first two and last two were admitted by Denonain into his text only within brackets. They may now be accepted as authentic.

    35.18. *for* man *read* 'tis thought, man
    37.14. *for* as the *read* as beyond the
    44.4–5. *for* delight . . . days; *read* delight: . . . days,
    64.31. *for* alms *read* alms only
    85.12. *for* Pliny, *read* Pliny, a tale of Boccace or Malespini, (orig.: a tale of
    Boccace or *Malizspini,*)

The following departures from Martin's text of *Hydriotaphia* derive from Browne's autograph corrections in the Avery copy of the first edition:

    95.31. admixture *Avery:* a mixture *1658*
    188.9. consisting *Avery:* consist *1658*

In a copy of the second edition (1658, quarto) of *Hydriotaphia* and *The Garden of Cyrus,* appended to the fourth edition of *Pseudodoxia Epidemica,* which once belonged to Browne's daughter Elizabeth Lyttelton and is now in the editor's possession, the author made numerous autograph corrections and a few additions to the texts. The most interesting of those which do not appear elsewhere are as follows:

    99.ult. crept into: crept they into
    115.15. a piece: yet a piece
    120.26. lay: therin lay

p. 197   Index
            Bible,
            Gen., *insert* 38, 60, 98,
            Exod., *insert* 23,
            Lev., *insert* 63,
            Eccles., *for* 130, *read* 131,
p. 198   Matt., *insert* 59,
            Mark, *insert* 4,
            Luke, *insert* 23, 66,
            Acts, *insert* 42,
            1 John, *add* , 60
          David, *for* 126, *read* 127,
p. 199   *insert* Favorinus, 144
          Hernandez, *for* 195 *read* 194
p. 200   Lot's wife, *for* 39, *read* 40,
p. 201   *delete* Phavorinus, 144
          Plato, *for* 167, *read* 166,
          Severus, Septimius, *delete* , 113
          Shakespeare, *for* 43, *read* 44,
p. 202   Trajan, *add* , 113